COMPUTER EXPERIENCE AND COGNITIVE DEVELOPMENT:
A Child's Learning in a Computer Culture

ELLIS HORWOOD SERIES IN COGNITIVE SCIENCE

Series Editor: Masoud Yazdani, University of Exeter

**COMPUTER EXPERIENCE AND COGNITIVE DEVELOPMENT: A Child's Learning in a
Computer Culture**
R. LAWLER, G.T.E. Laboratories Inc., USA
COGNITION, COMPUTERS AND CREATIVE WRITING
M. SHARPLES, University of Sussex

COMPUTER EXPERIENCE AND COGNITIVE DEVELOPMENT:

A Child's Learning in a Computer Culture

R. W. LAWLER, PhD, MS, AB
Fundamental Research Laboratory
GTE Laboratories, Waltham
Massachusetts, USA

ELLIS HORWOOD LIMITED
Publishers · Chichester

Halsted Press: a division of
JOHN WILEY & SONS
New York · Chichester. Toronto · Brisbane

First published in 1985 by
ELLIS HORWOOD LIMITED
Market Cross House, Cooper Street, Chichester, West Sussex, PO19 1EB, England

The publisher's colophon is reproduced from James Gillison's drawing of the ancient Market Cross, Chichester.

Distributors:

Australia, New Zealand, South-east Asia:
Jacaranda-Wiley Ltd., Jacaranda Press,
JOHN WILEY & SONS INC.,
G.P.O. Box 859, Brisbane, Queensland 4001, Australia

Canada:
JOHN WILEY & SONS CANADA LIMITED
22 Worcester Road, Rexdale, Ontario, Canada.

Europe, Africa:
JOHN WILEY & SONS LIMITED
Baffins Lane, Chichester, West Sussex, England.

North and South America and the rest of the world:
Halsted Press: a division of
JOHN WILEY & SONS
605 Third Avenue, New York, N.Y. 10158, USA

©1985 R. W. Lawler/Ellis Horwood Limited

British Library Cataloguing in Publication Data
Lawler, Robert W.
Computer experience and cognitive development:
a child's learning in a computer culture. —
(Ellis Horwood series in Cognitive Science)
1. Cognitition in children   2. Human information
processing in children
I. Title
155.4'13   BF723.C5

Library of Congress Card No. 85—5534

ISBN 0—85312—860—X (Ellis Horwood Limited — Library Edn.)
ISBN 0—85312—916—9 (Ellis Horwood Limited — Student Edn.)
ISBN 0—470—20193—2 (Halsted Press — Library Edn.)
ISBN 0—470—20194—0 (Halsted Press — Student Edn.)

Typeset by Ellis Horwood Limited
Printed in Great Britain by R.J. Acford, Chichester

As a young man, I stumbled upon a book I still find inspiring. It began this way:

> I am a human being, whatever that may be. I speak for all of us who move and think and feel and whom time consumes. I speak as an individual unique in a universe beyond my understanding, and I speak for man. I am hemmed in by limitations of sense and mind and body, of place and time and circumstance, some of which I know but most of which I do not. I am like a man journeying through a forest, aware of occasional glints of light overhead, with recollections of the long trail I have already travelled, and conscious of wider spaces ahead. I want to see more clearly where I have been and where I am going, and above all, I want to know why I am where I am and why I am travelling at all . . .
>
> N. J. Berrill
> *Man's Emerging Mind*

Berrill characterizes his book as one man's contribution to developing a scientific concept of man. This book is my imperfect contribution to that same end: it is in a tradition, begun by Norbert Wiener and Warren McCulloch, which rises directly to Berrill's challenge. The central goal of that tradition is the explanation of intelligence, both artificial and natural. Beginning with development as the central fact of mind, I attempt here to construct a computationally oriented view of learning around the microgenetic analysis of an ecological study.

to Gretchen
my friend and wife of twenty years
who has made this work possible
from its first conception
through its final editing

Contents

Foreword

Begun in research inspired by Marvin Minsky's statement of a goal, expressed as our need for a better theory about the emergence of the control structure of mind, this book has developed as an attempt to tie down some powerful ideas from the discipline of Artificial Intelligence (AI) and try them out on the interpretation of human behavior. The focus on detailed interpretation of the individual case makes this work more than a popularization of AI ideas because I offer the reader the chance to explore a major psychological issue, learning, through the analysis of how the mind develops from interaction with specific experiences.

Nearly every man of intellectual aspiration hopes ultimately to make sense of some part of life and to contribute whatever he can to mankind's proper study. Such is my ambition. Learning shapes the life of every man and transmits the experience of the race. A theme so pervasive and focussing on the distinctive character of man, the cultural transmission of experience, *must* lead to controversy. Should this work tax your tolerance, please bear in mind these words of Warren McCulloch:

'Don't bite my finger; look where I'm pointing.'

Introduction

... a stick thrust in water felt straight and looked bent to a Greek. The sun moved for the Inquisition, the earth for Galileo. Light is a wave for Schroedinger and a particle for Heisenberg. But even the last have had their Dirac. The seeming contradictions vanish in the grace of greater knowledge. We have learned that the answer depends upon how we ask the question. And we have learned to ask the question so as to get an answer of a kind that we can use . . . .

Warren S. McCulloch
Through the Den of the Metaphysician

The four central studies of this book are about Miriam, my daughter. The extensive detailed data collected in the study of her thinking and the attempt to use it all in interpretation represent an effort to tighten up the case study approach to permit empirically based descriptions of cognitive structures. The analyses of Miriam's learning form a unified exploration of how local changes in cognitive structure result in significant large-scale effects. The study was inspired in part by a suggestion of Flavell's (1963) to blend Piaget's focus on cognitive structures with the ecological emphasis of Barker and Wright and undertake 'a type of research endeavor which has not yet been exploited: an ecological study of the young child's mundane interchanges with his workaday world'. Because this book is not about a great man's thought but merely about the marvel of a normal child's learning, it depends for its general interest, in a technical way, on arguments about the lawfulness of psychic phenomena advanced by the psychologist Kurt Lewin. He argued that the individual case does not merely illustrate the general law; it embodies the general law. If mental phenomena are lawful in a strong sense, as physical phenomena are, one can arrive at the general law through detailed interpretation of the particular case[1]. The primary objective of The Intimate Study was to produce a corpus which could be analyzed in such a way as to advance our understanding of learning. Let me first describe what that corpus is and how it was constructed then explain some of the reasons and accidents that gave the project its specific form.

CONSTRUCTING A CORPUS

Activities and observations recorded

At the beginning of The Initimate Study, we were four in my family, two parents and two children, Robby, age 8, and Miriam, age 6. The specific objective we followed was to trace in fine detail Miriam's learning for the six months following her sixth birthday (April 9th through October 8th, 1977). This is the CORE of The Intimate Study; it is extended beyond this core period by later observations. I recorded her behavior in well-structured situations and followed her beyond the confines of the computer laboratory with naturalistic observation in the various settings of her everyday world. Miriam was under continual observation for six months.

When The Intimate Study began, Miriam was attending kindergarten (one making no substantial academic demands upon her). As the study ended, Miriam completed her first month of first grade. Miriam was an unschooled school-age child. I frequently visited kindergarten and was a part of her social world as well. When her friends came to play, on rainy days there was no place to escape them in our small dwelling; on sunny days, they often asked me to join them at the tree fort, in the garden, playing in the courtyard, or pushing them on the space trolley. We lived in the carriage house of an old suburban mansion. By distance and dangerous roads, in effect, the children were imprisoned in the mansion's grounds unless they could get a parent to act as chauffeur. Very occasionally, the children would visit friends or go shopping with their mother. But over the summer, most of Miriam's friends were away, and their mother preferred shopping alone. With very few exceptions, the only times Miriam spent away from home were in my company; most of those times were the hours at project Logo's Children's Learning Lab. Her young age, the limits of her world, and my having the time permitted us to share a common world for the period of The Intimate Study. The data collected during this period are grouped into four matters: profiles; sessions; vignettes; and the log.

The profiles

The profiles are a series of initial and terminal cognitive examinations. Through these, Miriam's capabilities and styles of thought may be compared with data in the psychological literature and with normal education skills through her performance of these specific tasks[2]:

1 See the citation 'Lewin: On the Pure Case' (p. 245).
2 Summary data from these experiments are presented in Appendix 1, 'Relating this Subject to Other Studies'.

- School tasks: reading and arithmetic skills.
- Piagetian tasks: one-to-one correspondence; class inclusion; continuous quantity; time; object volume; combinations; substance; weight; displacement volume; backspinning a ball; beam balance; multiple seriation.
- Stanford-Binet Intelligence Scale: test L-M at 6 years, 19 days.

Other materials of an idiographic character were collected but are not reported here.

The sessions

The sessions were mechanically recorded, all on audiotape and many on videotape. Processing of the marginally edited transcripts and working materials of these sessions is described below. These relatively formal, directed working sessions at MIT's Logo lab (approximately 70) and at home (approximately 20) exhibit more than four months of interactions between Miriam and me in a computer-centred environment. The data are as detailed as any critic could wish.

The vignettes

Richly interpretive, highly subjective, open to error and overstatement, these materials are essentially ephemeral literary constructs whose purposes are to document events in the social world of our family and to connect themes emergent in the more structured data. The vignettes are like snapshots of thinking or short stories that surfaced in the small society of our family. They are based on selective naturalistic observation of Miriam's behaviour beyond the range of mechanical recording and in situations where the recording itself would have been obtrusive. I attempted to capture all unrecordable and significant expressions of development Miriam exhibited during The Intimate Study. To the extent that they record observations by an ever-present scientist in the midst of the action, they attempt to elevate anecdotal reportage to the status of naturalistic observation through the claim that they record ALL thematically interesting behavior in those settings beyond the range of mechanical recording. Though imperfect, these data may still be accepted as additional, well-placed pieces in the puzzle, pieces that have in fact been essential in helping me grasp patterns in the development of Miriam's mind. Each vignette includes a short sketch of the point of view from which I judged the content significant.

The log

These daily notes for the last five months of The Intimate Study record how Miriam spent her time. The observations are quite variable in level of detail and quality. The objective was to note what Miriam was doing every half-hour or hour. Lacunae exist (occasions where I was asleep or otherwheres) and even a day or two may have been missed. No analysis of these observations has been attempted here.

Processing observations of the corpus

A description of our typical day during The Intimate Study will illuminate how the data were rendered in their first processed form. Early in the morning, the

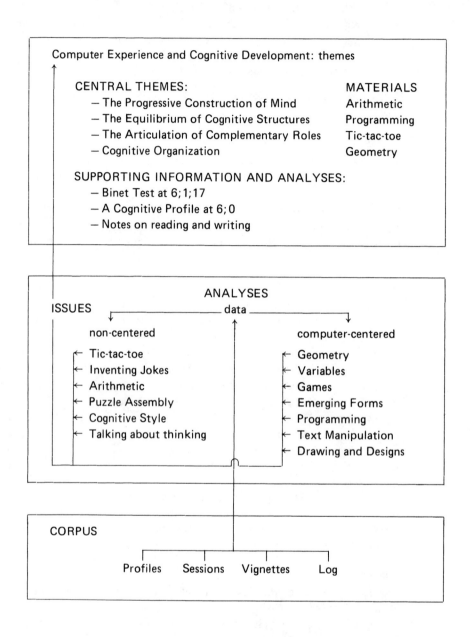

MIRIAM'S BEHAVIOR
During The Intimate Study

Fig. I – The Intimate Study and its interpretations.

children and I would ride to the Logo Lab and execute our day's experiment. Each session was mechanically recorded; printed output was collected and labelled with session numbers. We would drive home for lunch, following which the children would occupy themselves with their own amusements for the remainder of the day. I would spend several hours transcribing the recordings of Miriam's work in manuscript. After that, I composed vignettes, attempted to understand ongoing work, and planned future sessions. Usually this work occupied me until late in the evening. Throughout the day and outside the laboratory, I would interrupt this processing to note in the log what Miriam was doing. The essential value of the log was in returning me regularly to observe Miriam's activity. The lag time to transcription for recordings was usually kept down to several days at the maximum. For vignettes, the lag was more variable but usually under a week. Those days when the children did not want to work, I was able to catch up. Consequently, the data were processed to this rudimentary state in nearly real-time.

Figure I summarizes the elements of the corpus and how the materials relate to the analyses in this book.

The study of the process of learning is related to, but different from, the assessment of states of knowledge. I claim that The Intimate Study represents a sensible approach to studying the processes of learning, despite the manifest difficulty of the task and the method's vulnerabilities to criticism. Further, I claim there is no other empirical approach with such promise of telling us anything important about the accommodation of mental structures through experience in the language-capable mind. If the experimental task is too simple, observations may lead erroneously to a simple-minded view of mind. Even if the mind should prove to be a simple thing (which I doubt) its interactions with experience may be much more complex than studies in the Peterson paradigm or of cryptarithmetic would suggest (the former involves memorizing lists of nonsense syllables, the latter decoding puzzles where letters have number values).

Some reasons for adopting the method

There are at least three fundamental problems in exploring learning as insight. Major insights happen rarely; they cannot be scheduled; and they may not be recognized when they *do* occur. All three problems set major limits on any method which could possibly be useful for studying the accommodation of cognitive structures[3]. During the nine months wherein I followed Miriam's learning closely, she learned how to add. For her, this learning required four insights (one about every ten weeks!). This witnesses the rarity of such learning. Contrasting the small number of insights with the hundreds of pages of transcriptions which capture her calculation behavior exemplifies the 'noisy data' problem.

---

3 This is Piaget's term for the process by which cognitive structures adapt themselves to new experiences. I use it in the same sense and try to describe it, partly through exemplification.

An insight is something that happens in an individual mind; it is a private experience. There may be manifestations in behavior, e.g., a shocked look or a surprising question, but the best evidence available is the subject's witness as to the occurrence and significance of the event. Consider this example:

Where I was reading, Robby assembled a puzzle on the living room floor. He left off the puzzle and lay on his side, bending his body back and forth at the pelvis. When I asked him to stop squirming, he sat up and spoke to me:

> Rob: Daddy? You know all that stuff about 3 hundred and 60? (A reference to discussions of the effect of reducing an angle by 360 degrees.) I understand it now.
> Bob: Wow! How did you figure it out?
> Rob: Well, you know if you have an angle that's 3 hundred and 61? ... And you take away 360? It's 1, and that's like it's starting all over again.
> Bob: That's really great, Rob. When did you figure it out?
> Rob: Now.
> Bob: Just now? When you were squirming around there on the floor?
> Rob: Yeah. Squirming around helps me think.

Robby returned to his puzzle.

If Robby had not been willing and eager to reveal his thoughts, his understanding of this particular problem at this time would have been missed; more importantly, the evidence of the connectedness of his knowledge would have been missed as well. Had it not surfaced in our conversation, who would have guessed that his squirming around on the floor in a place and at a time remote from our formal sessions was a response to an earlier confusion based on work at Logo? I would not have realized his squirming was a simulation, with his own body, of operations performed by the turtle in experiments at the lab. Surely such symbolic behavior as this 'simulation' is evidence about how knowledge in one structure relates to another.

The preceding ideas and examples suggest why I adopted the methodology of The Intimate Study. Let me state as lucidly as possible the principles that study embodies:

1. The most significant form of learning is the accommodation of cognitive structures; under the assumption that insight is the phenomenological correlate of this accommodation, the functional objective of The Intimate Study is to explore the interaction of mental structure and experience when learning-as-insight occurs.
2. Because insight occurs rarely, the study must be long to assemble a sufficient collection of incidents of learning for analysis.
3. Because insight cannot be scheduled, the observations of the subject must be continual and protracted; the data collection must be an everyday part of the subject's life in which he participates willingly for his own reasons.
4. Because insight is essentially a private event, the subject must trust the

experimenter and be a colleague more than an object; reports from articulate introspection are a key source of information.

5. To the extent that insight involves the integration of ideas, it requires a rich interpretation of a sort typically not accessible to the subject; while the subject experiences it as personally significant, the experimenter will view it as theoretically significant.

6. Inasmuch as the experimenter has an imperfect theory of mind, is insensitive to the importance of specific incidents, or cannot comprehend the mass of observation as it is developing (these conditions are always true), the strategy of choice is to create a corpus of sufficient richness and permanence that it may be queried as subsequent interpretation proceeds.

7. The final point is primarily an ethical one. One should not establish a relation of trust in a prolonged and intimate study of cognitive development and then abandon the subject when the experiment is finished. Respect for the subject, even love, is appropriate; one must not take advantage of the subject[4].

Some critics will feel that the study is reduced in value by a lack of scientific objectivity. I don't feel that one should be overly concerned with objectivity, especially because it would prove impossible for a study at this level of detail[5]. Many of the ideas and objectives which guided the execution of The Intimate Study are novel and sound, but some are certainly at least partly wrong. So long as errors are not disguised, the harm in them is merely two-fold. First, the value of the corpus, compared to a perfectly executed study, will be diluted, and thus the conclusions will be less compelling than they might otherwise have been. Second, I will appear more stupid than I like to admit being[6].

Some of the accidents involved in the genesis of The Intimate Study are the following. For two years, Robby had come often to the Logo Laboratory and worked with me there, giving me his reactions to programs I made and ideas I wanted to try out. Those projects, thematically various and undertaken with no overall organization in mind, comprise a pilot to the The Intimate Study, in fact even though not in intention. That earlier work has impressed me with the importance of long studies, the usefulness of mechanical recording, and the value of an approach which could capture unscheduled learning. This latter idea is central to The Intimate Study: the accommodation of cognitive structures

4 When it began, this study was severely criticized with the argument that it might endanger the well-being of my child; some feared she would grow up feeling used by a father whom she loved. There has been no such outcome in this case. To fail to consider such a possibility, however, would be irresponsible in the extreme. No one should undertake such a study without the firm, personal commitment that the well-being of the subject is more important than any outcome or even the continuation of the study.

5 The arguments advanced in the citation 'Langer: On Objectivity' (p. 244) may help make this minority position seem not unreasonable.

6 I find some consolation in my favorite line by Anatole France from *La Rotisserie de la Reine Pedaque*: '... je ne me flatte pas de direr grand honneur des ces revelations. Les uns diront que j'ai tout invente et que ce n'est pas la vrai doctrine; les autres, que n'ai dit que ce que tout le monde savait ...'.

happens rarely but is the most significant form of learning. With this point of view forward in my mind, I stumbled upon Flavell's suggestion in a discussion of the stability of Piagetian stages, which I cite here in extension for its importance in forming the objectives and methods of The Intimate Study:

> The question which these investigations bequeath to us is the same one they were designed to answer: how do conservation and other Piagetian concepts develop? It might be said, parenthetically, that this question can in principle be divided into two: by what concrete methods deriving from what theory of acquisition can we most effectively train children on these concepts? and — what may be a different question — how are they in fact acquired normally — that is in the child's day-to-day cognitive bouts with the real world? It is not likely that the second question can ever receive a direct and precise answer because of the intrinsic difficulty of sorting out the myriad uncontrolled environmental pressures to which the child is exposed. But the very posing of the question in this way suggests a type of endeavor which has not yet been exploited: an ecological study of the young child's mundane interchanges with his workaday world, a kind of job analysis of his daily life along the lines of Barker and Wright's work (1951, 1955)[7]. This sort of study might suggest promising leads to pursue in the more conventional transfer of learning experiment; in view of the infertility of most training methods so far tried, no source of new ideas should be ignored.
>
> John Flavell
> *The Development Psychology of Jean Piaget*

The Intimate Study was an attempt to approach a variant of that impossible second question: what is the process of learning like in the language-capable mind. The study shared with ecological psychology the objective of specifying how components of mind relate to the specifics of experience. Such a challenge I considered an opportunity of the first order and one congenial to my interests and values, and to my obligations as well.

During the period of the study, my wife and I planned to have another child (now our daughter Peggy), and I expected the responsibility for the older children would be mine. How much better an idea if we three should undertake together a significant research project than that we should merely entertain or tolerate each other for the duration. The Intimate Study was thus an experiment 'with' children, not an experiment 'on' children. It was not undertaken to make them academic prodigies. Miriam and I shared a robust love and respect. Her brother occupied no less a place in my heart. They were willing to help me with my work because doing so implied we would spend a lot of time together. In function, we three comrades worked like a project team or task force. If I was first among equals because of my specific skills and depth of experience, nonetheless Robby and Miriam exercised considerable direction in our daily doings because my objective was to follow in detail *their* understanding of our work.

---

7 *One Boy's Day; Midwest and its Children.*

Some work bored them; some engaged and inspired them to products they are still proud of. I do not believe the work has damaged them in any way. On the contrary, our involvement in the project certainly enriched their lives. Such is my personal and ultimate conclusion.

THE FRAMEWORK OF IDEAS

It is a commonplace of relativism that every system of ideas is at root a metaphor from which its vision grows, branches, and is nourished. In such a view, the appropriate criterion for the value of a system of ideas is fecundity in application to cases we care about. Many people assume that computational descriptions offer no substantial advance to psychology but are merely the latest fad in the reformulation of age-old problems. On the contrary, with the founding of cybernetics Norbert Wiener and Warren McCulloch began a 'Copernican' revolution in the study of mind, one crisply phrased in this assertion: the laws of the embodiment of mind should be sought among those governing information rather than those governing energy or matter[8]. McCulloch, a neurophysiologist and logician, advanced an 'existence proof' for this position,

> ... a true mathematical idea: between the class of trivial combinatorial functions computable by simple Boolean logic and the too general class of functions computable by Turing machines, there are intermediate classes of computability determined by the most universal and natural mathematical feature of the net — its finiteness. This is pure mathematics. The theoretical assertion of the paper is that the behaviour of any brain must be characterized by the computation of functions of one of these classes ....

> Papert, 1965
> *Introduction to Embodiments of Mind*

This means less that 'the brain is a computer' than that it is possible in principle to create an adequate computational model of any brain. Notice that any model which described the organization and flow of information in a brain would describe identically what most people commonly mean by mind.

Near the end of his career, McCulloch spoke of turning psychology into *experimental* epistomology by attempting to understand the embodiment of mind. This task he understood as involving three problems: a physiological problem (understanding the brain), a psychological problem (understanding the mind), and a logical problem (understanding how to represent relations such as exist in both mind and brain). He required of this logic that it be able to represent both the organization of mind, in detail, and possible different states of that organization. His example was: descriptions of cognitive structures should be able to represent the mental equivalent of the fist as well as the hand. The step-wise trace of a program's execution (they are easy to acquire) bears such a relation to the text of the program; it represents one possible performance of a functioning program. It is *this* aspect of computational descriptions — that

---

8 For an accessible appreciation of their contribution, see the article by Stephen Toulmin in *The Horizon Book of Makers of Modern Thought*.

an execution trace can represent functioning in a particular case — that permits addressing specific problems, e.g. how a particular mind was changed by a specific experience[9]. Through the addition of functioning as an essential aspect of structure, representing the mind as progamming structures provides a specific way to make sense of Piaget's proposal that structure and development are correlatively generative; that is, new structure develops through the functioning of pre-existing structure.

Papert has proposed that the insertion of control elements into functioning structures is the 'missing link' in descriptions of knowledge needed to understand significant learning. I ask if one can apply the essentially mathematical ideas of McCulloch and Papert to solve particular problems of learning[10]. Could one use Papert's idea, which I call 'the elevation of control', to explain in detail an individual's mind as a system evolved through the experience of that individual interacting with his everyday world?[11].

Nothing comes from nothing; what are the circumstances through which minimal means can engender connections between preexisting structures? Going beyond Papert's proposal, I introduce in the following analyses another idea which can help explain the creation of new links and structures in the mind. Call it the 'relational conversion'. Imagine there exist within the mind large-scale cognitive structures competing with one another to solve problems. Each attempts to select aspects of the problem as presented to the mind on which its 'programs' can work. Assume that in order to prevent paralysing confusion, when one structure is able to appropriate a problem it is also able to inhibit competitors, as if by sending a message 'you must not confound *this* situation (which is my problem) with other situations'. Such a scenario is the basis, for the establishment of 'must-not-confound' links between disparate but competing cognitive structures. Learning, seen as significant structural change, occurs when one of these 'inhibitory' links is converted into a 'relational' link through an insight contingent upon a specific experience. This begins the coordination of disparate cognitive structures, a theme of interpretation throughout this book. It is a simple and direct explanation of how new structure can be created almost from nothing.

9 I do not claim to solve the problem of embodiment of mind, but I do hope to make some advance on the psychological front by applying some AI ideas, which comprise in general a kind of logic of functioning representations, to approach Minsky's goal of a theory of the emergence of control structure. I do not touch the issue of physiology; McCulloch's colleague Lettvin now argues convincingly that the complexity of even the single neuron is still beyond the reach of AI and that to claim any reality for models of the ensemble is very rash and unwarranted.

10 This book does not assume a knowledge of programming. I do refer to some ideas for representing aspects of thought which were almost inconceivable before the advent of computers, and I do apply computational ideas in a description of thinking and learning based on a significant corpus. But my work is never formal for the sake of formality, nor do I produce programmed models of mind. My inferences from the data of my studies are too fragmentary to permit the creation of functioning programs without excessive fabrication. To do so would be more deceptive than illuminating.

11 The idea is more subtle than the mere insertion of links into a semantic net. The key point is the joining together with minimal means of two structures which own an essential epistemological complementarity. For Papert's application of this idea to the analysis of Piaget's conservation phenomena and its relation to Piagetian 'groupements', see the citation 'Papert: On the Elevation of Control' (p. 247).

CHOOSING DESCRIPTIONS

A very simple model of how to do science proposes that hypothesis confirmation and disconfirmation is the central activity. One might then contrast two grand theories, draw inferences from them applicable to a single case, then test the implications of the two different theories as to which the evidence makes appear the more worthy of belief. A richer perspective is presented by Goodman wherein one recognizes that a primary factor which separates the true from the logical is the choice of categories through which things are described. This has precious little to do with any sort of valid inference, *per se*, and must be justified as right by some other means[12].

The distinction between valid induction and deduction, on the one hand, and how one divides the world with descriptions of things, on the other, does not imply that such choices about cutting up the world are theory-free or that studies which indulge in extensive exemplification are empirical in any mindless sense. How one divides the world with descriptions is the major decision from which theories and experimentation follow. But we can't get at the content of the world, the thing itself; we can only ask what are the natural chunks of reality, how can we analyze or cut up the world for our better understanding in such a way that pieces separate individually without disintegrating. The criterion for judging descriptions is productivity: does the cutting produce a useful result?

The rightness of my descriptions of knowledge in the mind and its development is a central issue. In the detailed studies, I have resorted to extensive exemplification of the cognitive context to justify my arguments about the character of knowledge in the mind and the processes of its development. The major issue in exemplification is whether or not one's examples comprise a fair sample — no matter from what material they are cut out[13]. What precisely are those things which the data-rich studies of this book exemplify? By the chapters, they are:

Chapter	The material of the study shows:
1:	that non-expert problem solving is more like 'bricolage' than analysis.
2:	how generally applicable skills can be understood as the controlled invocation of highly particular, domain-specific knowledge.
3:	that formal thought, in the Piagetian sense, is a competitor with concrete thought, not an emergent from its perfection.
4:	that social engagement can engender intermediate (metastable) structures with functional lability from which develop in turn mature structures with their own more powerfully adapted stability.

12 See, the extended citation 'Goodman: On Rightness of Rendering' (p. 236). The essence of Goodman's position on exemplification is that it comprises one of the three primary modes of meaningful reference (the others are representation and expression). The selection implicit in a thing's being a sample determines what are the aspects in virtue of which it exemplifies and is thus meaningful.

13 In Goodman's *Ways of Worldmaking*, see Chapter 4 (When Is Art?). Here, see also the extended citation 'Goodman: On Multiple Worlds' (p. 237).

>   5:   how essentially different representations are brought into regis-
>   tration with one another, a requirement for any developing
>   coherence of mind.

By choosing the exemplifying material with a focus on such themes, I am asserting that themes are primary issues in understanding human learning.

1

The development of objectives

... the more one examines life the firmer becomes the conviction that it contains no well-rounded plots and that a good deal of what we do has a higgledy-piggledy nature, slapstick in tone, which forces us either to be greatly sad or highly hysterical. Philosophy is merely the parlor interpretation of unplanned pandemonium in the kitchen. The philosopher attempts the Herculean when he tries cataloguing chaos.

Walt Kelly

INTRODUCTION

This chapter explores a person's developing objectives tracing the pattern of their changes through analysis of a limited empirical corpus. The issue confronted here is creativity in respect to objectives. That goals dominate activity is a central dogma of current work in the study of intelligence. However, any person who showed the goal-commitment typical of artificial intelligence programs would be judged a monomaniac. Human commitment is typically of a more limited sort. Consequently, I prefer to describe people as having not goals but objectives, indeed, large collections of objectives[1]. In special circumstances some people do develop commitment to and struggle to achieve very difficult ends; such behavior would be properly characterized as goal-driven.

My specific endeavor here will be to recount and explain some details of how a seven-year-old child drew the picture of a house and its setting. My general

---

1 In precise use, the word 'goals' generally implies struggle and hardship in achieving some end; the contrasting word 'objective' implies the attainability of the end. These and other contrasts are laid out in extensive detail in Webster's *Synonomy*.

purpose is to find and present specific sources of guidance, i.e. what led the child to do one thing rather than another. The two principles of creative projection I uncover and examine are simple elaboration, that is, applying some working procedure to some slightly more complex case, and objective formation proper through the frustration of an attempted elaboration. Tracing the developing activities of the project raises important issues about how problem solving in the current task domain relates to earlier experiences. The values of working through this analysis and its introductory material is uncovering a view of mind which is then applied to the problem of learning in the remainder of this book.

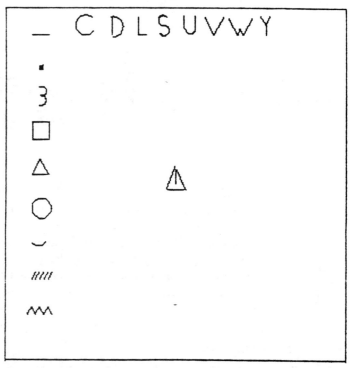

The DRAW program offered this menu of shapes for a child's selection[2]. The expectation was that children would enjoy assembling the designs of the menu into whatever shapes suited their fancy. When a child completed a shape, he directed the program to generate a Logo procedure for recreating that shape by specifying its name. My intention was that DRAW function as an introduction to progamming for children. DRAW uses procedure names with inputs to specify the sizes of the designs. For example, 'BOX [20]' makes a square 20 turtle steps on a side and 'BOX [20 100]' makes a rectangle 20 steps high and 100 steps wide. Robby was provided with a list of procedure names for shapes in the menu, but tha lack of clarity about how inputs were applied to shapes created some of the problems and even interesting incidents in the development of H7GS (the name Robby gave to his scene).

Fig. 1.1 – Menu of shapes.

2 The program was inspired by the drawing techniques of Ed Emberley (1972).

Background of the data collection

I had two purposes in preserving a better record of interactions with children: first to understand better the specific path of learning, and second to record their reactions to programs I developed for their use. The work was not an 'experiment' in the sense of being fashioned to test some hypothesis. This particular project began with my asking my son, Robby, aged 7 years 5 months (7; 5), that he test a new drawing program and give me his reactions (see Fig. 1.1). At the end of the project, I had an audiotape record of a multi-day computer project. The material is suitable for an analysis of objective development because the boy followed his own direction within the loose constraints set by the computer medium and the programmed environment. The story of how Robby made this drawing will not be presented chronologically but rather in an order chosen to highlight the ideas which the case material exemplifies. We begin with presentation of several related and simple cases of elaboration and the natural limitations of the process. Let us start then with a simple idea, but in the middle of a story.

CASES OF ELABORATION

The basic example

Near the completion of the drawing shown in Fig. 1.2, Robby said he wanted to put some grass near his house. After several trials, exploring the effect of the input parameters on the turtle's action, Robby completed the first line of grass at the base of the house. He then undertook the yard, first with three lines of grass (after which he saved his work as H4GS — House and Four Grasses) and then completed, with three more lines of grass, his final product, H7GS. In the explication of changes in Fig. 1.2, notice the stepwise progression and changing of one element at a time.

In this environment, elaboration is the process of repeating the execution of a successful procedure with some small variation of its application, for example in the location of the turtle or the value of an input variable supplied to the procedure[3]. With the grass of H7GS, the process of elaboration was terminated by exhaustion. There is no more room for grass; in this specific sense the application of the procedure to this little task domain is complete. The child's progressive mastery of the use of the procedure in the environment has turned a procedure, at first successfully executed in one specific case, into a tool usable more freely within a small domain of application. This is a very concrete form of generalization. Such a process of elaboration is not limited to task domains using computer procedures. For example, if one tells a child that numbers greater than twenty are formed by concatenation of twenty with the well-known smaller numbers, he should not be surprised that the child puts together what he's been told and begins counting with twenty-one and proceeds through twenty-nine, twenty-ten, twenty-eleven, etc. With this counting example, the child focusses on the most salient element and varies the adjunct terms. Although 'achieving mastery through consolidation of a working procedure' may be one reason behind the everyday phenomenon of elaboration, there are surely others. I am less interested in

3   See the extended citation 'Tversky and Kahnemann: On Anchoring with Variation' (p. 255).

reasons for elaboration than in the creativity of the process. Consequently, I choose here to set out some other examples which reveal the impact of concrete experiences on the process.

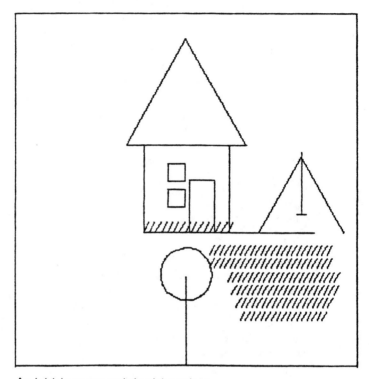

An initial success and six elaborations

This scene was made over three days in working sessions of approximately an hour's duration each. During the development of the scene, the shape menu was also on the computer display. The spaces above and to the left of Robby's scene were filled by the menu shown in Fig. 1.1. The details of successive elaborations in use of the 'HAIR' procedure to make grass are as follows.

Initial success: grass at the base of the house

ELABORATION	DETAIL
1	grass low on screen: changing initial turtle location
2	a little longer (changing an input variable value)
3	a little longer still; saving work on a disk file
4	grass moved left (near the tree)
5	moved left, made longer: no good, too close to tree
6	repeated higher (farther from tree); saved as H7GS

Fig. 1.2 — H7GS: 'House and seven grasses'.

Early in the project, Robby noted some of his intentions in the sketch of Fig. 1.3. In general, his plans revealed a process of repeating a successful procedure with a minor variation to achieve a richer, concrete objective, one more complex, more full of detail, more like the everyday world in which he lived. For example, the house he first produced has overhanging eaves as did the carriage house in which we lived at the time. The dormer windows — a dominant aspect of his planning — reflect forcefully the influence of the presence of such windows in that house, as well as being duplications with reduced proportions of the HOUSE itself. The detail of the windows — their being made of four panes — also reflects this casual inspiration of the created object by the concrete experience of everyday life.

Two aspects of these paper plans are noteworthy. First is the repetition of basic shapes on a diminished scale. Thus the house shape itself is replicated in the dormer window. The square of the house story next appears as the window and then as the individual glass panes. The second aspect is the concreteness of the drawings in the sense that his plan shared several specific features with the house we lived in. Finally, notice at this early planning stage the appearance of the grass motif which was only completed at the end of the project. See the text for a discussion of the role of deferred objectives in this project.

Fig. 1.3 – Paper plans.

I felt it necessary to dissuade Robby from undertaking these specific additions to his house because of all the complicated positioning that would have been required to achieve the dormers-with-four-paned-windows. He himself decided that making a doorknob for the door would be too tedious (he imagined here making a series of twenty-four 'forward and right' commands). Finally, the grass which he later added as the finishing touch of his H7GS design first appeared in this sketch (the five slanted lines with three arrows from them). I suggested to

Robby using the HAIR procedure to make the grass he wanted. Robby adopted the idea and elaborated it: 'I could put three grasses in here so it looks like a yard'.

If objectives are blocked, some appear to be lost but not all of them. We know from the final design of Fig. 1.2 that Robby ultimately achieved his objective of making a yard. The characterization of elaboration as one process of objective generation is accurate, but it is not the whole story. We now examine in detail how this simple objective of making a yard became deferred and by what sort of objective it was replaced. The reason we do so is to develop a richer sense of the interplay of multiple objectives over a long time scale and, we hope, a simple model which adequately describes that interplay.

DEFERRED OBJECTIVES

After I explained how to use two input variables to specify the height and width of a door, Robby expressed a desire to make a park, 'Before we go into the fancy stuff, why don't we put in the grass'. He pointed to his chosen design in the shape menu, and I told him the procedure name was SAW. Neither of us knew what relation the specific input bore to the size of the figure. Robby decided to execute SAW [10]. The object created was a single sawtooth of size smaller than the turtle-cursor. He erased that and tried, at my suggestion, SAW [100]. Robby wanted grass extending from the house to the edge of the screen. What he got surprised us both.

> Robby: Hey! That's one big blade of grass.
> Bob: Oh ... you know what happened, Rob? This SAW procedure tried to make the grass 100 turtle steps high. That's not what you wanted .... I think you'd better erase that .... Go ahead, Rob, rub it out.
> Robby: No, it's going to be a playground.
> Bob: Oh ... I get the idea. [This is not a suggestion, but my empathetic grasp of what his motives were.] You want to keep that, like the swing set out back in Guildford [the town we formally lived in].
> Robby: Yeah.
> Bob: We can still put some grass in.
> Robby: No. It's going to be a tar playground.

The tendency with which Robby protected this accidental addition to his house was shown even more forcefully in what followed. He could not see any good way to get the turtle to the top of the 'swing', save trial and error. I suggested erasing the swing and re-creating that appearance by executing TRI [100], because I knew that the turtle would finish the procedure aligned under the top vertex of an equilateral triangle. From such a position, reaching the vertex would have been simple. Refusing this suggestion, Robby proceeded to the vertex by moving and turning the turtle little by little, reaching it precisely but in his own way at his own pace. Thence he drew the swing and seat of Fig. 1.2.

Demon procedures

Robby's adoption of adding a swing to his house can be described as the activation of a demon procedure. In the lexicon of Artificial Intelligence, 'demon' names a procedure which becomes active under the fulfillment of specific conditions. Think of Maxwell's demon: a little man who watches a strictly limited set of conditions and leaps into action when those conditions indicate the opportunity is right to effect his objective. Robby's 'swing demon' was created by our moving to Massachusetts. At our former home, the swing set was Robby's delight. When we moved, he expected to disassemble it and bring it with us. The unforeseen obstacle was the resistance of our new landlords; they would not permit such a swing on their property. I propose, then, that Robby's adding a swing to the HOUSE he had constructed, when he saw its achievement as being within reach, amounts to a *symbolic realisation* of a prior, frustrated objective. I specifically disavow making the Freudian claim that such symbolic realization satisfies whatever frustrations are entrained in an objective's failure. My proposal is different, that the symbolic realization of prior frustrated objectives explains a significant portion of those everyday objectives which a person adopts as he operates in a relatively unconstrained task domain.

OBJECTIVES	SOURCES	DEMONS							ACHIEVED
Encode a House	Programming	HOUSE							–
	Project	I							–
Bring Swing set	Moving	I	SWING						–
First square	HOUSE demon	X	I						YES
Bigger Square	Bob	I	I						YES
Add roof	HOUSE demon	X						→	YES
Add eaves	Elaboration		I						YES
Window	Elaboration		I	WINDOW					–
Door	Elaboration		I	I	DOOR				–
4-pane window	Elaboration		I	I	I				–
Dormer windows	Elaboration		I	I	I				–
Door	DOOR demon		I	I	X				–
Door knob	Elaboration		I	I	I				–
Grass	Rob (procedure)		I	I	I	GRASS			–
Yard (of grass)	Elaboration		I	I	I	I	YARD		–
Door	DOOR demon		I	I	X	I	I		–
Grass	GRASS demon		I	I	I	X	I		–
Swing set	SWING demon		X					→	YES
Tree (of yard)	Elaboration			I	I	I	I		YES
Person (of Tree)	Elaboration			I	I	I	I		–
Window	WINDOW demon			X	I	I	I		YES
Grass	GRASS demon			I	I	X		→	YES
Window	WINDOW demon			X				→	YES
Window 2	Elaboration				I		I		YES
Door	DOOR demon				X			→	YES
Window 3	Elaboration						I		–
Yard	YARD demon						X	→	YES
Seven grasses	Elaboration								YES

'X' indicates that the objective surfaced and either was achieved or deferred.

This chart is reproduced from a detailed analysis of the material summarized in the text. See in the text 'A retrospective account' for an explanation of the source of the HOUSE demon.

Fig. 1.4 – Inception and fulfillment of deferred objectives.

This proposal — call it the *demon objectives* proposal — implies first that there might be a multitude of objectives which could be activated at any time. This is very troublesome. One might ask whether it be possible to make any sense at all of behavior — in terms of the operation of such demon procedures — given their potentially enormous number. It *is* possible to do so. Fig. 1.4 exhibits such an analysis in detail of the components of the design H7GS.

The demon objectives proposal is troubling, most especially because with the 'symbolic realization' of objectives almost anything can symbolize anything. Such vagueness is possible that any interpretation might work. It is at this point that I must invoke a commitment to empirical detail as the guidance which can save us from the excessive fancy of a theorist's imagination. If one examines what is unusual about the interpretation of objective formation implicit in Fig. 1.4, he will notice that it depends especially on two factors: first is the unusual closeness, in a problem-solving study, of the experimenter and the subject (no non-intimate of the subject could claim such understanding without ridicule); second is the time scale as a factor or enormous significance.

To clarify the importance of time scale, I present here a second demon-driven interpretation of objective formation, one based on related material from a protocol taken in an earlier project with the same child. It also introduces a new issue of major importance. Robby's attempting to apply a successful solution to the next more complex objective in that earlier project encountered an unanticipated obstacle and generated a demon — an objective he failed to achieve and which was deferred for activation at some later time. I propose that Robby's choice of drawing a house as his initial and primary objective in H7GS derives from the following specific failure in a previous project.

A retrospective account — a house that failed

I told Robby I was going to make a procedure for him to try on his next visit to the Logo lab. I wrote TRI, a procedure for generating an equiangular triangle of 100 turtle steps on a side[4]. Robby was a little confused as to my purposes but followed step-wise my drawing the figure on our chalkboard and my encoding the procedure on a 3 X 5 card. I followed TRI with TINY, which draw a similar triangle of 30 units side measure.

```
TO TRI                TO TINY               TO FOX
   FORWARD 100           FORWARD 30            CLEARSCREEN
   RIGHT     120         RIGHT    120          SETHEADING 90  TRI
   FORWARD 100           FORWARD 30            LEFT 60  TINY
   RIGHT     120         RIGHT    120          RIGHT 60 FORWARD 70
   FORWARD 100           FORWARD 30            LEFT 60  TINY
   RIGHT     120         RIGHT    120          HIDETURTLE
   END                   END                   END
```

---

4 The Logo procedures encoded throughout the text conform generally to that of Apple Logo. Where departures are made (usually for historical reasons), I will make it clear. Since Logo is a high level language, the differences between various implementations with comparable machine features are minimal.

Thereupon I told Robby the idea was to make a FOX out of these two triangles, in the way he had learned from reading Ed Emberley's books. This caught his interest. We began FOX[5].

We simulated on our home blackboard the action of a Logo computer turtle. I arranged initial conditions so that at the completion of TRI the turtle was horizontal at the left vertex, pointing across the top of the head. To put on the ear we had to have him point differently. 'How much is half of 120', Robby asked me, then said the turtle must 'LEFT TURN 60' after my answer. What do we do next? Robby: 'TINY'. His decision to turn left 60 degrees worked. The FOX had one ear. We returned the turtle to the horizontal, went forward 70 turtle steps, did a left turn 60, and invoked TINY. Our FOX was complete. Robby showed his mother the procedure we had 'planned out' for our next trip to Logo and brought her to the chalkboard to see the FOX we had drawn. My objectives were completed, but Robby developed his own.

An unexpected elaboration

Robby asked me for a 3 X 5 card so he could write a procedure for a HOUSE. It is hard to be certain why Robby chose a house as his next project, but it is not unreasonable that, having worked through a FOX picture by assembling two triangles, Robby was attempting to create a house from a triangle and a square. One could judge this objective to be the next more complex task, thus a simple elaboration. I tried to help, but Robby said he wanted to do it alone. As I was leaving the room, he asked how much was half of 90. This question echoed his earlier query when attempting to figure out how much the turtle should turn before drawing the TINY ear. Half of 120 was, by chance, a good choice in that case. Half of 90 was not so lucky a choice in this second case. When I returned from some chores, I found on the chalkboard this triangle, with Robby standing puzzled before it.

Robby asked if 40 was the right length for the slope of the roof. I informed him that by choosing 45 degrees at the horizontal vertices he had gotten himself into a tough problem — not even I could tell him what the right number was just by looking at the triangle. He argued that 40 should work because 'when you make triangles out of tinker toys, if you use two blue ones for the side, you use

5 Employing the figure assembly techniques described in Ed Emberley's books, Robby's practice was to make elaborate and extensive drawings at nearly every opportunity. His figure assembly skills were well developed.

the next bigger size, a red one, for the longer part; and 50 is like the next bigger size from 40'. Should I have told him about the square root of 2? I did say that with triangles, the next bigger size for the side depends on the angle, that 45 degrees made things tough but that 60 degrees was a good number and that's why the FOX had worked out so well. Robby was clearly in over his head. He decided he was going to stop because the problem was too hard and he had to leave for a birthday party. He folded his work and threw it in the trash whence I retrieved it later. You can see his drawing of the house he failed to encode in Fig. 1.5.

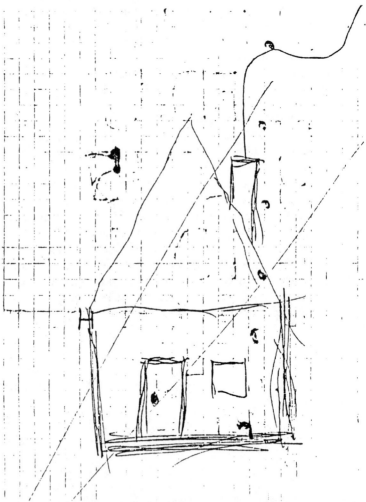

The main points of similarity between this failed-house of Robby's earlier programming project and the house of H7GS are: general proportions, existence of a door and window (and the doorknob which Rob also failed to get in H7GS); the scribble at the bottom of his drawing may have re-appeared as his first successful use of the HAIR procedure to represent grass.

Fig. 1.5 – A house that failed.

Shadow domains

In this incident, one can see exhibited the guidance of problem-solving within the task domain (Logo programming) by values appropriate to what I call a 'shadow domain'. Logo commands are typically formed by an operation (*what to do*) and an operand (*how much* of it). Note that Robby had a good sense of operations in that domain. He knew about going forward, about turning, about making procedures, but his use of these ideas was imperfect, in the sense of how to apply them to this specific problem. What recourse has he? He chose to operate in the task domain with operand values derived from the shadow domain, as his explicit analogy makes clear: he assigned distance values in this new domain, Logo language programming, on the basis of relations applying in a shadow domain, in this case the play world of tinker toys, to which he assimilated his coding judgements. Should this surprise anyone? Is not an operand — the how much or how many of an action — the finer specification of choosing what is to be done? If one is familiar merely with the operations of a domain, is it not reasonable that judgments of quantity and relation might still lag behind familiarity with operations? In precisely this sense and at such a specific point, the values of a shadow domain could be used to guide judgements in a task domain.

To understand problem-solving in a task domain, one must be sensitive to existing shadow domains — whatever they are and however many they may be. There exists some more profound relation that must be considered in the problem-solving environment than a simple assignment of external objects to internal categories. This more profound relation is an expression of the fundamental problem-deforming character of mind. The impact of such guiding knowledge on problem solving *must* be considered and *can* be considered; *this is a central postulate of my work.* Let us now attempt a deeper characterization of these shadow domains and the development of objectives.

REFLECTIONS
Shadow domains and cognitive structures

We have seen how this little shadow world of 'tinker toy' play entered into one child's problem solving in a programming task domain. One could label such a thing analogy and let it go as something vaguely understood. I choose, however, to pursue the character of such shadow domains by a more extended analysis of this example. Consider first that the guidance of problem solving by past experience *can only be* through the cognitive structures of mind. The child has constructed within his mind symbolic descriptions of his past little worlds of experience — call such a structure a microview[6] — which is useful not only in tinker-toy play but also as a model which provides guidance to him for solving newly encountered problems in different task domains. Three characteristics of this tinker toy microview stand out as especially noteworthy: the concreteness

---

6 The character, development, and interaction of such microviews is explored through the empirically based analyses of this book. A compact overview is presented in Chapter 7, 'The genesis of microviews'.

of the objects of the world; the usefulness of the knowledge about them for guiding problem solving; their procedural genesis.

With respect to concreteness, note that the rods not only have well-defined properties of length and assembly-relations, they are also specified by their color coding. The salience of such accidental properties as color (for objects whose most important relations in normal play use are geometrical) implies that microviews may be more experience bound and particular than is logically necessary. An implication of this fact is that the use of such microviews with particular problems encountered may be highly idiosyncratic. If the child preserves too much concrete detail of his past experiences, his problem-solving attempts could be more hindered than helped by such guidance. Is not this all too often the case?

The use of one body of knowledge, e.g. the tinker-toy microview, to provide explicit guidance in problem solving in a different task domain, programming in turtle geometry, emphasizes its model-like character. Robby called upon his knowledge about tinker toys — and that of number sequences simultaneously — to form an hypothesis about what might be reasonable operands for turtle geometry commands. At least two observations are appropriate here. First, such a style of problem solving helps explain the genesis of hypotheses in fact, whether or not one can feel logically entitled to use the information[7].

This observation raises serious questions about the value of any description of problem solving which focusses on a single task domain. If shadow domains play an important role in problem solving, if the invocation of knowledge appropriate to the microviews constructed from earlier experience guides problem-solving behaviour in novel situations, any study of problem solving sharply focussed on a task domain alone is vulnerable to the criticism that the task itself may inhibit the characteristic operations of natural intelligence. Secondly, if new microviews are constructed within the mind through problem-solving expriences and if the shadow domains of prior microviews guide problem-solving behavior in novel situations, can it be doubted that there must be a very potent 'genetic' influence of prior experience on the development of new cognitive structures[8]. This in turn suggests that it might be fruitful to think of the mind as having a control structure of invokable knowledge which embodies the genetic path of descent[9]. To the extent that any description of mind — however precise and formal — cannot encompass such an organization of knowledge, it is inadequate to represent human mentality even in the relatively simple area of problem solving. Any theory which undervalues the functional and developmental importance of such an organization of structures will misguide those who follow it, no matter how great its owner virtues may be.

7 There is a major issue here, the validity of induction which, like a hidden shoal, I would prefer to avoid. Note in the extended citation 'Goodman: On rightness of rendering' his reference to frantic attempts to justify the process of induction. Prefer, if you can, his more balanced view.

8 I use 'genetic' here in the specific sense of Piaget's genetic epistemology; I have no intention of raising or arguing in this place any questions of the relative influence of experience and biological inheritance.

9 What this might mean in practical terms and how one might gather evidence for or against such a conjecture are central issues dealt with in Chapters 2 through 5 of this book.

Generalization and classification

We can say a procedure becomes progressively generalized in application as it is used first with one variation then another. Thus a concrete procedure used within a task domain becomes a tool applicable over the range of that domain[10]. But the microviews in the mind may be more than collections of procedures. They have — or at least seem to have — existential implications. How can it be the case that a procedure could serve a classificatory function? To the extent that a procedure has become a tool which functions over a limited domain, the question can be put to it whether or not a specific object would serve a specific role in the functioning of the procedure. The question 'Is X a kind-of-thing?' can be reduced to 'Will X work in your procedure which applies to such kinds-of-things?' This is a commonplace question, one which every problem solver asks when seeking substitutes caused by some material shortage which blocks achievement of his objective with some ongoing procedure.

Generalization and objective formation

Given that one can understand how a provided procedure such as SAW, which Robby used for making grass, could be made into a tool through progressive variablization of salient inputs, we might next ask how created procedures such as HOUSE could also be turned into tools. The HOUSE procedure is context-bound in the following senses. Consider the HOUSE as portrayed in the picture of H7GS (Fig. 1.2). That HOUSE is composed of a large square and triangle with a door and two windows as essential features; call that HOUSE 'HDW' (for HOUSE-DOOR-WINDOW). 'HDW' does not exist independently of the specific design in H7GS. For the HOUSE 'HDW' to exist as a tool, its embodiment in a procedure would require extraction from the context in which it developed as a construct. Creation of such a tool would show generalization as context de-sensitization. Robby did not show this form of behavior. No one should be surprised at failing to see such an event: one should expect such generalization to take some time and to wait on the adoption of some objectives of greater scope wherein the development of such a tool would be useful.

A second, specific sense in which the HOUSE is context-bound is in respect of scale, i.e. the HOUSE, in however many instantiations it might appear, would always be the same size. Let me exhibit some Logo instructions to variablize a HOUSE, thus turning this object into a tool[11]:

---

10 If one pushed a vision of the child as scientist, one might want to argue that he is 'testing an hypothesis' about the application of his theory to a particular case. A slightly weaker position is that the child is exploring the range of application of his procedure. This is still 'scientific' in the sense of many physical laws, such as Hooke's law of elasticity, which they apply. More importantly, it emphasizes the abductive rather than inductive character of the inferences involved. See, however, my final characterization of Miriam italicized at the end of 'A cognitive profile' in the Appendix (p. 221).

11 A short technical note. The procedures invoked here, BOX and TRI, were written to take lists as inputs and implement default values for variables not specified; consequently their syntax is quite non-standard.

```
TO HOUSE.CONSTRUCT          TO HOUSE.TOOL :HOWBIG
    BOX [100]                   BOX [ :HOWBIG]
    PEN UP                      PEN UP
    FORWARD 100                 FORWARD :HOWBIG
    PEN DOWN                    PEN DOWN
    TRI [140]                   TRI [ (7 * :HOWBIG/5) ]
    END                         END
```

As an overview of the process of making tools from objects in this domain, we should expect the developmental sequence to consist of at least these three steps: creation of a concrete object for specific purpose; context desensitization of the procedure which produces the object; use of the procedure as a tool by its invocation from a higher level of control. The purpose, either explicit or implicit, of such an endeavor is to create components for some project of larger scope — which could only be imagined as possible given the achievability of its components.

Implicit in these forms of context desensitization, implicit in the repeated use of a procedure as a tool, is the creation of structure through the invocation of the procedure from a higher level of procedural control.[12]

The unified generalization proposal

I propose that the process by which a concrete procedure is transformed into a tool is the same process by which a demon is created, that the failed objective capable of symbolic realization is the cognate of the tool created from the achieved objective. Let us call this idea the 'unified generalization' proposal. Let us look more closely at the parallel. If one notices that any objective implies a structure, a temporal and serial structure of the process of pursuing that objective. First, actions achieved by procedures serve objectives. The structure of all actions have beginnings, middles, and ends. The simplest such action structures, wherein the middle has no significant complication, proceed nearly directly to achievement of the objective. The simplest elaborations are of such a form. When that process occurs (whatever it may be) which transforms the serial structure of pursuing an objective into components of control structure, there is no reason to suppose that objectives should be immune from the context desensitization that is implicated in generalization. This is precisely what symbolic realization of objectives requires. If you compare the little procedures for the HOUSE.CONSTRUCT and HOUSE.TOOL, you will notice that it is precisely the objective achievable by the procedure that is changed. In this specific sense, the symbolic realization of a demonic objective does not appear markedly different from the generalized application of a procedure which has been transformed into a tool. At this level of description it is possible to unify the problems of generalization and objective formation. A schematic represenation of the unified generalization proposal is presented in the box.

---

12 This is a central theme of the book; its more precise exposition and its role in learning appear more explicitly in Chapters 2 and 4 where it is discussed as the elevation of control. See also the extended citation 'Papert: On the elevation of control' (p. 247).

BEGINNING:
An initial objective becomes active
    — when its procedure appears achievable in a domain
OUTCOMES:
The initial objective succeeds:
    — this leads to a new objective through elaboration
    — the procedure becomes a more generalized tool
The initial objective fails:
    — this leads to a new objective through demon formation
    — the objective of the failed procedure becomes variablized, that is,
        symbolically realizable; at its furthest extreme, this permits
        detachment from the local context and procedure which created it
CONSEQUENCES:
Any new objectives can become an initial objective
The range of the procedures' efficacy is determined

A system such as that represented in the box is a creative, closed system. Objectives proliferate, some to be achieved after deferral, others to be permanently lost. Such a formulation shows how ideas and objectives may develop in a specific way in an individual mind. Nothing implies, obviously, that all objectives are determined exclusively by operations in such a closed system. For example, different bodily needs can provide starting points for diverse families of elaborated objectives (hunger, sex, etc.). Beyond the achievement of objectives, there may also be other motives for mental action. A second class might be represented by curiosity, seen as a primitive inclination to explore imperfectly understood phenomena; a third class might be purely expressive, as the poet G. M. Hopkins asserts:

> Each mortal thing does one thing and the same;
> Deals out that being indoors each one dwells;
> Selves — goes itself; *myself* it speaks and spells,
> Crying *what* I *do* is me: for that I came.

Constraining the behavior one examines by pre-setting objectives, as in typical laboratory experiments, inhibits the surfacing of those processes which reflect the nature of mentality as revealed through its self-control. The kind of analysis represented by the body of this paper, to the extent that it applies to behavior less constrained than laboratory samples, is truer to the nature of the mind. However unsatisfactory the conceptual machinery for coping with the analysis of such challenges as Robby's HOUSE, restricting oneself to simpler problems will lead to solutions entirely inadequate to represent important processes of the natural mind. If we fail to tackle such problems as Robby's HOUSE (which is constrained by the medium more than by any objective), we miss a major component of mentality, perhaps *the* major component. We might even see demon-driven structures as a searching of domains so limited that nearly all demons are inhibited. We might see isolated problem spaces constructed by experiments. We will miss not only solutions, but also profound problems of mentality.

How general are these ideas

One may ask, given that these notions are built on a few ideas and illustrations, whether or not the characterization of mind is sufficiently general to warrant interest and exploration. Against the goal-dominated activities of programmed intelligence, I hold out a contrasting characterization of human action, based on a much better broader base of diverse cognitive study than analyses of my children's problem solving.

Claude Lévi-Strauss describes the concrete thought of not-yet-civilized people as *bricolage*[13], a French word naming the activity of the *bricoleur* (a man who undertakes odd jobs, a sort of jack-of-all-trades or, more precisely, a committed do-it-yourself man). The essential idea of bricolage is the looseness of commitment to specific goals, the idea that materials, structures, and competences developed for one purpose are transferable, can very easily be used to advantage in the satisfaction of alternative objectives. Lévi-Strauss's appreciation of bricolage is sufficiently profound to the worthy of both quotation and extended examination[14].

> ... The bricoleur is adept at performing a large number of diverse tasks; but, unlike the engineer, he does not subordinate each of them to the availability of raw materials and tools conceived and procured for the purpose of the project. His universe of instruments is closed and the rules of his game are always to make do with 'whatever is at hand' .... *In the continual reconstruction from the same materials, it is always earlier ends which are called upon to play the part of means* .... This formula, which could serve as the definition of '*bricolage*', explains how an implicit inventory or conception of the total means available must be made ... so that a result can be defined which will always be a compromise between the structure of the instrumental set and that of the project .... The bricoleur may not ever complete his purpose but he always puts something of himself into it ....

In this description, one can appreciate the opposition of planning (the epitome of goal-directed behaviour) and the opportunism of demon-driven bricolage. This seems an idea profoundly antithetical to the goal-driven commitments of cybernetics and artificial intelligence. Observe, however, that the two are not discontinuous, that all activities can be seen as a mixture of the dominances of the polar tendencies represented here. The second point, not the less important, is that the relationship is not directional: there is no reason to suppose that planning is a more nearly perfect form of bricolage. If some inclusion relation must be sought, one could easily view planning as a highly specialized technique for solving critical problems whose solutions demand scarce resources.

13 For more detail, see the extended citation 'Lévi-Strauss: On Bricolage' (p. 250).
14 Pp. 17, 21 in *The Savage Mind*, University of Chicago Press, 1966.

BROADER CONSIDERATIONS

Over the past century, we have witnessed a widespread abandonment of the concept of 'free will,' an idea useful to individuals and society but one for which there is no sensible proposal at mechanical levels of description. Theorists of mind have striven to replace the individual who directs his thinking with some other alternative. Freud introduced fragmentation of the person into three active and competing homunculi: the individual becomes the body housing the Ego, Id, and Superego. For Freud, the apparently integral personality is a projection by society and the self on the resultant behavior of these three primitive forces and their processes of interaction.

Minsky and Papert, in the *Society Theory of Mind*, push the fragmentation and competition of the Freudian vision to its logical completion in the attempt to banish from the mind any trace of a mysterious homunculus[15]. Instead of three struggling fragments of self, they proposed societies of agents – each agent so simple it could be represented by a comprehensible computational process. For me, the image of mind as a society of computing agencies did not make satisfactory contact with the issue of how a person can feel himself to be related to the many subordinate processes from which others might see his behavior to emerge. Lévi-Strauss's characterization of bricolage seemed to fill the critical need – relating a computational theory to a more human image of man – and to go considerably beyond it.

To the extent that bricolage, and not planning, is the best characterization of objective-related human behavior in everyday situations, introducing the idea of bricolage into the AI community could permit the development of machine intelligence with some creativity in generating goals[16]. But further, and much more importantly, if behavior is seen as driven by a bricoleur's objectives and if one constructs his own mind out of concrete experiences, then the metaphor might be extended to bring Piagetian mental self-construction (currently the best theory of human learning) within the range of a non-demeaning mechanical vision of mind.

The functional lability of cognitive structures

Students of anatomy have named the adaptiveness of structures to alternative purposes *functional lability*. Such functional lability is the essential characteristic of the bricoleur's use of his tools and materials. I propose that bricolage can serve as a metaphor for the relation of a person to the contents and processes of his mind. Bricolage, as a name for the functional lability of cognitive structures, emphasizes the character of the processes in terms of human action and can

15 A research program and an assemblage of ideas while I was their colleague, the society of mind theory represents the intellectual backdrop against which my work may be seen as the major empirical investigation of learning developed in that MIT community during the late 1970s. Minsky continues his effort to produce a work which will make these ideas generally accessible as a theory.

16 An example bearing on this contention is the program AM which has succeeded in inventing the idea of number. The program is described in the thesis by Douglas Lenat, 'AM: An Artificial Intelligence Approach to Discovery in Mathematics as Heuristic Search'. For a perspicuous analysis of the successes of that program, see *Why AM and EURISKO Seemed to Work*, by Lenat and Brown (1983).

guide us in exploring how a coherent mind could rise out of the concreteness of specific experience.

Bricolage presents a very human model for the development of objectives, for learning, and even a model for the interaction of the texture of experience and the symbolic descriptions through which people think. This represents not a mere metaphor in some superficial sense but a radical idea[17]. Every new idea is a metaphor; what is important is its fecundity. An idea becomes a radical metaphor precisely to the extent that its ramifications are found to be richly productive, in practice, in other domains. Functional lability is witnessed in diverse other areas as well, for example in the process of physical evolution, and in the development of civilization. Consider these important examples.

Functional lability in the evolution of flight

How did dinosaurs turn into birds? A team of researchers at Northern Arizona University proposed an explanation for the development of powered flight which appears to be a significant breakthrough in our understanding of this major evolutionary change[18]. It is valuable for my purposes as a clear example of functional lability which emphasizes both the step-wise adaptedness of precursors and the locus of creativity.

A number of people have believed that powered flight derived from soaring as the membranes of tree-dwelling gliders somehow changed into muscular wings. The details of this scheme comprise the arboreal theory of flight. A competing theory, the cursorial theory, has been much strengthened by the breakthrough of Caple, Balda, and Willis. This team created a series of models of successive forms of 'proavis' and then established the progressive adaptedness of each of these models by coupling appropriate aerodynamic arguments with a cost–benefit analysis of specific behaviors. A sketch of their assumptions and arguments is as follows.

Assuming first that the ancestors of birds were insectivorous dinosaurs, the theory measures good adaptedness with the criterion of 'foraging volume', the space within which the creature might capture bugs in a given time. The greater the foraging volume, the better a creature could compete. Since bipedalism produces a higher reach and speed covers a greater area, one or both should be expected to develop. Well articulated, supple movement would provide more effective penetration of that foraging volume, as would the ability to jump at any point in a running course, so the well-balanced control of movement by itself would favor those creatures which possessed it. These issues of balance and control become increasingly important as running speed increases. The location of considerable mass in a biped's forelimbs which could extend far beyond the radius of the body would provide significant control. The conclusion is that 'wings' developed because of the adaptive advantage of better balance in the air and on landing after a jump, not for flight.

17 A philosopher I once knew, Hunter Mead, aesthetician and student of Susanne Langer, argued often with me the point that every philosophical system begins with a radical metaphor, a root from which it grows, branches, and is nourished.

18 My version is based on the article 'How Did Vertebrates Take to the Air?' by Roger Lewin in the Research News section of *Science* (July 1, 1983). The original by Caple, Balda, and Willis appeared in the *American Naturalist* (**121**, 455 (1983)).

Any flattening of these balancing forelimbs would provide lift[19], thus permitting the extension of this increase in foraging volume through gliding on limbs already powered to exercise control of attitude. A similar effect would be achieved by extension of proto-wings through the elongation of scales and their transformation into feathers. The effect of lift would be to increase stability and thus permit greater running speed, and thus greater lift again, both of which extend further the predator's foraging volume.

In summary, three different physical changes lead to positive increases in foraging volume: bipedalism, increased running speed, and controlled jumping at speed. Because of the physics of the world, limbs extended to control the trajectory during a high-speed jump experience lift. Since this lift increases with increased speed and since it also increases the stability of the running creature, a positive feedback condition develops where more speed produces more lift and this in turn produces more speed. The creature takes off. Once in th air, those very limb movements which facilitate trajectory control, when coordinated, serve as the power stroke of flight.

The character revealed in this example of evolution is one where opportunistic systems are constrained into paths of a step-wise development which pemit coupling of physical effects of the milieu. The magic comes from the functional lability of physical structures (the leg becomes an arm functional lability of physical structures (the leg becomes an arm becomes balancing mass becomes an airfoil) in a world where serendipity is possible and development irreversible.

Functional lability in the invention of writing

The Sumerians of Mesopotamia are usually credited with being the first people to write texts, about 3000 BC. The writing system had two basic character types: objects used as counters, numerical signs, were pressed into a clay surface; all other signs, pictographs and ideographs alike, were incised with the pointed end of a stylus. This invention is surely one of the central events in the history of civilization. It is possible to advance well-reasoned arguments that make this creation comprehensible. More specifically, with the domestication of plants and animals around 8500 BC, as Schmandt-Besserat observes:

> The new agricultural economy, although it undoubtedly increased the production of food, would have been accompanied by new problems. Perhaps the most crucial would have been food storage. Some portion of each annual yield had to be allocated for the farm family's subsistence and some portion had to be set aside as seed for the next year's crop. Still another portion could have been reserved for barter with those who were ready to provide exotic products and raw materials in exchange

19 Lift is the common name for the Bernoulli effect, the pressure differential created by airflow around an asymmetrical convex object. If such an object, an airfoil, is flat on the bottom and curved on top, it will experience a net pressure up.

for foodstuffs. It seems possible that the need to keep track of such allocations and transactions was enough to stimulate development of a recording system[20].

The recording system which satisfied these needs, one where specific clay tokens represented quantities, was very stable. It spread throughout the region of western Asia and remained current there for four thousand years. The second major step followed another cultural landmark, the emergence of cities.

> The development of an urban economy, rooted in trade, must have multiplied the demands on the traditional recording system. Not only production, but also inventories, shipments and wage payments had to be noted, and merchants needed to preserve records of their transaction.[21]

Most significant seems to have been the development of token-based contracts. These contracts are represented now by clay envelopes, usually sealed with the marks of two merchants, hardened by baking, and containing within them the numeric tokens representing the amount of goods exchanged. With such a contract in hand, a middle-man could transport goods from one city to another with a guarantee to all that neither the shipment nor the terms has been altered. But, since the contract was validated by remaining unopened, one could not tell what it said without destroying it; consequently, it became customary to impress on the outside of the envelope the shapes of the tokens contained inside. The tokens were pressed into the clay envelope with a mnemonic intention based on one-to-one correspondence; the marks they made came to represent the contents of the envelope. The external markings were not invented to replace the tokens sealed within the clay envelopes, but that is what, in fact, happened. And this replacement of tokens, signs of things, by symbols — the impressions they made

According to this scenario, writing was not invented to transmit ideas; but in the history of the West it has been a most powerful force in doing that, the primary means by which man has been able to extend communication beyond the circle of his immediate acquaintance, both in space and time. The functional lability of written symbols permitted a flowing of effects to derive from the adaptive development of writing's precursor, and accounting function, in response to a sequence of specific needs.

I see in this cultural example, and in Jacob's vision of evolution[22] the same processes of bricolage whereby an active agent applies pre-existing resources to new problems — through which process he defines what is novel in the problem and extends by modification his earlier resources. Occasionally these newly modified resources have a far wider application than their precursors. Such functional lability, developed through application to particular problems, is the root of creativity in evolution, culture, and personal development.

20 This citation and general view is derived from 'The Earlist Precursors of Writing' by Denise Schmandt-Besserat in *Scientific American*, June 1978.
21 Schmandt-Besserat, op. cit.
22 See the extended citation 'Jacob: On Bricolage in Evolution' (p. 253).

We can bring this broad-ranging claim down to earth in the case of cognitive development by trying to penetrate more deeply into the Piagetian notions of assimilation and accomodation.

BRICOLAGE AS PROBLEM DEFORMATION

People frequently confuse 'abstract' with 'generally applicable'. What one *does* could apply generally and merely seem abstract if problems in the external world are deformed to fit processing by highly particular structures of the individual mind. Piaget named such a process of problem deformation 'assimilation', taking that name at various times both from an alimentary metaphor and processes of linguistic change. If we move in the direction of more logical descriptions, the most apt way to characterize such a mind's logic in action is as proceeding less by deductive or indicative logics than by what C. S. Peirce named 'abduction'.[23]

> [Abductive inference] ... is where we find some very curious circumstance, which would be explained by the supposition that it was a case of a certain general rule, and thereupon adopt that supposition.

Peirce's theory of types of inference: simple examples:

DEDUCTIVE INFERENCE

the rule: All the beans are from this bag are white.
the case: These beans are from this bag.
implied result: These beans are white.

INDUCTIVE INFERENCE

the case: These beans are from this bag.
the result: These beans are white.
implied result: All the beans from this bag are white.

ABDUCTIVE INFERENCE

the rule: All the beans are from this bag are white.
the result: These beans are white.
implied case: These beans are from this bag.

Peirce's terms 'rule', 'result', and 'case' translate into a more concrete vision of the evolving mind as follows. The 'rule' becomes a cognitive structure, a model of a situation, what is known in the mind. The 'result' is the problem situation actually confronted. It presents immediate data such as 'these beans are white'. The implied case is the interpretation of the problem through the model.

---

23 Peirce, the major American philosopher of the nineteenth century, wrote popular articles as well as more technical work. His most accessible work, well represented by the essay 'The Fixation of Belief', is both profound and charming. The idea of abduction sketched below was introduced in his essay 'Deduction, Induction, and Hypothesis'. A technical analysis of his developing ideas of logical fundamentals may be found in *Peirce's Theory of Abduction*, by K. T. Fann.

Abduction is prior to deduction and induction. This formulation emphasizes that a primary aspect of problem solving is the adopting of a hypothesis
about 'what's what'. The perspective from which you view a situation determines
what problem you imagine you are attempting to solve. This is so less by choice
than by necessity: one can recognize the unfamiliar only by first misapprehending
it as something familiar, then progressively distinguishing it from things actually
familiar in the past. Thus, the core of abductive inference in human problem
solving is the deformation of problems to fit the recognizing processes of models
in the mind.

The best computational embodiment of such a view of mind is presented in
Sussmann's HACKER system (Sussmann, 1975), wherein a mental 'programmer'
perfects old programs and assembles new ones with the guidance of failure
information from its previous mis-appreciations of presented problems. Similarly,
the Merlin system (Moore and Newell, 1973) matches a target/goal description
against stored descriptions by some higher-level process making terms variable
until partial equivalence is achieved at some level of variation. In contrast, the
essential element of my vision of the evolving mind is that a number of active
descriptions apply themselves simultaneously, each performing its best match/
deformation, and those with sufficiently good match to the specific problem
go forward while other competitors infer nonsense and inapplicable results. It is
difficulty of applying generated conclusions that defeats the parallel effort of
the less successful competitors.

With such a vision of mind, it is possible to understand how generally
applicable skills arise from the coordination of diverse structures based upon
particular experiences with processes that are more like abduction than generalization[24].

Bricolage, as a name for the functional lability of cognitive structures, with
its focus on the interaction of pre-existing tools and available materials, helps to
explain the power of the particular in determining the course of development.
Here is a profound convergence, permitting a unification of points of view
through which the form of evolution of species, the rise of civilization, and the
pattern of development of the individual mind can be seen as the parallel results
of the same sorts of historically determinate processes.

Bricolage and cognitive structures

What are the practical advantages of discerning human activity as bricolage in
contrast to goal-driven planning? The first advantage is that it is more natural,
a more fit description of everyday activity than planning is. The second is that it is
more nearly compatible with a view of the mind as a process than is planning,
which seems to call for a single center of decision or a chain of decisions in a pre-
ordered form. The final and most important advantage permits a new vision of the
process of learning. Bricolage can provide us with an image for the process of the
mind under self-construction in these specific respects:

---

24 Chapters 2 and 4 show extensive, detailed examples of how such ideas can be applied in
   describing a specific mind and its development.

- if the resources of the individual's mind are viewed as being like the tools and materials of the bricoleur, one can appreciate immediately how they constrain our undertaking and accomplishing any activity;
- not only constraint comes from this set of limited resources; also comes productivity, the creation of new things — perhaps not exactly suited to the situation but of genuine novelty;
- the mind, if seen as self-constructed through bricolage, presents a clear image of the uniqueness of every person:
  - each will have developed his own history of conceptions and appreciations of situations through which to make sense of the world;
  - each will have his personal 'bag of tricks', knowledge and procedures useful in his past;
  - each will have his own set of different, alternative objectives to take up as chance puts the means at his disposal.

If viewed as claims, such statements are not easy to prove. However, they provide a framework for investing learning which could be valuable by *not* demeaning human nature through assuming it is more simple than we know to be the case. With such an intention, it is reasonable to ask if these ideas can be applied to a specimen of behavior — one able to sustain extended analysis — so that we may return with a richer and more precise application of how the development of objectives and learning create the self-constructed mind.

Implications for method

The image of bricolage, when extended from a description of behavior to a characterization of typical human thought, suggests how to explore human behavior for evidence about mind. It gives hints of what to look for in the search for the psychologically real (concrete experiences and their sequelae). It emphasizes the importance of following an individual's selection of activities and the need for sensitivity to cultural expressions in tracing the development of mind on a Piagetian scale of development. Given that such observation has provided a fecund method to study the development of objectives, should it not be extensible for the exploration affects the mind and how significant learning happens in concrete situations? After this analysis of Robby's project, such questions generated The Intimate Study.

2

The progressive construction of mind[1]

Pas de genese sans structures; pas de structures sans genèse.

J. Piaget

STUDYING NATURAL LEARNING

I follow Piaget's paradox 'There can be no development without structures nor any structures without development', arguing by example that one can understand learning with structural conceptions and that one can understand cognitive structures in detail by tracing their development. Focussing on changes in the organization of distinct and separate cognitive structures, I explain some significant learning as enhancements of performance which emerge from small changes in that organization. From the corpus of The Intimate Study, which is reasonably complete with respect to her behavior relative to addition, I have extracted the following story of Miriam's learning to add and on it erected an interpretation of how that learning happened.

My focus on the particularity of knowlege exhibits a primary stance of this research. I hope to avoid abstractions and the process of 'abstraction' by describing the emergence of broadly applicable skills from the interaction of highly particular knowledge with specific experiences. This objective was a basic motive for amassing so detailed a corpus. What we workers in the field all seek is a very specific and relatively precise theory of the emergence of a complicated organization of mind. Any such theory, to the extent that it argues behavior and development emerge from the interaction of competing cognitive structures,

1 An earlier version of this analysis appeared as Lawler, R. W. (1981), The progressive construction of mind, *Cognitive Science*, 5, 1–34.

would be a species of equilibration theory. It it is argued further that the control structure of mind embodies the genetic path of learning, such a sought-for theory would be an extension of the Piagetian vision of mind.

As a guide for the reader, Fig. 2.1 offers a chronology of calculations cited and the main insights Miriam experienced on her path to mastery of addition. Because the case material presented here deals with simple arithmetic, a reader might believe that our theme is 'addition'. This is too limited a view. Our theme is learning. But you can't learn about learning nothing; you can only learn about learning something. How to add is one of the 'somethings' which I observed this child master in our attempts to learn about learning.

AGE	EVENTS
(year;month;day)	
before 5;0;0	counting objects
before 6;0;0	playing with coins
before 6;0;0	15¢ + 15¢ = 30¢
6;0;9	17 + 6 = 23 by counting
6;0;9	89 + 14 = . . . (failure)
6;0;23	playing with computers
	typical calculations:
	100 − 20 = 80
	55 + 22 = 77
	55 + 26 = 70:11−76
6;0;26	Decadal view insight
6;0;28	ninety degrees is special
6;1;20	first instruction in paper sums
6;3;6	idiosyncratic addition (reduction to nines)
6;3;7	interrupt computer play
	for remote vacation
6;3;16	Serial view insight
6;3;23	spontaneous calculation with Serial world
6;3;25	resume computer play
6;4;28	60 + 90 = 500?
6;5;24	proving 96 + 96 = 192 by Serial addition
	and with 90 + 90 = known result
6;5;29	9 + 9 = 8 + 8 + 2 = 16 + 2 = 18
6;6;12	75 + 26 = 101 by Serial addition
	75¢ + 26 = $1.01 by coin equivalences
6;8;31	Conformal view insights
6;9;28	imperfect vertical sums
6;10;5	perfect vertical sums

(Underscore signifies continuing activity)

These activities, calculations, insights, and their calculations are discussed in the text.

Fig. 2.1 − Steps in the mastery of addition.

THE ORGANIZATION OF DISPARATE STRUCTURES

My commitment is to explore how disparate, i.e. separate and distinct, structures of knowledge interact and become integrated. What are the phenomena that argue there is such disparateness of related cognitive structures? The following example, which I offer to represent the general case, is based on material from late in the study and shows three different solutions to the 'same' problem. I asked Miriam, 'How much is seventy-five plus twenty-six?' She answered, 'Seventy, ninety, ninety-six, ninety-seven, ninety-eight, ninety-nine, one hundred, one-oh-one [counting up the last five numbers on her fingers]'. I continued immediately, 'How much is seventy-five cents and twenty-six?' She replied, 'That's three quarters, four and a penny, a dollar one'. Presented later with the same problem as a paper sum in the vertical form of addition, she would have added right to left with carries. Three different structures apparently could operate on the same problem. The evidence about the disparateness of structures is that Miriam did not, in fact, apply the result of the first calculation to the second formulation of the problem. Moreover, for a long time she did not relate paper sums to mental calculation at all. We may infer, further, that structures differ in their analysis of what the significant parts of the problem are and how those parts are manipulated to reach a solution.[2] One structure analyzes the problem in terms of multiples of ten and counting numbers. Another deals with coin denominations and known equivalences. The third deals with the columns of digits and their interactions. Ginsberg (1977), in dwelling on the 'gap' between children's formal and informal knowledge of arithmetic, witnesses that the disparateness of knowledge is more common than rare. Finally, observing that how a problem is presented affects which specific structure engages the problem confirms the disparateness of cognitive structures in general.

Fig. 2.2 exhibits a microview of counting knowledge, which I have labelled Count.[3] In answer to the particular problem of Fig. 2.2, which I posed in the initial test of Miriam's calculation skills, she said, 'Well, seventeen [then finger counting by the value of the second addend], eighteen, nineteen, twenty, twenty-one, twenty-two, twenty-three. Twenty-three is the answer'. This counting knowledge was limited in scope, so, although Miriam might add 89 plus 7 by finger counting, she couldn't add 89 plus 14. Her occasional use of hash marks — vertical strokes drawn on a piece of paper — instead of fingers to work out sums beyond ten testifies to the firm rootedness of this knowledge in one-to-one correspondence. (In arguing with her brother about a large sum, before the beginning of The Intimate Study, Miriam represented an addend by drawing hash marks on a paper napkin.)

A NEW WORLD OF EXPERIENCE

If some knowledge comes from experience, new experiences bear special scrutiny for the role they have in engendering new knowledge. One significant new element in The Intimate Study was Miriam's engagement with Logo language computer

---

2 This position is similar to one advanced by Goodman in *Ways of World Making*. See his discussion under the sub-heading 'Weighting' in Chapter 1 of his book.
3 For a general discussion of the structure and organization of microviews, see Chapter 7.

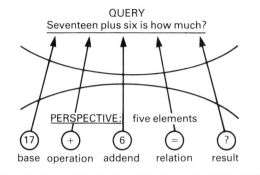

QUERY
Seventeen plus six is how much?

PERSPECTIVE: five elements

(17) (+) (6) (=) (?)
base operation addend relation result

Functions:	Examples:
Well-known results:	2 + 2 = 4, etc.
Procedures:	COUNT-UP:
	— Anchor at base value.
	— Increment the base, raising
	fingers until their count
	equals addend.
Cascades of activity:	(see Fig. 2.4)

(Arrows flow away from centres of control.)

The Perspective, a collection of active structured descriptions, analyzes a query into elements. Functions execute upon element values to produce output.

Fig. 2.2 – The Count microview.

systems.[4] Most of our working sessions occurred at MIT's Logo Project. Many involved play with computer systems using the Logo language. The central activity through which children have been introduced to Logo is 'turtle geometry'[5]. That children's mathematical world is a geometry of action. The child specifies commands, e.g. 'move forward some distance' or 'turn right through some angle', for execution by a computer-driven agent, known as the 'turtle'. The turtle exists in two forms: a small floor robot and a triangular cursor on a video display. The turtle is equipped with a pen which will, on command, draw a line as the turtle moves from one place to another. The commands of movement, rotation, and pen control provide a drawing tool — one significantly different from children's other experiences because of the pervasive quantification required by the use of the turtle commands.

4 Logo is used here with three different meanings: first as the name of a computer programming language; second as the name of the Education Research project of MIT's Artificial Intelligence Laboratory where much development of that language went forward; third as the name of the place which housed the Logo Project.
5 Further information on turtle geometry will be found in Chapters 3 and 5. Here our focus is on the calculation consequences of experiences with turtle geometry.

The specialness of 90 (as the number of degrees in a right angle) was unrecognized by Miriam early in The Intimate Study. For example, when directed in a game by her brother Robby (age 7 years, 10 months – 7;10) to turn 'right 90', Miriam (at age six years, 1 month – 6;1) turned her right foot about 60 degrees, brought her left to it and said 'one'. She repeated the action and counted with each 'two ... three ... four ...' etc. Robby gave her instruction in what 'right 90' means: 'look straight ahead and hold your arm out at your side; jump right around so your feet point where your arm is pointing'. The specific knowledge of what right 90 means and that two executions of right 90 are required to turn around are needed to make line-drawings in turtle geometry. When used in solving particular problems later, this specific result, 90 plus 90 equals 180, is a sign that Miriam's knowledge rooted in turtle geometry was implicated because that result was well known to her before she knew that 9 plus 9 equals 18. For example, at six and a half, Miriam mentally calculated 96 plus 96, using 90 plus 90 = 180, while days later she still calculated 9 plus 9 by deforming it to 8 plus 8 plus 2.

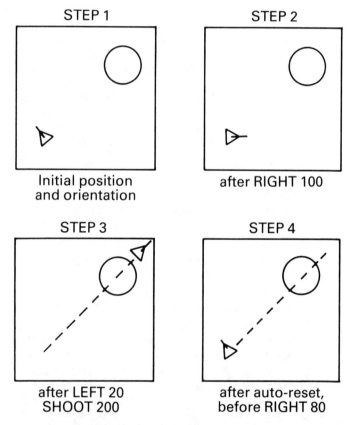

STEP 1

Initial position
and orientation

STEP 2

after RIGHT 100

STEP 3

after LEFT 20
SHOOT 200

STEP 4

after auto-reset,
before RIGHT 80

Playing this simple game led to Miriam's ability to calculate large sums mentally, e.g. 100 minus 20 equals 80.

Fig. 2.3 – SHOOT – A computer game.

The pervasive quantification of computer experience is evident in Miriam's early play with her favorite computer game, SHOOT. In Fig. 2.3, the square boundary represents the computer video display, the circle is a target, and the triangle is the turtle. The objective of the game is to get the turtle into the target using the Logo turn commands to aim and a SHOOT procedure to move the turtle forward into the target. A point is scored when the turtle lands in the target. Should the turtle miss (for example, by going too far as in Fig. 2.3), a trace is left on the video display and after a short time, the turtle returns to its initial location and orientation. In the incident depicted in Fig. 2.3 (around 6;1), Miriam first commanded 'right 100'. She judged the turtle had turned too far and compensated with a 'left 20'. The command 'SHOOT 200' took the turtle beyond the target, so it returned to its initial state. Miriam's next command, 'right 80', shows she compacted the two earlier turning commands to a single one. This required her mental calculation with the decades (100 and 20); I call such multiples of ten 'decadal numbers'. Frequent play with SHOOT involved her in performing mental calculation with such decadal numbers at nearly every turn. She did not indulge in mental calculation for its own sake; it was a subordinate task rendered meaningful by being embedded in an activity she enjoyed for a variety of other reasons.

Let's suppose that from playing with SHOOT and the experience of computer drawing Miriam was developing a new microview. Let's call this the *Decadal microview* because a primary characteristic of its activity was the mental calculation of sums using decadal numbers. Consider a typical calculation problem in this Decadal microview, '55 plus 22 is how much?' (This might arise where Miriam first turned 55 degrees then decided to turn further, 22 degrees.) The perspective exhibited in Fig. 2.4 analyzes the problem as she formulated it into elements; then a set of functions execute. First, the fifty and twenty are grouped, then stripped of their zeroes. The modified symbols (i.e., '5' and '2') are passed to the Count view from which a result, '7', is returned. By restoration of one zero, the '7' is reconstituted to '70', a number of the right order of magnitide. Similarly, the five and two are added by invocation of the Count microview knowledge. The two partial results are catenated to produce the answer, an operand value, which Miriam then used in the Logo command. The claim implicit in this interpretation is that catenation of separately achieved partial sums — both separately performed by the Count microview — was the key function of the Decadal microview.

What evidence is there that the invocation of the Count view was involved in calculating such results? Three kinds: first, Miriam's repertoire of well-known results did not include these decadal numbers; second, during calculations such as '50 plus 20', I often witnessed Miriam counting on her fingers; finally, Miriam's guessing pattern indicated she was manipulating symbols without fully understanding their significance. Consider this detailed example. To add the numbers '50' and '20' on one's fingers requires deforming the terms to other representable analogs, '5' and '2', by stripping off two zeroes. To reconstitute the Count view results for use in Decadal, a single zero is catenated with '7' to make '70'. The other one zero remains unused, stripped off and not later reaffixed; this is the 'extra zero problem', which caused frequent confusion as we see in the following. Adding 97 plus 64, Miriam separated the decades, added, and guessed. 'That is 15 tens ... 500?' Whatever the actual representation in Miriam's mind, such guesses show there was a second zero to which she was sensitive, whose non-representation in the result she couldn't account for; I take that as further evidence calculations proceeded as described.

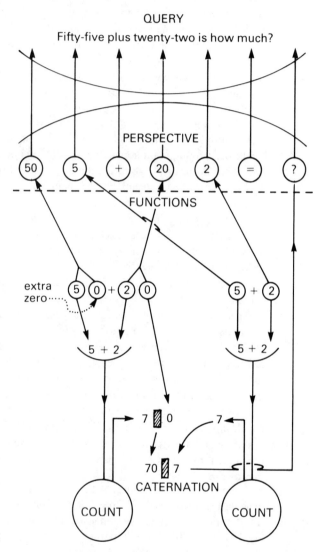

QUERY

Fifty-five plus twenty-two is how much?

(Arrows flow away from centers of control.)

When element values are assigned, decadal functions further analyze those elements, invoke Count view knowledge, and reformat the result for use.

Fig. 2.4 – Activity within the Decadal microview.

GENESIS AND STRUCTURE

The evidence for the manner in which the Decadal perspective analyzes a problem to elements is based on the interpretation of an incident where this new structure came into being, a moment of insight, and on a knowledge of the Decadal view's predecessors. The moment of insight occured at Miriam's age 6;0;26 while the children were playing with SHOOT. Miriam's older brother, Robby, demanded his turn — they were fighting over who would use the terminal — and Miriam ended up with the piano. She played the piano with her elbows while they argued about how much to turn the turtle; the numbers 50 and 53 were mentioned frequently. In the midst of this chaotic scene, Miriam inquired of Robby, 'How much is fifty plus fifty-three?' How could Miriam *not* know such a result? Is it not likely she knew fifty cents plus fifty-three made up a dollar three? It could very well be. The point is that Money view knowledge does not imply the existence of cognate Count view knowledge. Further, the ability to add on a small addend to a counting number name does not imply that such a number name as fifty-three could be analyzed into parts which could then be recombined after operations had been performed on them. More generally, the claim for the disparateness of microviews means we should not assume the existence of knowledge applicable in one task domain applies anywhere else. The functions of such microviews are only locally applicable. What is known by microviews has a very limited lawfulness, rather like Hooke's 'Law of Elasticity' which is defined as applying over that range to which it applies.

Robby answered Miriam's question, 'A hundred and three'. I take the *question* as evidence that Miriam did not know the answer and interpret it as a request for a specific result. Robby's answer brought with it an insight — that in the world of turtle geometry fifties can be added together and a unit cut off from one can be subsequently re-affixed by a simple catenation of number names. Miriam confirmed her insight a moment later by by asking, 'What is fifty-three plus fifty-three?' She answered the question immediately herself, 'A hundred six'. To appreciate her insight into the legitimacy of catenating decadal and unitary number names in a context of addition operations we must relate the incident to Miriam's antecedent microviews of Money and Count.

The Money view had its roots in Count, but it involved counting with a difference: denominations in coin values. Pennies, nickels, dimes, quarters, halves, dollars — these were the elemental things of Miriam's Money microview. The procedures were more complicated and various than those of Count. For example, Miriam would calculate her allowance (a nickel for each year of her age) by skip-counting (5, 10, 15, 20, etc.) under finger-counting control: each finger raised represented one year of her age. The well-known results of the Money view were highly particular. Miriam knew that 15 cents plus 15 cents was 30 cents because each five-pack of her favorite gum cost 15 cents and she knew she could buy two of them with her allowance. Similarly, the elements of denomination each involved some few well known results, e.g. two, three, and four quarters were 50 cents, 75 cents, and a dollar. Miriam also knew around age six some decadal sums from counting dimes, but there is no indication of extensive systematic knowledge of dime-based calculations. The perspective of the Money view superposed the denominations of coins on the countable objects of the Count view's perspective. Its knowledge comprised a speciali-zation of the Count microview perspective, extended in particular directions because of the accidents of the American coinage and Miriam's spending habits. Even though its genesis occurred before the beginning of The Intimate Study, we can describe with confidence the Money view as an experience-elaborated *descendent* of the *ancestral* Count view. The implication of this descent of one microview from predecessors is that the ancestral perspectives provide the initial structures for the elements of the descendent's   perspective. That is, 'what's what' in a microview begins with its likeness to what was recognizable in ancestral views and proceeds through further differentiations based on the lessons experienced in a particular environment.[6]

The perspective of the Decadal view embodies a specialization of the idea of denomination first introduced with the Money view. It is a specialization in the sense that the two supplement denominations are tens and ones. Decadal is a descendent of the Money microview. The application of the denomination idea to the decadal numbers representing angles in turtle geometry changed the elements to which the idea was applied from concrete objects, such as coins, to symbolic objects, i.e. to digits and names for large numbers of uncertain significance. The insight that the number names, used for counting as well as turtle geometry, could be separated as decades and units for addition, then recombined by catenation is, by itself, evidence that Decadal was closely related to Count, as well. The frequently repeated advice that she should consider Decadal sums as analogous to the well known results of the Count view demands that we describe Decadal as descended from Count as well as from the Money view. This common descent from two ancestors will be represented in Fig. 2.5 (discussed in the section 'Coordinating and Task-rooted Structures') by the channels of communication through which the Decadal view may invoke results of both ancestors. That is, *the control structure of mind embodies the genetic path of learning.*

THE INTRODUCTION OF PAPER SUMS

The Intimate Study began with Miriam unable to add 10 plus 20 as a paper sum in the vertical form. When I posed verbally the question 'How much is ten plus twenty?', Miriam answered with confidence, 'Thirty'. Her response to the first sum (a) below was quite different: 'I don't know ... twelve hundred?' (After this confusion, vertical lines were used frequently to emphasize column alignment.)

	at 6;0			at 6;9

```
        at 6;0                       at 6;9

      | 1 | 0 |      | 3 | 2 | 4 |     2 2 8 5 7
   + | 2 | 0 |    + | 2 | 1 | 2 |   + 4 7 3 4 5
     ‾‾‾‾‾‾‾‾‾‾      ‾‾‾‾‾‾‾‾‾‾‾‾‾   ‾‾‾‾‾‾‾‾‾‾‾
      |   |   |      |   |   |   |     7 0 2 0 2

        (a)             (b)              (c)
```

6 We can imagine such differentiation going forward piecemeal through the process of description emphasis proposed by Winston (1975) with the difference information whose natural contribution to the growth of memory was proposed by Minsky (1975).

Despite instruction that she should not 'read' the individual digits but should add within the columns and assemble a result from the columnar sums, Miriam added the addends to 'five hundred nine' for sum (b) $[2+1+4+2=9]$. We continued to use the vertical lines shown above to emphasize the column divisions. She received instruction for solving problems such as (c) by a procedure I call 'order-free adding' — one based on the very simple idea that it doesn't matter in what order one sums column digits so long as any column interaction is accounted for subsequently.[7] There were many single-digit sums which Miriam did not own as well known results and would calculate on her fingers, such as '8 plus 3'. After preliminary instruction, the typical problem Miriam confronted in order-free adding presented two multi-digit addends in the vertical form. Her typical solution began with writing down from left to right the well known results of column sums. Next, Miriam would return to the omitted subproblems and calculate them with her fingers. When this first pass solution produced multi-digit sums in a column — a formal illegality, as I informed her — Miriam had to confront the interaction of columns. I instructed her to cross off the ten's digit of such a sum and add it as a 1 to the next left column, that is, to 'carry the one'. With less than two hours of such instruction, Miriam succeeded at solving sums with two addends of up to ten digits; but she realized no significant gain, for the procedures were subject first to confusion and then to forgetting.

Why were Miriam's initial skills with paper sums vulnerable? Consider the three representative solutions below:

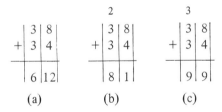

$$\text{(a)} \qquad \text{(b)} \qquad \text{(c)}$$

The first (a) shows no integration of columnar sums; the second (b) shows a confusion over which digit to 'put down' and which to 'carry' (with an implicit rule-like slogan behind the action). The third (c), a conservation response, is an invention of Miriam's which will be described more fully below. If you don't already understand the meaning of the rule 'put down the N and carry the one', why should you prefer that to a comparable rule, 'put down the 1 and carry the N' [as in (b) above]. Miriam was confusable in the sense that she chose, with no regularity and no apparent reason, to apply both these rules. Although frequently instructed in the former rule, she did not remember it. The rule-like formulation made no direct contact with her underlying microview structures. Without support from 'below', the rule could not be remembered. Miriam eliminated her confusion by inventing a carrying procedure that made sense to her, shown in (c) above. 'Reduction to nines' satisfied the formal constraint that each column could have only a single digit in the result by 'reducing' to a '9' any multi-digit column sum and 'carrying' the 'excess' to the next left

---

7 This procedure and Robby's early experiences with it are detailed in my unpublished paper, 'Order-free adding'.

column. (38 plus 34 became 99 through 12 reducing to a 9 with a 3 carried, i.e. added to the two threes of the ten's place.) Miriam's invention of this non-standard procedure (at 6;3;6) I take as weightly evidence characterizing her understanding of numbers and addition in the verbal form. (The latter we will discuss shortly.) About numbers we may conclude she saw the digits as representing things which ought to be conserved, as did the numbers of the Count microview. The achievement of columnar sums by finger counting or by recall of well known results further substantiates the relation of paper sums to numbers of the Count view. Let us declare, then, that these experiences led to the development of a cognitive structure, the *Paper-sums* microview, a direct descendent of the Count view.

Miriam did not understand 'carrying' as being at all related to place value. The numbers within the vertical columns did not relate to those of any other column in a comprehensible way. Despite my initial criticism of 'reduction to nines' — by asking if she were surprised or not that all her answers had so many nines in them — Miriam was strongly committed to this method of carrying. For Miriam, at this time, addition in the vertical form had nothing to do with the Money or Decadal sums she achieved through mental calculation. 'Right' or 'wrong' was a judgment applicable to a calculation only in the terms of the microview wherein it was going forward. I conclude then that the Paper-sums microview shows a diverging line of descent from Miriam's counting knowledge, diverging with respect to those other microviews which involved mental calculation.

The more general final point is that what 'made sense' to Miriam completely dominated what she was told. She could not remember a rule with arbitrary elements, an incomprehensible specification of what to put down and what to carry. Why is it that a rule 'put down the N and carry the 1' didn't make sense? How can we recapture a sense of what that must have seemed like? To her, a number represented a collection of things with a name: '12' was a name by which reference could be made to a collection of twelve things. Numbers may have seemed to her as words do to us, things which cannot be decomposed without destroying their signification. If you divide the word 'goat' into 'go' and 'at', you have two other words not sensibly related to the vanished goat. Similarly, from our common perspective, if you don't see the '1' as a '10' when you decompose a '12' into a '1' and '2', you lose '9'. Unless you appreciate the structured representation, the decomposition of 12 can make no more sense than cutting up a word. What appears as forgetting in Miriam's case is an interference of equilibration processes; that is, what makes sense in terms of ancestral cognitive structures dominates what is inculcated as an extrinsic rule. (I don't claim here to offer a theory of forgetting. Competition from sensible ideas of long dependability is a very good reason, however, for forgetting what you're told but can't comprehend.)

THE CARRYING BREAKTHROUGH

The 'carrying problem' was not restricted to Paper-sums and was, in fact, first resolved among the microviews of mental calculation. Although she could add double digit numbers that involved no decade boundary crossing, like 55 plus 22, Miriam's Decadal view functions failed with sums only slightly different, such as 55 plus 26. Sums of this latter sort initially produced results with illegal number names, i.e. $55 + 26 = 70:11$ ('seventy-eleven'). In playing with SHOOT, however, precision was not required. Miriam's typical 'fix' for this problem was to drop one of the unit digits from the problem and conclude that $55 + 26 = 76$ was an adequate solution. She could, of course, cross decade boundaries by counting, but for a long time this Count view knowledge was not used in conjunction with her Decadal view knowledge. Miriam's resolution of one carrying problem became evident to me in her spontaneous presentation of a problem and its solution (at 6;3;23). She picked up some of her brother's second-grade homework and brought it to me:

> Miriam: Dad, twenty-eight plus forty-eight is seventy-six, right?
> Bob: How did you figure that out?
> Miriam: Well, twenty and forty are like two and four. That six is like sixty.
>   We take the eight, sixty-eight (and then counting on her fingers) sixty-
>   nine, seventy, seventy-one, seventy-two, seventy-three, seventy-four,
>   seventy-five, seventy-six.

Here was clear evidence that Miriam had solved one carrying problem by relating her Decadal and Count microviews. When and how did that integration occur?

The corpus of The Intimate Study is sufficiently rich in detail that I have been able to trace to a moment of insight Miriam's integration of formerly disparate microviews. We were on vacation at the time. I felt Miriam had been working too hard at the laboratory and was determined that she should have a rest from our experiments. I was curious, however, about the representation development of her finger counting and raised the question one day at lunch (at 6;3;16):

> Bob: Miriam, do you remember when you used to count on your fingers all
>   the time? How would you do a sum like seven plus two?
> Miriam: Nine.
> Bob: I know you know the answer — but can you tell me how you used to
>   figure it out, before you knew?
> Miriam: (Counting up on fingers) Seven, eight, nine.
> Bob: Think back even further, to long ago, to last year.
> Miriam: (Miriam counted to nine with both addends on her fingers — leaving
>   the middle finger of her right hand depressed.) But I don't do that any
>   more. Why don't you give me a harder problem?
> Bob: Thirty-seven plus twelve.
> Miriam: (With a shocked look on her face) That's forty-nine.

Something about this problem and result surprised Miriam. I recorded this situation and her reaction in a Vignette; I did not appreciate it as especially significant at that time. My current interpretation focusses on this specific incident as a moment of insight.

It is the rich corpus of The Intimate Study, conjoined with its detailed analysis, that permits me to ascribe with confidence a particular change in cognitive structure to a specific situation. When such a status is assigned to an incident, the moment of insight can be judged as significant only in the context of an interpretation. Here is an abstract of the methodology. Notice through behavior evidence of two different states of cognitive structure. For example, Miriam was able to sum 48 plus 28 where previously she had dropped one of the unit's digits in such a problem. Proceed in the detailed analysis of the corpus (i.e. the examination of every item of overt behavior possibly related to the state change) to determine in what situations and how rapidly the change of state became manifest. When a moment of insight is assigned to an incident, such as the finger counting incident above, re-examine the corpus for conflicting or supporting evidence. One hopes, with a final interpretation, to find only supporting evidence, as the following. During the remainder of our vacation, Miriam pestered me to do some addition experiments. I tried to give her a rest, and her pestering intensified. As we drove back from our vacation, she made me promise to do an experiment as soon as we reached home: that day she brought to me the problem of 28 plus 48 described above. Miriam clearly owned some new knowledge she wanted to employ.

How should one characterize this insight? Precisely what was it that Miriam saw? In the Decadal view, the problem 'thirty-seven plus twelve' would be solved thus, 'thirty plus ten is forty; seven plus two is nine; forty-nine'. The Decadal view would have produced a perfect result. Miriam had recently become able to decompose numbers such as 'twelve' into a 'ten' and a 'two'. This marked a refinement of the Count view perspective. If we imagine the calculation 'thirty-seven plus twelve' proceeding in the Count microview — with the modified pespective able to 'see the ten in the twelve' — Miriam would say 'thirty-seven [the first number of the Count view's perspective], plus ten is forty-seven [then counting up on her fingers the second addend residuum], forty-eight, forty-nine'. Such a Count view calculation also yields a perfect answer. We are not surprised that the answer is the same as that of the Decadal view, but I believe the concurrence surprised Miriam. One can say that Miriam experienced an insight (to which her 'shocked look' testifies) based on the *surprising confluence of results* from apparently disparate microviews. 'Insight' is the appropriate common word for the situation, and I will continue to use it where no confusion is likely; but its range of common usage extends so far as to prohibit its technical use. So I introduce a new name, the elevation of control, as the technical name for the learning process exemplified here. The *elevation of control* names the creation of a new control element which subordinates previously independent microviews, in the sense of permitting their controlled invocation; some experiences of insight are the experienced correlates of control elevation.

The character of control elevation is revealed in the example. The numbers 37 and 12 were of such a magnitude as would have normally engaged Miriam's Decadal microview. She had just been finger counting (a Count view function) and Decadal could calculate the sum as well. If both microviews were actively calculating results and simultaneously achieving identical solutions, the surprising confluence of results — where none should have been expected — could spark a significant cognitive event: the changing of a non-relation into a relation, which is the quintessential alteration required for the creation of new structure.[8]

The sense of surprise attending the elevation of control is a direct consequence of a common result being found where none was expected. The competition of microviews, which usually leads to the dominance of one and the suppression of others, also presents the possibility of cooperation replacing competition. So we see, in the outcome, Decadal beginning a calculation and Count completing it. This conclusion, however much it is based on a rich interpretation, is an empirical observation. Where we expected development in response to incrementally more challenging problems, we found this form of insight: cognitive reorganization from the redundant solution of simple problems.

COORDINATING AND TASK-ROOTED STRUCTURES

The elevation of control, a minimal change which could account for the integration of microviews witnessed by Miriam's behavior, would be the addition of a control element permitting the serial invocation of the Decadal view and then the Count view. Let us declare at this moment of insight the formation of a new microview, the Serial view.[9] The perspective of the Serial view analyzes a problem into a 'part-for-Decadal' and a 'residuum'. 28 plus 48 would be regrouped as a part of Decadal (28 plus 40) and a residuum (8). The functions of this view first invoke Decadal; upon return of the Decadal partial result, they invoke Count to complete the sum.

Structurally, the Serial view is similar to its predecessors, but functionally and genetically it is quite different. Microviews whose perspective elements are descriptions of things, speculations about the relations of which may be verified or disconfirmed by straightforward experiments, are *task-rooted*. We may note that the Count view is rooted in one-to-one correspondence, the Money view is committed to a coinage-rooted perspective, and the Decadal view handles problems of a magnitude encountered in the scale of angles. These three are task-rooted structures (and the Paper-sums view is another). The knowledge which such views constitute is constructed through experience by elemental description refinement in a perspective descended from an ancestral view. The well-known results of such task-rooted views may be determined by accident, as Miriam's knowing that 15 cents plus 15 cents sums to 30 cents derived from the price of gum and the amount of her allowance. Other results are less accidental. That is, Miriam knew 90 plus 90 equals 180 because this sum (whose quantity and

---

8 See, in this connection, the discussion of 'relational conversion' in Chapter 7. In Lawler, 1979, I advanced the same argument, first that the boundaries between microviews are defined by networks of 'must-not-confound' links which function to suppress confusion between competing, related microviews; second, that the conversion of these repressive links, established by experience, to more explicit relational links, generates 'new' control structure at moments of insight.

9 One wants to avoid the creation of something from nothing. The creation of inhibiting relations between microviews to suppress confusion does the real work of structural creation. The relational conversion, in which an inhibiting relation is turned into one of richer semantic content, permits the smooth transformation in functional capability to another behavior over what otherwise would appear to be an unbridgeable gap.

representation are cultural accidents) embodied a significant action (turning around) in worlds of experience. We can state the observation more generally this way: the particular knowledge of a microview may be accidentally determined, but the microviews themselves are not accidental; they come to embody what is epistemologically profound in the experiences which inspire their construction. I return to this point in the penultimate paragraph of the chapter.

The Serial view is not a task-rooted microview and is different from such a one in several ways. Recall that task-rooted microviews may have merely a single ancestor, as the Money view's sole ancestor is Count. Microviews such as Serial which coordinate others must have at least two ancestors. Further, the elements of the Serial view's perspective are not descriptions of things in the world of common experience but are descriptions of the perspectives of the coordinated microviews. The Serial view functions by invoking the subordinated microviews and not by recall of locally well known results or execution of local procedures. Whereas the generation of the task-rooted views involves both insights about what are the significant elements of microviews and progressive familiarization with what can be done to them, the Serial view is so simple as to be complete at its inception. Finally, the problem confronted at the moment of insight (37 plus 12) did *not* require the insight to solve it. In this specific sense, the cognitive development was 'accidental' as opposed to being experience-driven. In a second sense, it was not accidental at all, for it depended upon the simultaneous engagement of robust ancestral knowledges. I will return to this issue at the end of this chapter.

Although the Serial view is achieved as a minimal change of structure, its integration of subordinated microviews permitted a significantly enhanced calculation performance, one so striking as to support the observation that a new functional level of calculation emerged from the new organization. This is especially evident where knowledge is articulated by proof. Consider this example (at 6;5;24). Miriam and Robby, himself no slouch at calculation, were making a clay by mixing flour, salt, and water. They mixed the material, kneaded it, and folded it over. Robby kept count of his foldings. With 95 plies, the material was thick. He folded again, 'ninety-six' then cutting the pile in half, flopped the second on top of the first and said, 'Now I've got ninety-six plus ninety-six'. Miriam interjected, 'That's a hundred ninety-two'. Robby was astounded, couldn't believe her result, and called to his mother to find if Miriam could possible be right. Miriam responded first, 'Robby, we know ninety plus ninety is a hundred and eighty. Six makes a hundred eighty-six. [Then counting on her fingers] One eighty-seven, one eighty-eight, one eighty-nine, one ninety, one ninety-one, one ninety-two'. We can see the Decadal well-known-result (90 plus 90) as a basis for this calculation and its relation to her counting knowledge. Both these points support the argument that Miriam's new knowledge was specifically of controlling pre-existing microviews. Robby was astounded — and we too should try to preserve a sense of astonishment in order to remain sensitive to how small a structural change permits the emergence of a new level of performance.

The advent of the Serial view marks the furthest reach of Miriam's mental calculation skills during The Intimate Study. Fig. 2.5 summarizes the development of the mental calculation cluster of microviews. The genetic structure, the descent of a microview from its ancestors, is preserved in the functioning control structure of the mind. Task-rooted and control microviews compete among themselves in a race for solution, a race open to bias by the presentation of the problem, and they invoke the knowledge of ancestral microviews where appropriate. (Such is conceivable even when an invoked ancestor is simultaneously a competitor.) The structure is of a mixed form, basically competitive but hierarchical at need. This vision of mind, the system of cognitive structures, presents disparate microviews of knowledge based on particular experiences. The elevation of control acts to integrate the disparate microviews. Most striking is the observation that the moment of insight resulted from solving a problem for which either of two competing microviews was adequate. That is, the elevation of control was *not* necessity-driven but rather derived from the surprising confluence of results where no such agreement between disparate structures was expected.

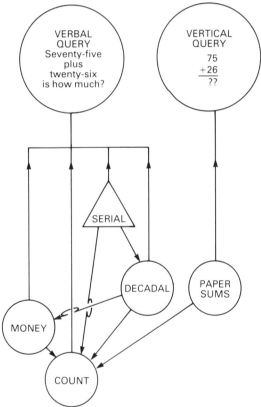

(Arrows flow away from centers of control.)

The Serial view both invokes and competes with the Count and Decadal views; the control is 'basically competitive but hierarchical at need'. Arrows between views exhibit paths of invocation which result from derivation of the descendent (higher) microviews from the earlier (ancestral) microviews.

Fig. 2.5 — The organisation of five microviews.

PAPER SUMS AND MENTAL ARITHMETIC

The core of The Intimate Study came to an end without Miriam's having learned to add, in the narrow sense of using the standard algorithm in the vertical form, but she did learn to do so subsequently. In the intervening month, she returned to school (first grade) and confronted these typical calculation problems: $2 + 3 =$ [ ]; if John had 7 cents and bought a nickel candy, how much would he have left?[10] When a severe winter storm kept us snowbound for a week, we extended The Intimate Study (around 6;9) for those days with several experiments during which Miriam leaned to add, in the narrow sense.

The objective of these late sessions was to lead Miriam to a vision of carrying as making sense in terms of her appreciation of the representation. In the midst of one session, I posed the problem 'How much is 14 plus 27?' by writing in the vertical form (a). Miriam calculated the answer mentally and wrote '41' on the chalkboard. I continued, 'I want you to look at the problem a different way (writing $10 + 4$ and $20 + 7$) (b). Can you see the 10 in the 14? Can you see that 10 plus 4 is 14?' Miriam responded, 'Sure', and writing '$= 14$' and '$= 27$' she concluded, 'and the answer is forty-one; we did that already'. I tried a different tactic:

$$
\begin{array}{lll}
14 \rightarrow & 10 + 4 = 14 \\
+27 \rightarrow & +20 + 7 = 27 \\
\hline
41 & 30 + 11 & 41 \\
& 30 + 10 + 1 \\
\text{(a)} & \text{(b)} & \text{(c)}
\end{array}
$$

Bob: Now how much is the ten plus twenty?
Miriam: Thirty.
Bob: [writes '30 +' in the answer line of (b).]
Miriam: Plus ... Oh [tapping '4' first then '7'] seven and four.
Bob: How much is that?
(1) Miriam: Thirty-seven, [then using her fingers] thirty-eight, thirty-nine, forty, forty-one. [Points to the answer in (a)] '41'.
Bob: How much is seven and four?
Miriam: (Pause) Eleven.
Bob: Will you write down the '11'?
Miriam: (She does so.) Eleven.
Bob: Is there a ten in the eleven?
Miriam: Yes. Equals forty-one [writing '41' in (c)].
Bob: What you have to see, Miriam, is that the eleven there is a ten plus a one [writes '10 + 1' under '11' in (b)].
Miriam: Yeah?

10 Miriam was offered the choice of doing more advanced work. She chose the standard material (even though she complained privately to me of boredom) so that she would not be separated from her friends or be marked as different from them.

Bob: And whenever you get a ten in something like an eleven or fourteen, you have to add it with the thirties [writes a second '30 +' before the '10 + 1' in (b)].

Miriam: Why not the twenties?

(2) Bob: So thirty plus ten —

Miriam: (Interrupting) Is forty.

Bob: And then plus one —

Miriam: (interrupting) Is forty-one.

Bob: Does that make sense now?

Miriam: Yeah.

Bob: Does it really make sense, or are you just humoring me?

Miriam: I tell you it really makes sense.

In the dialogue cited (transcribed from videotape), Miriam's Serial view knowledge was active at (1) above on the distributed form of the problem (b) to arrive at the result she already knew to be correct. After my pointing to the 'ten in the eleven' at (2) above, Miriam could see that the results of vertical form calculations could be the same as those of mental calculations. This amounted to an insight that the Paper-sums view related to the Serial view in a significant way.

After I set down the next problem [see (a) below], Miriam's Serial view knowledge produced the result '93'. Congratulating her for a correct result, I erased her answer, drew in the columnar division lines of (b) and asked her to calculate the result differently. She wrote an '8' in the ten's column, scratched it out and wrote in '93'. I stopped this attempt to bypass the problem, wrote an '8' and a '13' in the answer line of (b) and asked:

$$
\begin{array}{cc}
\begin{array}{r}
37 \\
+56 \\
\hline
93
\end{array}
&
\begin{array}{c|c|c}
+ & 3 & 7 \\
& 5 & 6 \\
\hline
& 8 & 13 \\
& 10 & 10
\end{array}
\end{array}
$$

(a)   (b)

Bob: Can you tell me why this [the '8' and '13'] makes sense?

Miriam: It makes sense because there's a ten (writing '10' under '13'); plus three is in the thirteen.

Bob: I'll buy that.

(1) Miriam: And if there's a ten, you add it to the eighty.

Bob: And what do you get?

(2) Miriam: [Tapping the '3' of the tens column in (b).] Is this a thirty?

Bob: Yeah!

Miriam: [Writes a zero to the right of '8' in the tens answer cell of (b).] Plus ten is ninety-three, and the answer's ninety-three.

At point (2) in the citation above, Miriam asked me, for the first time, about the place value of a digit. This is the moment where she has an insight into the nature of the representation which permitted her thereafter to do addition problems in the vertical form. Seeing that the '3' was really a '30', she transformed the '8' to an '80', to which it made sense to add the '10' of '13'. (I interpret the 'eighty' of statement (1) above to be the intermediate result, 'eighty', of the Serial microview calculation. Notice that Miriam appended the '0' to the '8' only after establishing that the '3' was a 30.)

During the core of The Intimate Study, Miriam's Paper-sums knowledge was so remote from her knowledge of mental calculation that she did not imagine results of cognate problems should be the same. In the preceding incidents we have seen Miriam making sense of the Hindu—Arabic representation — as that intersects with the standard addition algorithm — by connecting it coherently with her dependable knowledge of mental calculation. Fig. 2.6 names *Conformal* the structural element connecting the Paper-sums view of mental calculation. The implication of the name is that the knowledge of the Conformal view is a mapping, a set of correspondences between aspects of some calculation views and others. Which views? Which aspects? The most significant insight was that the '3' of '37' was really a '30' as is the 'thirty' of 'thirty-seven'. This is a part-to-part correspondence of elements in the perspectives of both the Paper-sums view and the mental calculation views. If we pursue the question 'which views?', we must conclude the description of the place value of Paper-sums columns relates to perspective elements of the Decadal view while the coherence of results relates the Paper-sums and Serial views.

From the *correlation of perspectives*, my name for the process which joined the Paper-sums view through Conformal to the microviews of mental calculation, Miriam could see that the results of the processes *should* be the same and thus, the manipulations of the paper-sums problems could make sense. The learning exhibited by the correlation of perspectives is different from that of the elevation of control in respect of the resulting structure. The Serial view intervenes directly in the functioning control structure of the mental calculation cluster. The Conformal view represents a species of knowledge essential in integrating disparate microviews — knowledge whose use is constructive but otherwise non-functional. Since the Conformal view does not enter into the control structure of the calculation microviews, we should not expect it to have functions within its own structure. The perspective of the Conformal view is a set of equivalences, e.g. a digit in this tens place is equivalent to a Decadal element.[11] This knowledge of other microview perspectives permits the coherent registration of one with another.

The crucial insight into the tens place value did not establish instantaneous coherence. First came the conclusion that the results of addition should be the same in Paper-sums and mental calculations, then came a working out of the value of the other places. For example, in her next two problems (77 + 23 and 137 + 256) Miriam used her mental calculation procedures to effect the carries required (arriving at the answer 'tendy', i.e. one hundred, for the first) but could not explain why this made sense in terms of place values. In subsequent

11 What is the relation between such equivalence in this mathematical domain and in those of logical classification? Miriam's performance on the class inclusion task of the Piagetian repertoire suggests that the solution of the inclusion relation — on the level of language processing — preceeds (and may thus enable) the establishment of such correspondence relations between related applications of the same numerical symbol system.

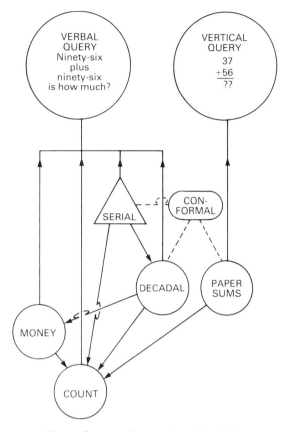

(Arrows flow away from centers of control.)

The Conformal view perspective relates elements of three other
views; this relating was needed for the subject to make sense of
vertical-form addition in the Paper-sums view.

Fig. 2.6 – The relation of the Paper-sums microview to others.

sessions, we worked over a series of problems and applied a re-naming step to
carrying. I criticized the rule 'put down the N and carry the 1' as not making
sense. We began renaming and marking the actual value of the carries, as Miriam
had marked the actual place value of the '8' in the tens answer cell above. Thus
Miriam's 'tendy' was renamed one hundred and the carry to the hundred's
column was as '100'. Similarly ten hundreds was renamed one thousand. Miriam
declared that this system made sense, though her execution required the fixing
of several procedural 'bugs'. Thus, in the sum (a) below at left, Miriam treated
the carry into the tens column as a ten and the 4 and 5 as units; she ignored the
carry into the hundreds column (in reaching 11) and probably disregarded place
values entirely in the thousands.

```
         0                              0
    1000 100  10               10001000 100  10
   | 4 | 7 | 3 | 4 | 5 |        | 2 | 2 | 8 | 5 | 7 |
 + | 2 | 2 | 8 | 5 | 7 |      + | 4 | 7 | 3 | 4 | 5 |
   -------------------          -------------------
   | 7 | 0 | 1 | 9 | 2 |        | 7 | 0 | 2 | 0 | 2 |

          (a)                            (b)
```

Miriam had shown me this result (a), believing it correct. When I pointed out her errors, she was so angry she refused to do any more calculations. Thus the second sum, (b) above, written on a clean chalkboard, was ignored for days, until Valentine's Day, when Miriam executed the sum as a surprise present for me. Since that time, Miriam's addition in this form has been essentially correct. Her confidence in her understanding was witnessed by the spontaneous extension of her addition skill to multi-addend multi-digit sums two months later.

SUMMARY AND REFLECTIONS

I have dwelt on one child's learning to add as a worked example of a productive method for investigating and interpreting learning. The contribution of this analysis is the notion of separate microviews, derived from particular experiences, joining into a powerful organization through structure-relating knowledge. Such relational knowledge is seen as different in application but not in kind from task-rooted knowledge. This analysis is a single, early step toward a computational theory or learning of general applicability, one wherein the specialization and refinement of perspectives expand and diversify the application of existing knowledges to new experiences, while the counterbalancing processes of control elevation and perspective correlation permit the progressive integration of disparate microviews into a coherent mind. It is from the balance, the equilibration, of such countervailing processes of knowledge application-extension and integration that Piaget's dialectical spiral of cognitive development appears. We can conclude that what is commonly called learning is the enhanced performance which emerges from changes within and between active microviews of knowledge.

We have seen four examples of significant cognitive development (see Fig. 2.7). The Decadal and Paper-sums views were related to tasks Miriam worked at, i.e. they are task-rooted microviews whose perspective elements describe things of our common world. The Serial view is a control view whose perspective elements are descriptions of subordinate microview perspectives; the sort of thing Serial 'knows' is that Decadal can handle in general problems of the form 'decade and units plus decade'. Similarly, elements of the Conformal view's perspective are descriptions of elements in the perspectives of microviews it relates. These last two microviews coordinate the activity of perspectives of the microviews their perspectives describe. We have observed that the perspectives of the task-rooted microviews derive from the extensions and specialization of ancestral perspectives to make sense of experience in a new domain. Recall how the Money view descended from Count and how Decadal was a specialization of the Money view which was powerful in application because the Decadal denominations (decades and units) fit the culturally embedded representation of the Hindu—Arabic number system. We have argued for the competition of microviews in the formation of the coordinating views and noted the empirical result that the insights occurred when there was a surprising confluence of results where none was anticipated.

MICROVIEW	CALCULATION EXAMPLES	INVOCABLE ANCESTORS
COUNT	$17 + 6 = 17$ (finger-controlled counting) 18, 19, 20, 21, 22, 23. 23 is the answer.	—
MONEY	75¢ and 26? That's three quarters, four and a penny, one-oh-one.	COUNT
DECADAL	RIGHT 100 and LEFT 20, that's 100 minus 20. That's like 10 minus 2. 80's the number I need.	COUNT MONEY
PAPER-SUMS	37 8 and 13. 13 doesn't fit. Put down +56 the 1 ... no. Put down the 9 and carry the 4, that's 129. Is 129 right?	COUNT
SERIAL	Thirty-seven and fifty-six. That's like 3 and 5, eighty. Eighty-seven, eighty-eight, etc. (finger-controlled counting).	DECADAL COUNT
CONFORMAL	37 8 and 13. The 8 means 80, and the +56 10 in the 13 should be with it, so it makes sense that this vertical sum should have the same result as the other way of calculating.	none

Fig. 2.7 – A summary of Miriam's addition microview.

We should ask about those incidents of insight, because they derive from an unexpected confluence of microview outputs, to what extent the occurrence was either accidental or necessary. The particular incidents themselves have very much the flavor of accident, especially in the case of the Serial insight. Is it possible to argue that there was some sense in which Miriam was 'fated' to make the discovery which integrated the Decadal and Count views for processing problems of a certain range of complexity? We could argue, for instance, that the cultural embedding of the number representation would present any child with a multitude of problems over time which would promote her stumbling into a serial-like insight. Likelihood, however, is not necessity. Is there such a thing as a mathematical structure which was, in any sense, pulling Miriam's cognitive development along a specific path? It is not necessary to make such an assumption. What marked the stability of Miriam's learning was the conjunction of ancestral microviews: the structure of the representation which we impute to Miriam is an emergent from her experience; its stability is based on the integrability of several experiences. That is, having multiple points of view is not magic; it was their fitting together that produced the stability. We have seen microviews of computation, each of whose perspectives analyzed problems into different elements for calculation. The significant aspect of number that results in developing complex and stable cognitive structures is not that there are 'really' such things as 'mathematical structures'. Rather, the nature of number makes· it amenable to calculations which go forward by anchoring thought at some element's base-value and varying that base by some other term.[12] What the specific bases of number used in a particular calculation may be matters far less than that some base is necessary. It is this epistemological aspect of number's structure (and its conformability to human thought processes) which permits a variety of views of experience to arise separately and subsequently to be integrated into a coherent and complex understanding.

12 See the extended citation by Tversky and Kahnemann, 'On anchoring with variation' (p. 255). Their work established the more general result that anchoring with variation plays a significant role in the mental calculation of mathematically sophisticated adults and first suggested to me the value of following the separate development of mental calculation and paper sums.

3

The equilibration of cognitive structures

There is a more important question than the truth of the theory propounded by Piaget, that of its necessity: if by some unfortunate chance, this theory turns out to be false, what would be the next development?...
I even think I could anticipate the answer: it would be the establishment of a new theory which would likewise be an equilibration theory.

Papert, 1976[1]

Major, rapid changes in problem-solving behavior do occur. These robust, well-documented phenomena have been referred to as stage changes by Piaget and the Genevan School of psychologists.[2] Surely such changes must be addressed by any theory of human learning. Piaget has proposed[3] that such stages occur from the closure of logical operations over all domains of experience, in consequence of which the mind is able to go on to a more advanced stage. In contrast, I have argued that learning is primarily a local process, in at least two senses: much of the knowledge constructed by any person is task-domain-specific; second, although significant integration effects surely are an important kind of learning, it appears they can be described as the linking of domain-specific cognitive structures into clusters. It is possible to limn such structures and to trace events of structural organization through the fine-grain analysis of detailed

---

1 This is a free translation of Papert's comments at a colloquium on the 80th birthday of Jean Piaget.
2 The phenomena have been largely discovered and documented by Piaget and his collaborators over many years.
3 In *The Psychology of Intelligence*, 1947.

case studies as in Chapters 2 and 4. Given such a fundamentally atomistic desscription of mind, one should inquire how large-scale unformities, such as stages manifest, could ever come into existence and how transitions between them could occur.

Probing the issue of stage changes, both theoretically and empirically, is a primary theme of this chapter. The means I have taken to explore this issue empirically is an intervention, an attempt to develop structures of a child's mind which would permit her to perform in a fashion typical of children twice her age through introducing her to skills of programming. The epistemological status of programming experience — as the potential generator of a cognitive ideal for formal thought — permits this material to address directly the issue of the development of the formal stage of thought as described by Piaget. The material of this chapter exemplifies how formal thought may be seen as a change in the balance between dominant and long-existing sub-dominant cognitive structures.

My introducing Miriam to computers and to programming was an 'intervention' in her life, a natural experiment whose outcome I committed myself to observe and record. I know a lot about programming and enjoy it, as I enjoy using computers to make learning environments for children. It seemed perfectly natural to me that my children should be among the first to use the things I made. Moreover, since I was a member of a computer subculture committed to the study of learning, Miriam's entry into that environment seemed an opportunity to examine the path of natural learning under cultural pressions which I well knew. Further, at the time we began this project, computers were rarer than they are today, and it was possible for me to know precisely the limits and occasions of Miriam's computer use. The corpus of material on which the analysis is based is essentially complete with respect to its topic of programming experience.

PIAGET AND PAPERT

This work is in a tradition committed to understanding the human mind through observing and analyzing the growth of knowledge in minds over time; in this sense, it is in the Piagetian tradition. A central theme for Piaget — perhaps even a word such as 'quest' is appropriate — was to discover if, when, and how 'necessary' truth relates to the contingencies of experience. In contrast, my quest, one I have shared with Papert, has a different central commitment: to understand the power of ideas. The quest generates these questions:

- what might an idea be?
- how do ideas function?
- how do ideas come to exist and change?
- how do ideas relate to one another?
- what could it mean for an idea to be powerful?

This quest, as Piaget's, implicates the study of how knowledge grows in individual minds and how that developmental path is affected by the nature of the idea, by the context (both physical and social), and by the previous development of the mind.

For Piaget, the structure of mind was best represented by his algebraic descriptions. For me, the structure of mind is quite a different thing, the 'frozen' control structure of the functioning embodiment of knowledge. I take as given the fragmentary quality of experience and the disparateness of microviews reflecting that experience. My attempt is to explain the development of knowledge witnessed in behavior as the interconnection of disparate microviews at moments of insight. This endeavor was influenced early by the 'society theory of mind',[4] at first a joint program undertaken by Minsky and Papert in the mid-seventies and now a work by Minsky nearing completion. The difference in representation is crucial. Minsky and Papert claimed that the information sciences offer a repertoire of intellectual tools which will render problems of mind more tractable.[5] While the AI community has invested much effort in the construction of computerized mental models, my focus has been more on the fecundity of computational ideas in their application to concrete problems of cognitive development. The ideas of control structure, concrete descriptions, and learning through debugging are central in my work as they are not in Piaget's, but I use these ideas as means to an end — which remains Piagetian in essence — to understand the structure and genesis of knowledge.

Stages versus cognitive ideals

Papert's clearest example of a powerful idea, if I understand him right, serves to distinguish his work and mine from Piaget's formulations, specifically in respect of what a 'stage' is. In Piaget's work, a stage is a period of time during which a mind deals in a characteristic fashion with problems encountered in all domains; when the mind completes the application of powerful operations to all domains, then it becomes possible for it, in effect, to impose a theory-in-practice on this concrete theory and deal with all of experience in a more formal abstract way. My description of a stage, developed through conversations with Papert, recognizes its existence as a robust phenomenon but eliminates its significance as a theoretical construct for psychology. A stage is no more than the achievement of a common level of performance across those clusters of cognitive structures which are potentially able to be influenced by a specific cognitive ideal. In Papert's example, when a pre-operational child conserves number and recognizes — for the very first time — that it is possible to know with deductive certainty, the knowledge of number is a concrete exemplar by comparison with which all other problem solving is ad hoc and unsure. If the child is then personally impelled to seek 'conservations' of something in her other domains of experience, the knowledge of number for her is both a powerful idea and also an ideal. The

---

4 Piaget discussed the mind as a society of independent agencies at the end of *The Psychology of Intelligence* (1947), but which ideas are taken seriously and where one takes them is an issue more important for any work than the historical precursors of ideas.

5 Whether or not this claim is true in any strong sense remains to be seen. It repeats the claim of Kurt Lewin that the physical concept of 'field' would be similarly useful. Followers of Lewin have succeeded in providing a mathematical basis for his proposal, but the specific program has been largely abandoned. See the discussion in the extended citation Langer: 'Against Physicalism' (p. 240).

speed or delay with which she can invent new conservations (the Piagetian issue of *decalage*) is an artifact of her overcoming accidental checks to the spread of an epistemologically powerful idea.

Can one trace the spread of such a powerful idea in a child's mind? An existence proof of sorts is needed. This has not yet been done for the conservation of number, but it could be done with the method of The Intimate Study. Whether or not such studies are 'scientific' depends on one's theory of doing science. The appropriate criterion at this stage is not replication of results but the disentangling of sequences and relations in observations where the ratio of signal to noise is very low, the paring down of experience — considered in all its complexity and detail — to a crisp model which can disambiguate the causal and circumstantial precedents of major phenomena.

An alternative to tracing the diffusion of number conservation in the mind is to ask if there exist comparable phenomena; what could be another such powerful idea? From such an inquiry arises Papert's conjecture that the Piagetian formal stage follows the concrete stage because the experiences which might generate its ideal are not a part of everyday culture, everywhere in the world, as are those which lead to number conservation. Papert has speculated that the experience of computer programming, in the immediate future, may come to serve just such a role. It would be a strong result if someone remote from the formal stage developed through programming experience characteristics of thought related to those typical of formal thinkers. This study has produced such a result. In addition, beyond this narrow but important claim, the study exemplifies how the equilibration of cognitive structures is a profound and obscure fact about which experiments ought to reflect.

PROGRAMMING AS AN EXPERIMENTAL DOMAIN

The programmable computer is something new under the sun. A computer differs significantly from a book in that it can embody the functioning of intelligence without the need for a living reader or interpreter. Three aspects of computer experience could well lead our children to develop minds different from those we developed at comparable ages. First, concrete experiences with programming variables may lead children to conceive of objects in a more formal way, as specific instantiations of possible objects more than as given things. (See Lawler (1982a) for a detailed explication and example of this point.) Second, the experience of using programmed repetition and the nesting of programmed repetition may lead children to think more systematically. Finally, the experience of teaching a computer new procedures may lead children to formulate more explicit theories of their own learning, consequently enhancing their reflexivity of thought. Such changes would amount to a significant increase in the analytical ability of very young children.

Practical as well as theoretical factors advance the value of studying how people learn about programming. Writing and debugging procedures are concrete activities in which a subject's formulation of a problem and changes in analytical ability are clearly revealed. The flexibility of programming permits enough variation to show differences in individual thinking while offering tasks sufficiently constrained that they can be related to preselected issues. The computer presence permits a milieu where children can and will engage in long projects which intermingle significant direction and their own setting of objectives. These practical features create an experimental learning environment which can be more natural than a typical psychological laboratory.

Although my choice to study Miriam's learning of programming is theoretically well justified, it is justified also by the results as well. This chapter provides a detailed and lucid example of what it is like for a person to learn something that is essentially new; it provides also an example of what equilibration could actually be like in practice if achieved by competition among different microviews of knowledge; finally, it throws some light on the interaction between factors of cultural influence and personal activity in learning. I will first present the basic experience of Miriam's learning about debugging, then turn to its extensions in her life (seen both through anecdotal material and through specific experiments), and finally, to what conclusions we may infer from the material.

PRE-PROGRAMMING COMPUTER EXPERIENCES

Miriam was introduced to computers at the age of four years. The environment I created for her was one of Logo subsystems EEL and ZOOM. EEL was the precursor of the DRAW program described in Chapter One, a shape assembly system.[6] ZOOM was a single key command interface. In both EEL and ZOOM, as one made a drawing, the interface saved the steps of that process and at a later command generated a symbolic procedure to recreate the drawing; I called such an approach for novices 'concrete programming'.[7] In neither of these interfaces did Miriam compose symbolic procedures before executing them. As The Intimate Study began, I introduced Miriam to text composition and editing through procedure generator.[8]

Writing her first procedure: details

Miriam was not introduced to procedure writing until Logo Session 20 (age 6;1;30). I had waited for the right opportunity, one of a special sort, one wherein something she had done and judged her own creation could be extended to a result of which she could be proud. I waited for such an opportunity with confidence. My experiences with other children showed that this environment was rich and epistemologically stable; rich in the sense that a child could recreate on the computer images of objects which were personally meaningful; by

---

6 EEL is an acronym for Ed Emberley's language; the inspiration for this system was provided by Emberley's *Make a World* book, 1972.

7 A paper describing ZOOM was included as an appendix in an NSF final report of the Logo Project. The work in which I advocated concrete programming, 'TURTLE: Learning by Doing', was omitted from that final report by administrative error and remains an unpublished work.

8 See 'An introduction to writing', Lawler, 1980. Excerpts from that article are included in the Appendix.

epistemologically stable I mean that the combination of a child's own direction and my knowledge would lead to a situation such as the one that is described below.

Miriam had previously used a procedure generator, TIMES, to create simple iterative procedures. TIMES generated procedures with a kernel, that is, a repeated portion, of her chosen commands and a control structure based on her response to a stop-rule generation query. (See Lawler, 1979, for more detail.) The typical kernel of the procedure was [FORWARD DISTANCE-QUANTITY RIGHT ANGLE-QUANTITY]. When I began the computer portion of Logo Session 20 with the request that we 'do something new', Miriam proposed a kernel with the component [FORWARD 1000]. When I criticized, 'That's not new. That's just a big number', Miriam suggested a different set of operations FORWARD and LEFT. After keying [FORWARD 20 LEFT], she changed her mind, deciding to use BACK and LEFT. Erasing LEFT she keyed BACK in its place. She judged this an error, but I advised her to keep the back operation with an operand 10, and then to execute some small right turn. I did not know exactly what would come of this move, but I did know that such a kernel would generate arcs with spiny edges. Since Miriam had no specific objective, she was willing to follow my suggestion; she concluded the procedure generation by specifying that an input variable should control the number of iterations of the procedure and named her procedure D123. When she tried to execute D123, Miriam had to work through the problems.

> Bob: It says D123 'needs more inputs' ... It's looking for you to tell it something but it needs more information. Do you know what it needs to know?
> Miriam: How much ... [Keying] D, 1, 2, 3, space, 30. [As the procedure executed 30 iterations of the kernel, the turtle moved from the home position at center screen to the upper right-hand corner of the screen and stopped.] ... Out of bounds. [This is her speculation based on the turtle's closeness to the screen edge.]
> Bob: No. I didn't go out of bounds. It stopped near the edge .... You've got a question mark, and it doesn't say, 'Out of bounds'.
> Miriam: Goody!
> Bob: 30 took it right up to the corner. [Realizing that a RIGHT 90 plus another execution of [D123 30] would return the turtle to the home position] ... Want to see a good trick?
> Miriam: [Negative noises.]
> Bob: No? It could really be neat.

Miriam was sufficiently uninterested that her only concern was determining the flavors available in the soda machine. At this point, I could well imagine the shapes made with D123 in Fig. 3.1 and I knew Miriam's delight in drawing flowers. We continued:

> Bob: Would you like to make a flower petal? ... I will tell you how to do it. Do a right turn 90.
> Miriam: [Keying RT 90] New line.

Bob: Now type D, 1, 2, 3, space, 30.

Miriam: [Keying as directed, Miriam begins to whine when the petal is not of the sort she considers prototypical] No. I sort of meant two flower petals in a circle.

Bob: Now wait a minute. Type D, 1, 2, 3, 30 again .... Now right turn 90 and D, 1, 2, 3, 30.

Miriam: [Keys as directed, then breaks into a broad smile as the two-petal flower of Fig. 3.1(a) appears.] ... How about a stem?

Bob: Shall we get two more petals, so there's one big flower in the whole picture?

Miriam: Yeah. It's going to be mine.

This expression of a claim to ownership is a clear indication that Miriam had adopted as her own the objective of making a flower from D123. The procedure will be hers, because it will be made from a subprocedure she created with an input value she selected. She can see how her procedure makes parts that assemble to a recognizable entity (a petal) and how the petals will make a flower. The flower is hers, even though its first imagining was mine and the knowledge to effect it was mine. This was the point of opportunity.

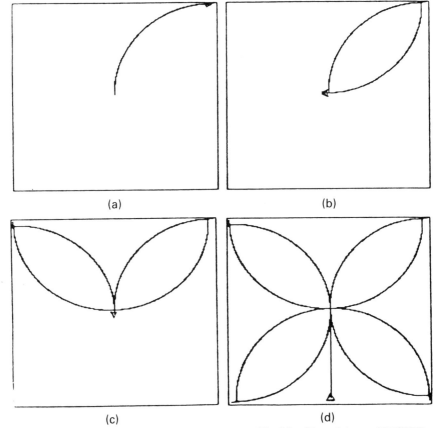

(a)

(b)

(c)

(d)

Fig. 3.1 − Four pictures of FLOWER.

As in much of our work that she found engaging, while I provided the initial impetus and direction, Miriam gradually took charge. Thus in the following segment of dialogue where I began directing Miriam at the keyboard, on her complaint that she was doing all the typing, we changed jobs and she assumed a more dominant role.

Bob: O.K. The first thing we did: D, 1, 2, 3, space, 30. What was the second thing we did?

Miriam: R, T, 90.

Bob: [Keying] 2 for the second thing. R, T, 90. What was the third thing we did?

Miriam: D, 1, 2, 3, space, right — no. Space, 30.

Bob: How much of the picture did that make?

Miriam: One of the petals.

Bob: So that's the end then, right? . . . and we type END.

Miriam: Now we type PETAL. P, E, T, A, L. . . .

Bob: New line. What do you think of that?

Miriam: That's all it does?

Bob: One petal. If we're going to make a flower, what do we do?

Miriam: Type: PETAL, PETAL, PETAL, PETAL.

Bob: [Beginning a new procedure] Space TO space FLOWER. What's the first thing we do? [Keys [1, space] and waits] You just said it: PETAL. What's the second thing we do? [Keys [2, space]] Same thing we did last time. P, E, T, A, L. What's the third thing? [Keying]

Miriam: Same thing.

Bob: The fourth thing? [Keying]

Miriam: Same thing.

Bob: The fifth thing?

Miriam: It's not the same. 100. Back a hundred 90.

Bob: 190. And what else did you do?

Miriam: Nothing.

Bob: Are we finished now when we make our flower that way?

Miriam: Yes.

After I saved her procedure on peripheral storage, Miriam printed twenty copies of her FLOWER, which the next day she distributed to her kindergarten class for coloring. She was obviously proud of work she felt was her own.

Writing her first procedure: reflections

One's grand flights, one's Sunday baths,
One's tootings at the weddings of the soul
Occur as they occur . . . .

The Sense of the Sleight-of-Hand Man

My delight in this work is clear; but should I be smug? What could be more accidental than the details by which this flower came into being? I had no idea that the kernel [FD 20 BK 10 RT 3] would lead this way. Surely Miriam did not select 30 as an input variable because 30 times 3 degrees would be an effective right angle. Was it not another accident that [RT 90 D123 30] not merely returned the turtle to the home position but did so in an orientation permitting simple repetition of the sequence [RT 90 D123 30] to draw four non-overlapping petals?

My sense of the contingent aspects of this session is different, rather more that these accidents provide a measure of the flexibility required for the easy operation and happy outcomes of developments almost inevitable in computer microcultures. Programming is the specific skill which transforms computer technology from a provided toy into a tool, and more, into a medium wherein one can exercise his imagination in the progressive construction of amazingly complex but comprehensible artifacts. At the MIT Logo project we expected those children participating, who were typically ten years old, to write procedures and to understand what they were doing. If they hang around Logo computers long enough, children *will* learn to write procedures. I believe this is true for young children also. In this specific case, Miriam directed me in writing a procedure. but it is clear that she understood well the successive agglomeration of one petal to the next and that the final step was different. This outcome was happy in the sense Miriam understood the FLOWER procedure (this does not imply she understood the subprocedure, D123). But it was happy in another sense also. She did not resist this learning at all. PETAL was a minimal extension of her procedure D123. Everyone knows that petals make flowers, so FLOWER was her own as well.[9]

Black boxes and human reflection

Miriam never, either before or after writing the FLOWER procedure, executed D123 with any other input value than 30. The procedure seems to have been subsumed by its use as a subprocedure (it was not executed separately again), but I infer it maintained an identity in Miriam's mind from her later suggesting the name 'E123' where a new procedure name was required. What we witness is the *functional isolation* (not logical closure) of knowledge about this procedure by its subsumption. That is, though personally created, it became a 'black box' in the mind, something usable but not understood in detail (Miriam did *not* understand D123, the subprocedure which made PETALS for her FLOWER). The failure to achieve objectives because of unanticipated interactions among such 'black boxes' creates the need for debugging programs.[10] This situation can be taken as the archetype of such concrete experiences as impel and make valuable the reflective ability of the human mind.

9 If I seem to dwell overmuch on the ownership of knowledge, there is a good reason. Think of learning as intellectual incorporation. If knowledge is not made your own, whose is it? On the margin of my mind, I find the flotsam of a shipwrecked Virgil, 'Terque quaterque beati'; these words mean nothing to me and serve only as an ever-present mockery of my classical studies. Does not such learning, recalled but not incorporated, go contrary to that coherence for which most vigorous minds struggle? Or is fragmentary comprehension an inescapable aspect of the human condition?

10 A program *bug* is an element or the interrelation of elements which do something not intended. Some bugs are bad, some are beautiful. Debugging is the process of removing bugs from programs. This often, but not always, requires analysis and a deeper understanding of a program and its parts.

PRECURSORS OF DEBUGGING: PRETTY FLOWER

Miriam's typical hand-drawn flower consisted of small circular petals surrounding a larger circle; it was quite unlike the flower created by her first procedure. Because making a flower of circles would involve Miriam in a classic turtle geometry bug, I proposed the project of making a different flower design. During the execution of her 'Pretty Flower' project, Miriam achieved a particular insight which showed her that one could understand and even explain emergent features of designs based on knowledge of what the subprocedures did. Knowing that the product results from the processes of its parts is an idea prerequisite to debugging, and understanding how a complex figure is created by the functions of the procedure steps is evidence that one does own that idea.

Miriam was initially apathetic, but her interest picked up when I generated a circle-making subprocedure C with a kernel [FD :DISTANCE RT 15]. She selected the input '12' as making a suitable flower heart [C 12], and '4' for making petals [C 4]. I composed a 'BUMP' procedure [BK 12 RT 15 BK 12 RT 15]

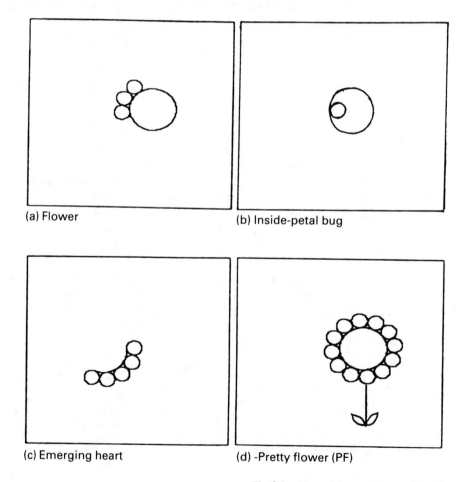

(a) Flower

(b) Inside-petal bug

(c) Emerging heart

(d) -Pretty flower (PF)

Fig. 3.2 – Four pictures of 'Pretty flower'.

for moving the turtle along the arc of the circular flower heart to that place where the next small circular petal should be placed. During the first session we drew a flower with our C and BUMP procedures but wrote no superprocedure to do so. (See Fig. 3.2(a).)

Instead of debugging

In the next session (Logo Session 49) using the same procedure, C, for the flower heart and petals, Miriam immediately encountered an 'inside petal' bug. (The turtle must turn 180 degrees to draw a petal outside the heart's circumference. See Fig. 3.2(b).) Miriam's reaction to this bug shows the character of her pre-analytic debugging.

> Bob: How do we make a petal?
> Miriam: I said C, space, 4. [She keys.]
> Bob: We got a bug there [the 'inside-petal' bug of Fig. 3.2(b)] .... Do you know how to get rid of it?
> Miriam: Press stop.
> Bob: [Presses 'stop' key twice] Didn't work .... Let's clear the screen and try again. Take a look at it closely now. You see the bug is that the petal is inside the heart of the flower.
> Miriam: Yeah. I forgot.... [Speaks to herself] B, K, and.... [Keys CS] C, space, 12.... C, now, outside.... [to herself] B, K, space.... [Keys also 12.]
> Bob: That's part of the BUMP procedure.
> Miriam: [Keys RT, pauses.... Keys space 15, and continues B, K, space, 12.]
> Bob: [When she completes the BUMP kernel] That's pretty good, Miriam. You remembered that very well. Let's see if it fixes the bug you have.
> Miriam: [Keys C, space, 4, and new line.]
> Bob: We still have it halfway in.... Shall I show you what the problem is?
> Miriam: Yeah.

The proposed second fix is vaguely associated with the circumstances of the bug, but the precise connection of bug description, analysis, and fix is nowhere present. The first fix, 'press stop', an appropriate response for some POLY procedure overruns, is even more inappropriate than the second fix in this circumstance. I conclude that both proposals are a kind of context-specific floundering. I fixed the bug; Miriam later gave no evidence of learning from this how to do so.

With the inside petal bug behind us, we completed the pretty flower by keying [C 4 BUMP] over and over. I proposed generating a 12-fold iteration of these Logo commands as a PETALS procedure. Miriam did not object. We are both surprised at the result. (See Fig. 3.2(c).)

> Bob: P, F. [He keys] ... Hey! It's in a different place.
> Miriam: But it's the heart!
> Bob: It still has a heart. How did the heart get there?
> Miriam: It goes around, in still a circle, and the middle of it.
> Bob: How did the middle get there?
> Miriam: See. It went around in a circle to make the little circles.

The BUMP procedure traced the twelve arcs of [C 12] as it was used to navigate from the location of one petal to the next. Thus, the circle of the flower's heart emerged from the process of adding the petals and was not needed for more than the original guidance in constructing the procedure. Miriam was surprised and delighted, but not mystified. The phenomenon continued to attract her and led (in Logo Session 52, 6;4;11) to this more lucid explanation:

> Miriam: [As the procedure begins to execute] Know how it gets that circle in there? ... See. Like it attaches the little circles, and has to make a little line to the next one, and that means it makes a circle in there [gestures to the heart of the flower].
> Bob: That's absolutely correct.... It's the BUMP procedure that goes over from the bottom of one petal to the next?
> Miriam: Yeah.

Miriam spontaneously explained the emergence of the flower heart to me three times. The event marked an insight that clearly was important to her. Her understanding of the emergent effect was possible because she was familiar with the parts the superprocedure ran to create the whole. This citation does not exemplify debugging, but it shows analytical development in that the explanation the phenomenon requires is available only through attending to the relations between the steps of the procedure and the resulting figure. The computer environment can foster an analytic mode of thought both because problems arise requiring debugging and because one encounters emergent effects whose explanation 'lies only one level of detail down', i.e. is directly accessible in the encoded steps of the procedure whose execution creates the effect. Such emergent effects become accessible to a person's understanding if she is familar with all the elements from which the design emerges, if, in the best case, she has created and used those elements herself.

Although Miriam concluded the project with a procedure, PF, of which she was justifiably proud (she later used it as a decoration on letters she wrote to friends), the debugging cited to this point is non-technical at best. The outstanding incident in composing Miriam's PF procedure was the shooting of her 'first bug'. The description of the components of debugging seen in this incident will serve us later as a standard for measuring Miriam's gradual acquisition of the skill of debugging her computer procedures.

Shooting her first bug

After three days of work creating a flower drawing procedure, Miriam made a final test and found a bug. She had drawn, with the turtle commands in immediate mode,[11] a stem of good proportion, 85 steps long, but had failed to encode in the procedure a [FD 50] command she had executed. Thus her flower appeared with a short stem, 35 steps. Here's how Miriam shot her first bug:

11 Integrated editing is a feature of many programming languages, including Apple Basic, where lines of code prefixed with a number are inserted in the program definition while those with no number prefix are executed immediately. Such execution is in 'immediate mode'. Logo on the PDP-11 had an 'integrated editor' which made it possible to execute commands of the language while defining a procedure. This feature is lacking from most current microcomputer implementations of Logo.

Bob: Looks pretty good to me.

Miriam: No.

Bob: Oh-oh. We got a bug, huh?

Miriam: Yeah.

Bob: What do we do about it? ... What's our bug?

Miriam: The stem is too short.

Bob. The stem is too short. How long is our stem? ... It's a 35 ... I know the trouble. We left out the 50. Remember?

Miriam: Oh yeah.

Bob: You did the 50, but we didn't write it in.

Miriam: Rats!

Bob: Can you fix it?

Miriam: How?

Bob: You remember what happened when you keyed the line 2 and the blank? And the old one went away and the new one got there?

Miriam: Yeah?

Bob: Key a new line 5.

Miriam: [Keys] 5, space. [Keys the new line character, replacing the FD 35 command with a blank line.]

Bob: Would that fix it? ... That just made the FORWARD 35 go away. Now your stem will be no-long at all. It will be zero long.... I guess you'd better have a new line 5 that tells the turtle to go forward the right distance.

Miriam: [Keying] 5?

Bob: Yeah. Space. And how far should he go? ... You had a 35 but you left out the 50. So it should be, —

Miriam: [Interrupting] Hold it.... 85 ... C, S, new line. P, F.

Bob: O.K. Let's see what's happening now.... Is that perfect?

Miriam: Yep.

Bob: Beautiful, Miriam. You shot your first bug.

Reflecting on this dialog, we see the debugging process as analyzable into six steps:

Steps		Key to preceding dialog
1. bug acceptance	Miriam:	No
2. bug description	Miriam:	The stem is too short
3. bug analysis	Bob:	We left out the 50
4. conceiving the fix	Bob:	replacement editing
5. implementing the fix	Bob:	5 FD 50
6. testing the fix	Miriam:	keys CS, PF

We notice that in this incident, although Miriam is credited with shooting the bug, steps three to five were dominated by my knowledge and guidance. Because of Miriam's interest in and success at analyzing this failure (at least in part), subsequently I offered her a didactic introduction to debugging.

Inasmuch as Miriam was immersed in a computer microculture, we must inquire about the extent to which her knowledge of debugging came from general influences of the culture and to what extent it came from particular events of instruction. More importantly, we should also ask what was the character of each component. Before we trace her learning through the detail of these instruction sessions, I should relate incidents which show what sorts of debugging knowledge she absorbed from the microculture of my family and her Logo acquaintances and convey its character.

THE SOCIAL CONTEXT OF DEBUGGING;

As a member of the Logo project at the MIT AI lab, I was part of a computer culture which welcomed children as members. It is natural then to ask how much the ambience of that microculture contributed to Miriam's learning about debugging. In my judgment, that contribution was limited in kind but substantial in import. The focus of our microculture was definitely on solving problems. The activities we engaged in and the terminology we used involved three major aspects: the discovery of interesting problems, the localization of failures, and the solving of advice. Call the first 'neat phenomena' and think of the skipping forward and rolling backward of a backspun ping-pong ball. The second we called debugging. The third we referred to as 'giving hints' and 'knowing good tricks'. The following vignette exhibits 'giving hints' as socially provided insights:

> One of Miriam's proudest achievements since her sixth birthday has been learning to ride her bicycle successfully without training wheels. She borrowed Robby's crescent wrench and removed the wheels herself. For several days thereafter, her procedure was as follows: sit on the seat and try to push off; try to get both feet on the pedals before the bike falls over; at the first indication of instability, turn the wheel in the direction of the fall and stick both feet out to catch oneself.
>
> The procedure is not bad; it's nearly perfect, in fact. The only flaw was that the bike would fall over after going about three feet. Luckily for Miriam, at this point she received some good advice from our neighbor Jim: 'If you start off fast, you won't fall over'. When Miriam told of this hint, I agreed that Jim's advice was absolutely correct and added that for problems that look hard or mysterious, if you get one good hint you may find they are not hard at all. Miriam joined Jim's good advice with a lot of practice. The advice provided the breakthrough she needed, and with the practice she has refined her skill so that now she rides ably.
>
> This evening Miriam met Jim again in the courtyard, showed him her latest achievements with the hula hoop and then went on to tell him she could ride her bike, that she was really good at it, and his 'one good hint' had taught her how to do it.
>
> Vignette 11; age: 6;1;14

Not only had Miriam learned about cycling, but she also adopted from me, because of this personally important example, a stance toward communicating ideas. The terminology surfaced later when Miriam expressed dissatisfaction with a swimming instructor: 'That lesson was terrible. She wants you to get your face wet all the time. I'll never learn to swim from her. She can't give any good hints!' This very simple, children's learning theory focusses not on 'basic skills' but on the insights necessary for understanding neat phenomena.

Even if a microculture is not didactic in its intentions, to the extent that 'neat phenomena' are what people want to share with others, the microculture is in fact very intrusive. For instance: among the tests Miriam performed at the beginning of The Intimate Study was one involving the backspinning of a ping-pong ball.[12] From that time on, whenever Miriam held a ping-pong ball, she would try backspinning it. I brought a hula hoop for a follow-up experiment to explore how easily she could generalize backspinning to a superficially different object. I let Miriam play with the hula hoop in the meanwhile. First the Logo Project secretary, then a graduate student, then another child independently and spontaneously tried to show Miriam how to backspin the hoop before I could perform my experiment. After the experiment, Miriam played in the hall while I packed up our paraphernalia for the trip home. Marvin Minsky came by and inquired, 'Miriam, have you seen this good trick yet?'

In the course of a few days, while the materials were at hand and she was sensitized to the phenomenon, Miriam encountered four separate situations of potential informal instruction. Can one control such informal exposure? I think not, especially in a rich environment and an active culture, because a lively intelligence, sensitized to an engaging phenomenon, will notice its manifestations with only the slightest exposure. Since controlling exposure is not possible the problem becomes methodological: how to be in the right place at the time when insight occurs; how to recognize a significant development and document its occurrence in detail sufficient to support subsequent analysis and interpretation.

I believe the design of this project, as an intensive protracted, naturalistic study of a bright child in a supportive environment during a recognized period of rapid development focusses on a rich domain of developmental data. The breadth of this study with respect to the child's life in the home, at play with friends, and under tutelage (at MIT), being both intrusive (thereby perturbing the structures of her mind) and extensive (opening to observation situations not usually attended to) offers a better hope of following the fine structure of developing ideas than does any method restricted to sampling ideas in more limited contexts.

I turn now to debugging as an important element in this children's learning theory. The purpose of debugging is to correct procedures that do not work. The function of describing the 'bug' is to localize the failure so that the bug can be fixed, excused, or avoided.

The use of debugging is by no means confined to computer procedures, and can be productively extended to everyday activities. Consider the following example:

> Over the past few weeks Robby has shown an interest in playing frisbee.
> Miriam has tried to play with us, but has been so inept that the game always
> became a squabble. We three played in the courtyard in a 20-foot triangle.

12 See Piaget, 1974, *The Grasp of Consciousness.*

Miriam was supposed to throw to Robby, but even when she did her best, she came nowhere near him. Robby tried to evict Miriam from the game, but could not because the frisbee was hers. I asked if maybe we could fix the bug? Miriam agreed. I described the bug as a 'holding-on' bug. We slowly executed her throwing motion, and I noted the point in her swing at which she should let go of the frisbee. On her second throw, and thereafter, Miriam was able to aim the frisbee in Robby's direction.

Vignette 70; age: 6;4;14

The second frisbee bug, frequently manifest, was one Robby described as a 'too-low' bug for which Miriam developed her own fix. This simple example shows how the microculture's focus on the identification, labelling, and analysis of failures can penetrate to a child's everyday concerns. More complex examples exist — such as the attempt we three made at folding paper boats following step-by-step instructions from *Curious George Rides a Bike*. There Miriam defined the 'no tuck in' bug, the 'I don't know what to do next' bug, and the 'last step pull apart' bug. Neither of these examples shows any explicit analysis by the child following description of the bug. Indeed, the children needed help, and that was precisely the kind of help this microculture provided. Both do show the kinds of incidents which can sensitize someone to an issue, and they exemplify the way a microculture focusses on aspects of a situation. It is not unreasonable to believe that this sort of focussing increases the salience of characters prominent in these situation-aspects and thus constitutes the way in which a microculture gives shape to, i.e. informs or structures, the perspectives of individual minds.

No badness in bugs

Miriam's labelling the 'no tuck in' and 'last step pull apart' bugs exhibits her acceptance of a debugging terminology and focus, but more is required to show its congeniality. One night at dinner Miriam struggled with a pork chop. Both lost — it skidded off her plate and onto the floor. 'Miriam!' her mother and I exclaimed. 'You know what, Dad?' We waited. 'My pork chop's got a jump on the floor bug', Miriam concluded, and we burst out laughing. This joke is clear evidence that Miriam was immersed in and very much at home in a microculture where procedural description and terminology were prominent.

Despite such jargon permeating the microculture of our family and the Logo Project, there is no evidence that Miriam absorbed anything more than a super-ficial use of the term 'bug' as a neutral label for a specific problem. Was there here an idea she could apply in problem solving? Was there here an idea that could ramify into other cognitive structures? The answer is 'no' — but we need to pass through considerably more analysis for that conclusion to be acceptable.

DEBUGGING INSTRUCTION

Miriam's satisfaction at receiving credit for 'shooting' her first bug presented an opportunity to pursue the theme of debugging. The first selection of the following excerpts shows the extent to which analysis, as a method of problem solving, is retrograde to the choices of circumstantial thought. The subsequent selections indicate what Miriam did in preference to analyzing the problem and permit reasoned speculation about the possible sources of guidance she accepted in her thinking.

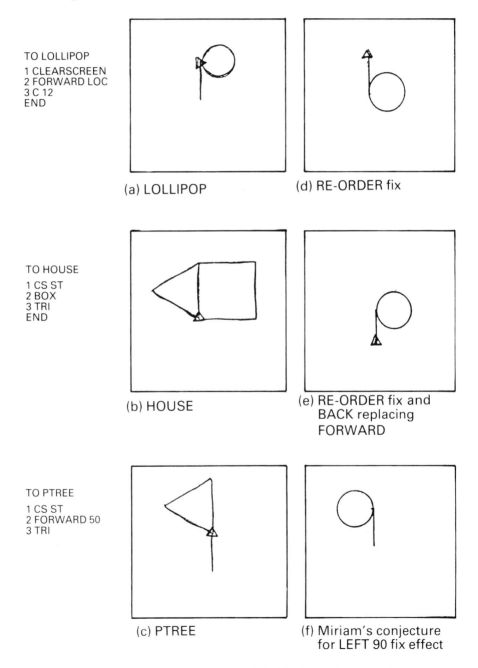

TO LOLLIPOP
1 CLEARSCREEN
2 FORWARD LOC
3 C 12
END

(a) LOLLIPOP

(d) RE-ORDER fix

TO HOUSE
1 CS ST
2 BOX
3 TRI
END

(b) HOUSE

(e) RE-ORDER fix and
    BACK replacing
    FORWARD

TO PTREE
1 CS ST
2 FORWARD 50
3 TRI

(c) PTREE

(f) Miriam's conjecture
    for LEFT 90 fix effect

Fig. 3.3 − Three Buggy procedures and fixes.

What did we do? I asked Miriam to fix three malfunctioning procedures, ones that I told her were characteristic of faulty procedures made by other children in the lab. The drawings in the initial 'bug'-ridden state are shown in Fig. 3.3. LOLLIPOP and PTREE exhibit interface bugs. The typical *interface bug* is the omission of a needed operation between two separable parts of a procedure; execution of an inappropriate operation between part-creating operations is also an interface bug. A *fix* is the operational sequence needed to make a bug disappear. The simplest fix for the LOLLIPOP procedure is a [LEFT 90] inserted between the FORWARD command and the invocation of the C (circle) procedure. HOUSE exhibits a *setup bug*, that is, one which results from incomplete specification of the initial conditions from which a procedure will execute. The easiest fix for the HOUSE procedure is a [RIGHT 90] inserted before invocation of the BOX subprocedure. The interface bug of PTREE requires two commands for its fixing, [RIGHT 90] and [BACK 50], inserted between the FORWARD drawing the trunk and the TRI (triangle) of the tree's habit. Miriam worked at these three debugging problems during two consecutive sessions (Logo Sessions 52 and 53), the first of which followed her direction, while the second was more didactic. I introduced the theme of debugging to Miriam by a reference to her fixing the bug in the PF (pretty flower) procedure by encoding a command she had left out.

Rejecting the problem

Although enthusiastic initially, as soon as the first bug became manifest Miriam quickly turned quite negative:

> Bob: We'll start off with one that's supposed to be a — [invokes the procedure. See Fig. 3.1.]
>
> Miriam: [Interrupting] Lollipop. . . . Rats! I hate that lollipop.
>
> Bob: You do? . . . Well, can you fix it and make it a good one?
>
> Miriam: No.
>
> Bob: Let me — [Prints the procedure on the terminal] . . . .
>
> Miriam: [Covers her eyes] No.
>
> Bob: What's wrong with it? . . . What's the bug?
>
> Miriam: I'll get rid of that lollipop. Do clearscreen, show turtle — Then I'll go forward 100. Then, but the circle's got to [twisting motion with her hand], got to go in the right place.
>
> Bob: Can you make a good lollipop, the way it should be? . . . You want to do that?
>
> Miriam: Yeah, but . . . can I do it the way I want?

Her request meant that she wanted to make 'her own' lollipop instead of fixing the flawed procedure. Why did Miriam reject the problem? It is clear that she understood the bug in the sense of being able to describe how this lollipop was different from what a lollipop should be. Miriam accepted the task of drawing a good lollipop but rejected the analytical problem. I believe she did not know what to do or even how to begin analyzing the failure.

Epistemological stability

Miriam immediately undertook writing her own procedure, PLP (pretty lollipop), revealing her plan as she began coding: 'Forward a hundred, then do my C (circle) procedure'.

> Miriam: P, L, P [keying the name to test the new procedure], new line. [The same buggy lollipop appears. Miriam laughs.]
>
> Bob: You've got a bug there. That's the same bug the other guy had.
>
> Miriam: [Laughing] I know.
>
> Bob: What are we going to do?
>
> Miriam: Can't fix it.
>
> Bob: You can't fix it?
>
> Miriam: No.

This 'good luck' of mine that Miriam recreated, as her own, the bug just rejected witnesses the epistemological stability of turtle geometry. Bugs encountered are common and persistent until understood. Miriam described the failure. Did she analyze the problem? No. She appeared at first to reject it (because she did not know what to do), but this rejection was only temporary. Her 'No' above was immediately contravened.

> Miriam: No. Hey! We'll put the circle in and then put the stem in.... I'll show you.... [keys clearscreen] ... I will do like C, space, 12. Right? [The shape appears on the screen when she keys new line] ... B, K, space, 1, oh-oh. [Keying. When Miriam hits new line, the bug again is manifest. She looks shocked.] Rats! [A smile of frustration] Look what happened.... It did the same thing again.

The essence of Miriam's fix was a pure re-ordering of the two component steps. Has the bug been analyzed? I think not. Trying to give her a hint, I asked Miriam to pay particular attention to where the center of the circle was, in relation to the stick and the turtle at the end of the procedure. As she watched the turtle draw the circle and complete the lollipop, she said incorrectly that the center of the circle was above the turtle. Miriam's failure to appreciate how the center of the circle drawn related to the turtle's initial position makes more firm the conviction that the procedures were not being analyzed in a specific sense of examining the functions of each step and their interactions. I interpret these preceding session transcription excerpts to imply that although Miriam could take direction from my analysis and employ it, she could not herself analyze even this very simple procedure.

Inferences

We could describe Miriam as following a 're-ordering' heuristic, but what would than mean? Labelling does not specify where the advice came from. One might imagine that Miriam's mind contained a separate microview of debugging knowledge (somehow or other accessible to other problem-solving microviews) in the fashion of Sussman's HACKER system (1975). I would prefer to avoid such a claim because it raises the impossible question of how such a structure of general applicability would communicate with all those other structures which might possibly benefit from its advice. An alternative is that such general problem-solving guidance is accessible in the same way as other 'invocable' knowledge, through the genetic path. This is possible because general guidance can be seen not as *generalized* knowledge but as *undifferentiated* knowledge.[13] If such a view is acceptable, general guidance does not come from some segregated debugging facility but bubbles up to current problems form the most primitive ancestors of all knowledge.[14]

Two rejections

After our break, I took a more directive role.

> Bob: Let's print out pretty lollipop and do it. [He keys, and the shape of
>   PLP, identical to Fig. 3.3(a), appears.] Now what's wrong?
> Miriam: It's stupid.
> Bob: Can you describe to me what's wrong? It's not enough to say that it's
>   stupid.
> Miriam: Unh-uh ... I guess the lollipop is being broken.
> Bob: That's re-interpreting what's happened, Miriam. Let's fix it.
> Miriam: Rats.

We witness here two different ways of rejecting the problem: first, by putting it down, a matter of valuation; second, by excusing appearances. Accepting such an excuse as adequate undercuts the 'need' for analysis. The cheerful abandoning of one objective for another when the knowledge-tools are not available for problem solving is a clear example of the kind of cognitive performance which is suitably described as bricolage.

Doing something different

I attempted to lead Miriam into a separate analysis of the procedure:

> Bob: [Printing the text of PLP] We will EDIT, that is, change, pretty lollipop.
>   Is there anything wrong with the clearscreen [step 1]? No. We know
>   what that does and what it is for —
> Miriam: But.... [Raising up her hand, a gesture indicating she has a new
>   idea]. I think I can do it, Daddy.... You know that EEL [the shape
>   manipulation program used earlier]? We could use that slash or dash
>   and like, turn it. And we could use a circle.
> Bob: Can you change this procedure to make the lollipop go to the right
>   place?
> Miriam: It really is a good lollipop. Know why?
> Bob: Why?
> Miriam: Someone bent the stick.

13 For arguments about how the genesis of new knowledge relates to residual control structure, see Chapter 7.
14 What might be the general structure of such an information network is a question addressed in Chapter 5, 'Cognitive organization'.

The suggestion to use EEL is a clear example of competitive microview intrusion. Miriam did not complete the analysis of PLP. Stymied, she advanced a completely different and inappropriate proposal for solving the immediate task of making a good lollipop drawing. With that alternative blocked, excusing appearances dominated analyzing the failure.[15]

As Miriam took over the keyboard, working on PLP, she exhibited a second form of 'doing something different'. Her inclination was to add a fifth line. When I pointed out she could change lines, she rejected my attempt to offer a hint and elected to change line 3 [C 12].

> Bob: What are you going to do?
> Miriam: I'm going to, ah ... say 13 [i.e. type C 13; instead she keys C 31].
> Bob: What's that going to do? I don't get it.
> Miriam: It's something different.
> Bob: It's something different, but will it fix the bug?
> Miriam: No. I want to see what it does. ...

Miriam's wish to 'do something different' soon expanded and she asked to abandon LOLLIPOP for some other task. We did so.

Discussion

What do we make of this detail observation? Two things, a case and a characterization. The case I wish to make is that Miriam did not understand the debugging of procedures at all. By this I mean specifically that although she could describe a bug as a failure with respect to an objective, she did not analyze bugs; she did not translate such descriptions into the potent operations of the debugging set out earlier. The gap in Miriam's knowledge was that no step of bug analysis intervened between bug description (in terms of divergence from an objective) and conceiving of the fix to be implemented and tested. The fixes did not take guidance from an analysis of the bugs.

We can characterize Miriam's behavior in these debugging exercises by specifying two factors. First, when she rejected a problem, the rejection was either a devaluation of the problem ('It's stupid'), a reinterpretation of the failure ('It really is a good lollipop.... Someone bent the stick'), or the election of some alternative problem (e.g. HOUSE or PTREE instead of LOLLIPOP) in the blind hope it might prove more tractable. The second factor is the sources of guidance which the problems accepted. The source or sources must be inferred from the fixes proposed. Consider Miriam's attempt to deal with the lollipop bug in terms of the procedures of the EEL interface. This is another example of guidance deriving from the essentially competitive interaction of microviews. Since this issue is treated extensively in Chapter 2, here we will focus on that guidance which is succinctly formulated as a general statement of advice.

---

15 It must be granted Miriam did not analyze the failure of PLP at this time. The strongest claim one could make is that she did not *because* she could not. Such a claim cannot be proven, for Miriam might have *preferred* to do something different. A weaker claim, supported, I believe, by evidence in the following protocol excerpts, is that she did not analyse PLP *and* she *could not have done so at this time*.

I want to propose a way of thinking about very general problem-solving guidance that is different from generalization of past solutions. Such very general guidance is exhibited by the re-ordering fix (draw the circle before the line) and the random fix (do something, anything, different). If we pursue interpretations where structure results from genesis, function from structure, and genesis from function, it is a puzzle how this generalized advice could be generated, and further, how it could be made available to a microview with a problem. These considerations lead me to propose that such advice is not generalized by a process of abstraction. Rather, it is undifferentiated in the sense of pertaining to the most fundamental microviews about physical reality. Let me be specific with this example. I have seen Miriam's infant sister with a large ring in one hand and a small ball in the other, trying to cram both into an open box. Frustrated when trying several times to insert the large ring first, she succeeded by re-ordering, i.e. she inserted the small ball in the box and tolerated a conclusion with the large ring sitting on top of the box. There is no need to believe the baby owned elaborate descriptions of the objects or reasoned before-hand that the acceptable solution would be achieved. If this re-ordering fix is a good trick known even to a one-year-old, it should remain available as supportive guidance, invocable through the genetic path unless countermanded by experience in descendent microviews. The second advisement ('do something, anything, different') can similarly be attributed to those knowledges of reality constructed in infancy.

TAKING INSTRUCTION

Miriam put me on the defensive with an incipient complaint: 'Is this shooting a bug again?' I took the blame for her pique at the previous day's session by admitting I had asked her to solve hard problems without explaining adequately what she should do. Thus we plunged into a more didactic mode. For example, I stated explicitly that whenever you begin debugging, 'the first thing you want to do is print out the procedure'. To this Miriam replied with a bored 'Yah'.

Miriam agreed I should show her how to fix the buggy lollipop — then immediately proposed her 're-order' fix again. When I would not let her reject the problem by starting over, she expressed antipathy ['Grumble-foo'] and proposed another 'random' fix, changing [FD 100] to [BK 100], which — when added to the re-order fix — made the original bug once more manifest (see Fig. 3.3(e)). At this impasse, I proceeded to fix the bug as a demonstration, giving the failure its type name, 'interface bug':

> Bob: This kind of bug is where something should happen between going forward and making the candy part for the top of the lollipop. Let me show you what to do. [She agrees.] This is a kind of bug where at 3 we should do a left turn 90.
> Miriam: Daddy? . . . Why won't the lollipop be pointing, ahm, ah that way? [Gesturing toward our left] That would be silly. Know why? . . . 'Cause then the lollipop would be crooked. [See Fig. 3.3(f) for my recon-struction of her conjecture.]

Despite Miriam's resistance, I altered LOLLIPOP, inserting a LEFT 90 command in step 3. Execution gave Miriam ocular proof that the fix was correct. When I asked her to describe the difference between the perfected procedure and the original, Miriam said, 'They didn't put it in, um, the left 90'. For the first time, at this juncture, Miriam saw an example of debugging applied to a problem she herself had accepted and long failed to solve. It appears that this incident marked the establishment of a debugging ur-concept.

A first extension

We turned to debugging the HOUSE procedure (see Fig. 3.3(b)) and Miriam took over, directing me to list the procedure:

> Bob: What's wrong with that house?
> Miriam: It's sideways. . . . They forgot something, too.
> Bob: What did they forget?
> Miriam: Ah, there should be something different. Right? . . . at number 3.

Could it be any clearer that Miriam is imposing the organization of the previous solution on this new problem? I prevented her following this tack by distinguishing the HOUSE bug as a setup bug, different from the previous interface bug, and continued into a second debugging demonstration.

> Bob: Let me show you a simple way to fix this bug. . . . Then we'll come back and you can tell me how to fix number three. The problem – you can look at this problem as saying the house is turned on its side . . . If the turtle were pointed in a different direction, then the house might get straightened out. How should we make the turtle turn?
> Miriam: I don't know. Like R, T, . . . ? R, T, space, [Miriam keys 90; Bob keys HOUSE and Miriam keys newline; the house appears correctly oriented.]
> Bob: What do you think?
> Miriam: I did it!

Miriam took a lot of credit for fixing this bug. In the remaining exercise, debugging PTREE, I let her have more opportunity to earn such credit.

One step forward

I asked Miriam to draw a picture of what PTREE should look like before we turned to the computer:

> Bob: You type in PTREE now. Is PTREE gonna look like this? [Holding up her drawing.]
> Miriam: [Keys PTREE] Unh-uh.
> Bob: No. So there's a bug there. [See Fig. 3.4(a).]
> Miriam: How do I do it? Oh. I get it. I get it. I get it. . . . You type RT 90. [Laughing.]

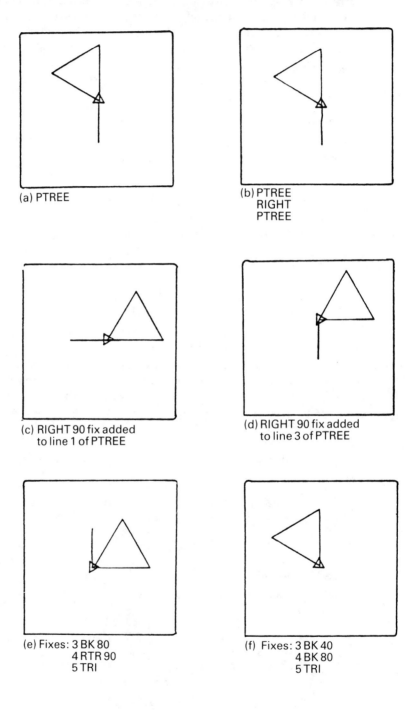

Fig. 3.4 – Six Fixes for the PTREE procedure.

Bob: You think that will help? It might. O.K. Let's edit. [Miriam rises to keyboard] Oh, I'm sorry. You want to type RT 90 before we edit the procedure?

Miriam: Yeah. [Eager interest. Keys RT 90.]

Bob: You think that's gonna fix it?

Miriam: Yeah. [Does keying to execute PTREE. See Fig.3.4(b).]

Bob: What happened? [Same result as original because clearscreen sets the turtle's heading to zero.]

Miriam: We forgot to edit.

Notice especially that Miriam's two observations, the RIGHT 90 fix and the 'we forgot to edit', both come out of the problem's immediate context, in contrast with the re-ordering fix so prominent with LOLLIPOP. RIGHT 90 was the previous successful fix; its failure here is excused by the fix's not being integrated with the procedure through editing.

The source of guidance

If there had been any uncertainty about what provided the guidance for Miriam's RIGHT 90 fix, that question was answered definitely as Miriam continued with her next proposal:

Miriam: I think I'll do something... Ed the first one.

Bob: You're going to change line number 1? The first step of the procedure? [Miriam agrees.] ... What do you want to do, Miriam? What do you want to accomplish?

Miriam: I want to try to do it like the house.

Bob: You think this might be a SETUP bug? [Miriam shakes her head 'yes'.] ... What other kind of bug could it be?

Miriam: I dunno. [Keying] CS, space, ST, then RT 90.... New line? ... [Keys PTREE. See Fig. 3.4(c). Turns to me laughing.]

Bob: Well, that was a good try. It didn't work, but it was a good try.

Miriam: Right, I got the tree thing up [the triangle is oriented with a horizontal base].

Bob: Well, hey, that's pretty good....

Miriam: I give up. I can't do it.

The RIGHT 90 fix to line 1 appears to have been the only one in Miriam's repertoire at this moment. The guidance is as concrete as can be. It is possible to see in Miriam's quick admission of failure a non-obvious advance. That is, having a specific but vague idea of the form of a solution, she no longer tried the 'general' and remote forms of guidance witnessed in the previous Logo Session.

Another step

I redirected her and recalled the LOLLOPOP bug fix.

Bob: This kind of bug is not a setup bug. This kind of bug is an interface bug, like the one you had with LOLLIPOP. Is that a good hint? [Miriam

agrees.] ... I'm going to take out the RIGHT 90 and we'll rerun PTREE
so it's back the way it started out.... Now, when I say it's an interface
bug, that means there's something left out — —

Miriam: [Interrupting] Oh. I get it.

Bob: — — between the forward and the TRI.

Miriam: [Keys 3, space, and turns to me] I don't know what to do.... Hold
it.... [With hands over the keyboard letter R, looks at me]

Bob: You're going to do another right turn? ... [Miriam keys RT] ... and a
space, please. [Miriam keys space, 90.] Want to give it a test?

Miriam: [Keys PTREE. See Fig. 3.4(d)]   Too bad.

Miriam's lucky conjunction of the 'line 3' fix of LOLLIPOP with the RIGHT 90
fix of HOUSE (the immediately preceding problem) got her halfway to the two-
operation fix required for PTREE — — but she did not recognize the outcome as
showing progress.

Bug re-description

I tried to help Miriam see that the last fix was a major step toward a solution.
Notice here how the re-description of the bug at this point changes directly
into first, an objective for action (at (1)) and then into a specification for a
fix (at (2)).

Bob: You know it's an interface bug and you've nearly fixed it. It's almost
fixed. (Pointing to TRIANGLE) You've got the tree now in the right
position, so you can describe the bug differently. How would you describe
the bug differently? How would you describe the bug now?

Miriam: I don't know.

Bob: Well, where should the tree be? Where should the trunk be? ... Is that
a hint?

Miriam: Unh-uh.

Bob: Look at your picture. Here [on picture] you have the trunk right in
the middle of the tree, but up there [on screen] is the trunk on the
middle of the tree?

(1)   Miriam: Move the loop over.

Bob: Good idea, How are you going to do it?

(2a)   Miriam: Ah, I don't know.... Back up the turtle.

Bob: O.K. That's a good idea. Let's print out PTREE and you decide where
to back up the turtle.

Miriam: [Keys 3.]

Bob: Step 3 ... Are you going to keep your RIGHT 90 in there?

(2b)   Miriam: Yeah.... B, K, space, 80.

Bob: What about your right turn 90?

Miriam: I'll make it [line] 4, then make the TRI 5.... [Completes keying
PTREE and new line; a bug is manifest; she then turns to Bob with an
uncertain smile of amused frustration — see Fig. 3.4(e).]

Bob. That's not bad.

Miriam: I moved the stem only.

Miriam's rudimentary analysis was vulnerable because a two-step fix was needed, and she failed to consider the interaction of steps.

Completing PTREE

The moment was a critical juncture in Miriam's debugging of this simple problem. She had begun to analyze the problem in terms that she could see as sensible. The mal-ordering of steps was a complication which pushed her back into floundering. Sensing that her commitment to solve the problem was declining, I gave her the solution to preserve the sense that this microdomain of experience was truly comprehensible and within her cognitive reach. From this point on, the remaining developments were refinements. It is worth noting, nonetheless, that Fig. 3.4(f) shows the outcome of a final erroneous fix. Miriam had decided that [BK 80] (line 4) was too much, and in trying to modify that command she encoded [BK 40] as line 3, thus wiping out the right turn. When I listed the procedure and pointed to it, she analyzed this erroneous fix: 'I left out the wrong thing'.

Exercises summary

If we rise now out of the detail observations, we can see several conclusions stand out. First, the sense in which analysis is retrograde to circumstantial thought is clear. Starting anew is preferred to analyzing another's failures; even more, it is preferred to analyzing one's own failures (thus egocentricity as an affective element is not implicated). Second, the knowledge that Miriam is shown developing about debugging is as concrete as any thought can be, down to the specific operations and step number insertions of solutions put upon unanalyzed problems. Third, we have seen that it is possible and necessary to distinguish between guidance that derives from immediate and remote cognitive ancestors. Further, this more remote guidance may have the quality of 'general' advice because it is fundmental, i.e. implicated in the microviews of infancy and thus able to bubble up through the genetic path. Finally, the clear progress we witness in Miriam's debugging knowledge from 'shooting her first bug' to the complications of debugging the PTREE procedure involves a characterization of the problem (bugs occur because someone left something out) and having a non-empty repertoire of possibly effective actions based on previous, particular experience.

THE PERSON PROJECT

Near the end of The Intimate Study, our work became more project-oriented. Breaking up a project into parts has a programming analog — using a super-procedure to control parts or subprocedure written separately. Because this 'structured programming' is more vulnerable to effects from setup and interface bugs than is serial coding, I introduced Miriam to a simple procedure-stub generator to observe the effects of the previous instruction.

MAKEDO, the procedure-stub generator, was intended to be seen initially as analogous to MAKE, the Logo operation used to assign a value to a variable.

MAKE declares the existence of a variable. Since it declares the existence of subprocedures, MAKEDO also has implications for control structure. When invoked, MAKEDO asked three questions: what are you going to make; what is the name of the first part; what is the name of the next part. The last question is repeated until the keyword END is entered. MAKEDO generates a super-procedure with the name of the thing you are going to make, whose content is a serial invocation of the procedure stubs named as the first and successive parts of that thing. For example, Miriam declared that she would make a person whose parts were head, body, arms, and legs. MAKEDO generated this super-procedure and four associated procedure stubs (one example shown):

SUPERPROCEDURE	TYPICAL SUB-PROCEDURE
TO PERSON	TO LEGS
10 HEAD	1 PRINT [LEGS STUB]
20 BODY	END
30 ARMS	
40 LEGS	
END	

MAKEDO was very primitive and was intended to serve only as the simplest of introductions to top-down design of procedure structures. Implicit in the generation of such a simple procedure as PERSON is the potential for interface bugs, whose manifestation and fixing we now trace. In what follows, my role was primarily one of consolidating ideas Miriam raised and worked out.

When we began to edit the HEAD stub, Miriam chose to use her C [circle] procedure as a basis. Notable was her avoidance of the 'inside ear' bug. (This can be seen as a 'preventive fix' to a well-known bug, known from her Pretty Flower project as the 'inside petal' bug.) The specificity of her knowledge is clear in her anticipation of this bug's possibly recurring at the second ear — from which we may infer that she did not understand how the bug derived from the sense of the turtle's turning. When Miriam suggested drawing the eyes, nose, and mouth, I dissuaded her, to avoid complicating navigation on the head circumference, and advised proceeding to the next subprocedure, BODY. The stage was set for the next major bug manifestation.

Body-on-the-ear

I proposed that Miriam make a box body, but she preferred a circle of size larger than the head and encoded [C 16] as the body. With an impending bug, I dissuaded her from attempting to add arms before testing the conjunction of HEAD and BODY.

> Bob: How 'bout we see how we're doing now? Type PERSON and see what our PERSON is. . . . What happened?
> Miriam: [Smiling] Made a mistake.
> Bob: You got a bug. Ooog.

Miriam: Ooog. [Laughing] . . . Ooog.

Bob. Is that a big problem?

Miriam: I think we better do it, i.e. execute [PERSON] to show everything when we make the other parts. So we can see what to do.

Bob: What's our bug like here? We got the head fine. But this is a very funny person, 'cause his body's connected to his ear.... Let me ask you something. Can you understand why the body's up here? At the ear?

Miriam: Yeah. 'Cause I didn't back him up [i.e., the turtle] down to the neck.

Bob: How can we do that?

Miriam: [Laughing] We should have said [BUMP BUMP BUMP].

Miriam did not describe the bug in general terms (e.g. the body is on the ear); she described the bug in terms of omitted operations which translate directly into a fix. This description witnesses her analytical understanding of the bug. That is, she relates the steps executed to their effect on the entire drawing.

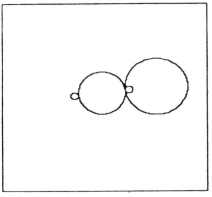

(a) Body-on-the-ear

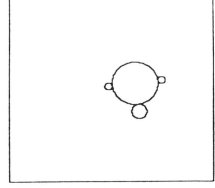

(b) Hair-on-the-neck bug

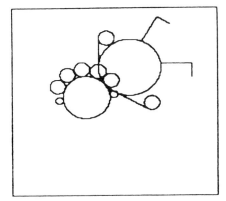

(c) Going-flying bug

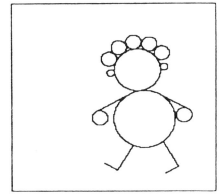

(d) The perfect PERSON

Fig. 3.5 – Bugs in the PERSON procedure

The perfect PERSON

The final phase of the PERSON project was an elaboration wherein Miriam added 'hair' to the HEAD procedure. The specific elaboration was not a new theme. While originally drawing Pretty Flower, Miriam at one point saw the petals as curly hair and noted she could add face parts. She selected the HEAD procedure as the one to nodify and executed it. Unable to figure out how to insert curls on the turtle's first pass between the ears, Miriam chose to do so on a second pass by extending the HEAD procedure. BUMPing up past the right ear, she began commanding and coding curls, i.e. [C 4]. After she placed and encoded the first curl, I asked Miriam to test. When HEAD executed, a bug was manifest, a curl at the neck (see Fig. 3.5(b)):

> Miriam: Noooo! [Complaining, smiling]
> Bob: What's the matter? ... Oh, I see, We've got a bug there. I think it's a sort of, must be a SETUP bug.
> Miriam: Yeah, We forgot to make the BUMPs that we bumped him up to the ear.

Notice that here also the bug description is presented in an analyzed form which translates directly into a prescription for a fix, not, for example, as 'he's got a curl on his chin'. Miriam added the remaining curls with no problems.

After the HEAD was modified with its complement of curls, testing made manifest Miriam's last bug:

> Bob: You cleared the screen. What are you typing, PERSON? ... There's the ears.... Here comes the hair.... What are we getting? ... [Bug manifestation; see Fig. 3.5(c).] Hey! Wait a minute.
> Miriam: DUMMY! [Big smile and laughs.]
> Bob: What's the problem? ... That doesn't look right.
> Miriam: [Speech too fast and excited to be comprehensible] The turtle [...] and we didn't get him down to where he should be to make the neck!
> Bob: What happened? We didn't do what, sweety?
> Miriam: Get him down to the neck.
> Bob. Oh. Gee.
> Miriam: I guess he's flying.
> Bob: I don't think so. No. I think that's a *bona fide* bug, Miriam. Let me get a look at that.... Holy smokes.... You think you can fix that?
> Miriam: Yeah.

It is the same old interface bug, but great fun in a new guise. But beyond that, and what I find most striking, here, of all the debugging incidents, is the joint appearance of two views of the problem. First, Miriam describes the bug as an omission of ours, a debugging response she has achieved in the Logo Session just described. Still present but now secondary and presented as a joke is the kind of excuse that formerly comprised Miriam's primary response to an uncomprehended problem. I consider this *prima facie* evidence for the reality of competition among active mental structures. It marks just the kind of change in dominance that differential development of competing active structures should be expected to bring about. When the final bug was fixed, we went on to test PERSON. Miriam said, 'I hope it works', and I asked, 'Do you think it will or won't?' Her reply: 'I hope it will and I think it will ...'. This note of cautious conviction seems to offer the right tone on which to close a description of debugging experiences.

PRELIMINARY CONCLUSIONS

I originally had expected text-editing experiences and the establishment of TEXT microviews[16] would prove ancestral to programming knowledges. This did not happen. Nor did Miriam's extensive use of computer design generators lead her into any analytic debugging. The main lines of cognitive structure creation and filiation are very clear in the preceding subsections. Miriam's experience with the TIMES procedure generator led her to construct a FLOWER microview in her mind. In turn this was ancestral to a PF (pretty flower) microview which was ancestral to a PERSON microview. Most important is the development of the ANALYTIC view that Miriam constructed out of her debugging experiences. Two aspects of its development stand out. First, her debugging knowledge was applied with power in the PERSON project (recall, for example, how she avoided the potential inside ear bug with no prompting whatsoever). Second, the unnaturalness of analysis to Miriam's mind could be clearly witnessed by what she did instead — rejecting the problem, excusing the result, and applying primitive heuristics. However, once Miriam formed an idea of what it might mean to analyze a failure, she was able to extend that idea and then apply it in the PERSON project to such an extent that even her descriptions of the failures were cast in operational terms.

The challenge now confronted is how to describe the application of the debugging knowledge of the ANALYTIC view to her programming PERSON. I can best approach that problem by examining the specific precursors of her use of analysis. Let me separate those precursors into critical incidents and sensitivities. The microcultural focus on procedural description and emergent forms sensitized Miriam both through terminology and through the valuation of certain phenomena. But a sensitivity is not the same as an insight. Consider that critical insight where Miriam saw that the execution of the PETAL sub-procedure created the heart of the flower as an emergent. Miriam was clearly sensitized to emergent phenomena — she had observed spiral arms ('those curly things') emergent in POLYSPI designs and found them pretty — but during the core of The Intimate Study she never understood where they came from (see Chapter 5). The heart of Pretty Flower was an emergent of a procedure *whose steps she had encoded*. She *did* understand it and her twice-volunteered explanation of how the heart appeared testifies how important the incident was to her. I can formulate her insight thus: the steps of a procedure can explain the results of its execution. This may seem so obvious as to appear inane, but Miriam

16 Such as might arise from the experiences described in 'An Introduction to Writing', (Lawler, 1980 and excerpted in the Appendix).

never showed she appreciated that truth previously. Her earlier considerable difficulty with reading procedures and understanding them argues she did not. Notwithstanding this critieal incident of the emerging flower heart, her intro- duction to debugging showed Miriam could not use that insight in debugging until she owned an ur-concept of what a bug might be: a 'bug' is 'something they left out', specifically a LEFT 90 in step 3 (this was immediately sup- planted by a RIGHT 90 in step 1). This ur-concept did not derive from her prior experience, was not a product of any specific conflict among internal structures, but was surely a case of her learning by example.

If we can accept this last observation as a fact, we should ask what its signifi- cance is. I consider it further evidence about the sense in which analysis is not natural for a mind such as Miriam's. Logo Session 52 is eloquent testimony that Miriam's analysis of procedures, a form of symbolic descriptions, was not a spontaneous invention; the PERSON project, however, witnesses that the idea of analysis in this form is natural in the sense of being easily extensible once it has been grasped. On the other hand, the extension of debugging comprehension required for use with PERSON may not have been great — debugging should apply easily to other programming projects. The more important question is whether or not the idea of analysis Miriam acquired through her programming experience was easily extensible and useful in other domains of her life.

THE RAMIFICATIONS OF DEBUGGING EXPERIENCE

To the extent that it is a precise (albeit limited) language for describing procedures and their interaction, the jargon of programming should be applicable and useful wherever the analysis of procedures, their interactions, and their failures is of concern.

Jumping rope

Two incidents show how effective was the carry-over of procedural description into Miriam's everyday life after the official end of The Intimate Study. The first shows how she could take advice, the second, that she could give it.

At Logo, too, Miriam's current interests are primarily physical skills. She plays with the computer (Wumpus, and lately some new facilities I've shown her), but her first choices are the hula hoop or jump rope. An incident occurring last night gives evidence of what may be the outstanding conse- quence of her learning during The Intimate Study — what I refer to is her sensitivity to instruction and advice couched in procedure-oriented terms. Miriam had convinced an older friend, Margaret, to turn a long rope for her jumping, the other end being tied to a doorknob. Miriam tried hard and long to jump into an already turning rope. She attended carefully to the rope and at the right time moved toward the center — but only a short distance in that direction. In consequence, she got her head inside the space, but the turning rope regularly caught her on the arm. Miriam had no good answer when I asked if she could recognize the specific problem. I asked if she could take some advice and said she should jump onto a line between Margaret and the doorknob. Miriam could not. I drew a chalk mark on that line. Miriam took the chalk and drew a box to jump into. Now she was ready.

Her first attempts failed because she jumped into her box without attending to the rope. Then she regressed to watching the rope and moving only a little. Finally, I said, 'Miriam, you've got a bug in your SETUP procedure. You're doing only one thing at a time. You have to do both things at once'. On her next try, Miriam jumped into the turning rope successfully. I did not see her thereafter exhibiting either of her two earlier bugs (too little movement or not watching the rope). This incident occupied about three minutes.

age: 6;7;30

Miriam clearly could understand and apply advice couched in such terms to domains of experience remote from the computer context in which they were introduced.

The second incident shows that when Miriam was cast in the role of instructor, she could use this programming jargon to communicate advice about failing procedures. The 'Physical Skills' experiment (age 6,5;25) was designed to turn the tables on the all-knowing experimenter (me). I never learned to jump rope as a child; Miriam's skill was considerable. Since I needed exercise, it seemed a most natural, 'real-life' experiment that we should see how well Miriam could debug my utterly inadequate flailings. I explained she was the day's instructor, and we began. (Note: this experiment was recorded on videotape; Miriam's analysis of my failures below are accurate.)

Bob: Miriam, why don't you watch the way I do it and tell me what I need to know.

Miriam: You're jumping too soon. [The 'too soon' bug; she demonstrates.] ... I watch it. When I see it touch the ground, I jump.

Bob: Let me try it now. [Starting] When I see it touch the ground I jump? [The rope catches him around the ankles] No. I'm still not doing it right. What's my problem?

Miriam: [Holding her hands at shoulder level] You hold it up when you're jumping. [The 'pull up' bug.]

Bob: [Tries again — high bounce] Hey! I got one foot over.

Miriam: [Laughs] Wanta see me? ... [She jumps] ....

Bob: Watch. Here we go again. [Starts jumping.... rope catches on the ankles.] Is it better to use one foot or two feet?

Miriam: I started out like this. [Miriam jumps in 'slow motion': one foot on ground at a time.]

Bob: Like walking? ... [Tries it: it catches on right foot.] Sort of walking over?

Miriam: Then I began doing it a little faster.... And next, when I wanted to do two feet — I keep my feet together.

Bob: [Tries: knees flex at horizontal and straighten as rope hits floor and is pulled in; as heels rise, rope hits ankles.]

Miriam: You had that pull-up bug.

Bob: [He tries again with Miriam watching closely.] No.

Miriam: You're jumping too low [The 'too low' bug.] and too soon.

Bob: I've got a too soon bug.

Miriam: And a low bug.

Bob: And, ah ... which should I fix first?

Miriam: The too low bug.

Bob: You watch now and tell me what I'm doing wrong here. [Bob jumps successfully five times, i.e. Bob simultaneously fixes the too low and the too soon bugs.]

How naturally Miriam slipped into failure analysis (debugging my procedures)! She specified three distinct bugs, implicity prescribing the fix by her bug descriptions. This incident provides clear evidence that she and I shared a potent language for communicating procedure-related knowledge.

Mega-cognitive consequences

Beyond this influence, the effect of Miriam's immersion in a computer micro-culture may well have had consequences of a meta-cognitive sort, through raising to salience as themes of discussion issues that are not so forward in other micro-cultures. For example, one day I succeeded in obtaining for a colleague the keys she had locked in her office; at supper that night (age 6;4;21), Miriam asked 'Daddy, how did you ever think of going under the floor? (The computer center had a raised floor.) Was it because you remembered how good a time we had before when the floor was up?' This shows that Miriam was capable of reflecting not only on her own thought processes, but mine as well, and even more had formed her own hypothesis to explain my thought process in this instance. Beyond reflecting on the process of thinking, the children even fell, in a jocular way, into reflecting on the structure of mind, thus:

> Over the past few weeks, in the context of repressing her desire for things she can't have, Miriam has spoken of having an 'eraser mind'. When asked to explain, she proposed the image for thoughts as ideas written on a tablet of paper and subject to erasure.

> As supper drew to a close this evening, Miriam cited the existence of another mind (a 'liver-hating mind'). Remarking my surprise at the thought of her having an eraser mind and another kind as well, I asked if she had any further minds. The topic lay unheeded for a while and I withdrew from the table. The children picked up the theme as a game between themselves. Miriam: 'I know another mind I have, a "remembering mind" ..., and another, a "stay away from sharks mind".' Robby asked if she had a 'talking mind'. 'Of course', responded Miriam, 'it has a voice box in it'. (This was a reference to the Votrax voice box attached to the computer system.) Robby continued: 'You must also have a learning mind, or all your other minds would be empty'. Miriam agreed and claimed that her learning mind was the biggest one of all. Expanding his theme, Robby said he had an 'electric mind' whose function was to manufacture electricity, 'for that's what every-

thing else runs on'. In response to Miriam's objection that she had no wires inside, Robby pointed to a wall socket and explained that the electricity was carried through the bones to outlets, such as the ones on the wall, where it was made available for local distribution.

The purpose of all this detail is to raise an essential issue for the question of reflexive thought: what experiences could children have that would permit them to develop ancestral reflexive microviews? The computer microculture is one where such experiences can occur. If a person reads a procedure of her own creation which embodies what she thinks, is it not natural to make the (not necessarily correct) inference that there must be something like that procedure inside her head? It is this intimate conjunction of computer procedures as the products of human thought processes that advances computer-based microworlds as exemplars for human thought. Since computer procedures are incrementally perfectible through debugging, since debugging is a central concern and'·theme of computer cultures, engagement in such a microculture should invigorate reflexivity of thought if experience affects the mind at all. These stories, with their specific detail, are meant to suggest how such changes in experience may become manifest in behavior. We do not expect six-year-olds to think as adolescents do, but we may expect different experiences with a reflexive component to alter the balance of structures dominating their behavior.

EQUILIBRATION AND STAGES

Problems can only be confronted when they are assimilated to the cognitive structures of the mind. Thus problems may be deformed inadvertently because the mind has no adequate representation and cannot deal with an aspect of the problem whose very existence it cannot recognize. Further, they may be deformed in a representational sense to structures developed through analogous microviews of experience. Even in the case where the cognitive structures are not adequate to the problems confronted, the structure of the mind is typically richer and more complex than the specific tasks it confronts at any time. In what follows, we will see not merely microviews of knowledge which dominate problem-solving behavior but also the existence of sub-dominant microviews which do not normally dominate behavior but which with intervention do so. Having seen what Miriam learned about programming, I turn now to the issue of how that new knowledge entered in equilibrium with the dominant structures of her mind.

Stage reconfiguration

The robust regularities of behavior discovered by Piaget and witnessed by years of extensive experimentation are emergents from the development and functioning of the computational processes of the mind. My central concern is to describe in detail functioning structures which could replicate the growth of knowledge as we are able to witness it in a human's interaction with the world. If the stages discovered by Piaget are less than logically necessary in their embodiments in human minds, it should be possible to change them. One might imagine analyzing the stage-defining behavior and recombining them in some different configuration. The possibility of doing so I have named 'the stage reconfiguration conjecture'.[17]

Even if it is *possible* to reconfigure the components from which stages emerge, doing so may not be *easy*. The robustness of Piaget's results in different cultural settings suggests how difficult effecting such a change might be. Even more, the logical possibility does not at all imply that an attempt to do so may be feasible in *any* particular case. At a public lecture, Papert suggested that performance on the bead families task[18] might show some effects from computer experience bearing on systematicity of thought. This 'offhand' but serious public proposal was less a theory-falsifying prediction than a suggestion of what sorts of effects might be seen if the general viewpoint was more or less correct on the large scale. I added the Piagetian bead families task to the repertoire of experiments which Miriam underwent at the beginning and end of The Intimate Study, not to test the hypothesis but to explore and comprehend what might or might not be a major phenomenon in the future.

A quasi-standard experiment

Where Piaget offered his subject piles of colored beads and asked him to make all combinations of those beads, I gave Miriam piles of cardboard pieces cut in various shapes. Our experiment then used 'shape families' to explore how a child goes about making combinations.

Initially, Miriam's dominant way of conceiving of the task was similar to the examples Piaget describes as 'crossed juxtaposition'. This confirms that Miriam's dominant structures were similar to those for children about eight years.[19] After I asked her to figure out all the possible ways of putting two shapes together to make a family, Miriam made the arrangement of Fig. 3.6.

> Bob: Can you tell me what your procedure is? It looks like a very interesting one.
> Miriam: I don't know what it is. I'll tell you when I'm done.
> Bob: Will you be certain that you got all the couples you can possibly make?
> Miriam: Yes
> Bob: How will you be certain? How will you know?
> Miriam: I'll just look. [Starts working on a third column.]

When Miriam had completed the arrangement of Fig. 3.6, I began intervening, relating her experiment to computer-based activities. What is important to notice is how Miriam responded to these interventions and how capable she was of doing so.

---

17 I called this the 'stage reconfiguration hypothesis' in Lawler, 1979. I believe this hypothesis was first advanced by Papert.
18 From *The Origin of the Idea of Chance in Children*, Piaget and Inhelder, 1951.
19 See the discussion of Miriam's mental age in the two sections 'A cognitive profile' and 'Binet IQ test' of the Appendix.

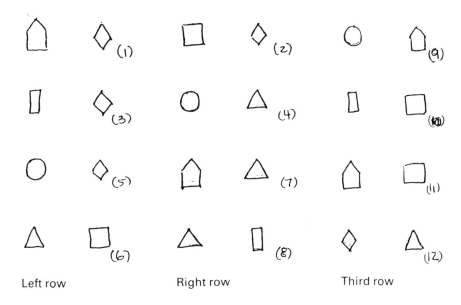

Left row   Right row   Third row

(Order of placement in parentheses)

Fig. 3.6 – Placements in the Shapes Families Experiment.

Bob: Let me give you a hint. Can I?

Miriam: Yeah.

Bob: You did that very well. You found a whole bunch of them. But there might be some we missed.... Do you remember the idea of making shape families?[20]

Miriam: Yeah.

Bob: You take all the shapes that are pretty much the same, and you change just one part.

Miriam: Uh-huh.

Bob: Can you do something like that? With these pieces of cardboard here? Let's pick one piece, say, the triangles. Can we be certain that we have every one that has a triangle in it?

Miriam: Yeah ... Take each one and put one down. [Places two shapes, a triangle and a house.... Places triangle.]

Bob: And a triangle and a what?

Miriam: Circle. [Places it next.] ... Triangle and diamond. [Placing them in column.] ... Triangle and a bar. [Placing them.] ... [After a pause] Ha ha! ... Another. [Places triangle and square.]

Bob: You've got a triangle and each different piece. Would it be fair, do you think, would it be a good couple if you had two that were the same?

---

20 This is an explicit reference to activities of a Logo Session wherein we generated collections of related POLYSPIRAL designs by changing one variable of three input to a procedure.

Miriam did not immediately apply this advice to the collection of triangle couples. Instead she volunteered to start a new collection.

> Miriam: I'll start with the houses now. [Places house—house couple] Houses.... Circle.... House and rect — diamond. [Placing those; then Miriam reaches to top of prior column to place two triangles; places house and square in the houses column.... Pause, no action.]
>
> Bob: Sounds like you're gritting your teeth there. What's going on?
>
> Miriam: [Picks up triangle] It's hard to think of what to do next. [Places house and triangle next to triangle and house] ... [Noise] Mmmm. Just one more.
>
> Bob: You're trying to get it so you have the same number in each bunch? Is that it?
>
> Miriam: [Perceptible but small head nod of agreement] Ha ha! I think I've got it.... Yep. I've got it. I've got it. I've got what's missing... [makes singing noises and places house and bar in the houses column].

The pattern in these episodes is the common one of Miriam's behavior. Once started in a specific direction, she takes over and makes the solution her own by extending it.

It is easy to suppose that Miriam would have been content to generate the permutations of these six shapes taken two at a time. A second major intervention cut off that path, channeling her behavior into a different way.

> Bob: Let's stop for a minute before you go on.
>
> Miriam: I want to do the sqaures now.
>
> Bob: I'm glad you want to do that. Can you hold on for a minute? ... [Touching two houses at bottom] Let's say this is the house family [running finger up the column, tapping each pair] because every one of these has a house. [Miriam assents.] Let me ask you. Do you have a duplication bug? ... Do you know what I mean?
>
> Miriam: No.
>
> Bob: A duplication bug, Miriam [reaching out to touch the triangle of the triangle—diamond couple] is when you've got one member in this family, that's the same as a member in this family [touches circle of house—circle couple], like if you had [touching triangle and square of triangle—square couple] a triangle and a square.... And over here [in a third column] you had a square and a triangle, say, that would be a duplication bug. Can you check to see if you've got a duplication bug?
>
> Miriam: Ah hah! ... I have one.... Found it.
>
> Bob: Can you get rid of it?
>
> Miriam: [Picks house—triangle from house family and throws it aside.]

After Miriam exhibited her understanding of the 'duplication bug', I then pointed out to her that the second family had one less couple than the first. Would that I had bitten my tongue! Had it been Miriam's observation that the second family had one less couple, the following extensions would have been more convincing. She went on:

Bob: Take a look at these two families again. Do they have the same numbers in?

Miriam: Unh-uh.

Bob: The house family has one less, because of the duplication bug.

Miriam: Now I'm gonna start with these squares. I can't do two things. I can't have one of these [touching house of house—diamond couple] or I can't have a triangle. Each one will be a little less.

Miriam completed the family of four 'square' couples, then went on to the 'bar' (or rectangle) family by laying out three bars in a vertical column before filling in the variable element of each couple. When asked, for example, why she laid out three rectangles, Miriam replied, 'You can't have a triangle, house, or a square'. After setting out five 'families' of couples made from six different designs, I posed the problem of completeness:

Bob: You got 'em all now?

Miriam: Yeah. I can only do one more pile.

Bob: What's that?

Miriam: [Putting them in place] Two circles.

With the specific intrusions documented here, this six-year-old performed on the task as children normally do only at age 12 or after. I do not claim that this shows a 'stage reconfiguration'. I do claim, on the basis of this evidence, that Miriam had developed different microviews of knowledge to which she could deform presented problems as matters of accident and microcultural intrusion dictate. These data show that Miriam owned sub-dominant structures at age six similar to those which normally dominate behavior at 12 or later. Other children may also have important experiences which provide specific foundations for analytic thought long before the resulting structures develop such vigor as to dominate their problem-solving behavior. These results suggest that the epistemological quality of particular experiences determine the development of analytic capability, *not* age and *not* completing the closure of concrete operations.

The 'shape families' experiment has established that one should conceive of task performance not just in terms of what the child does. One should inquire both directly and through interventions what she is capable of to explore the sub-dominant structures which may subsequently come to the fore. Only through consideration of sub-dominant structures will incremental explanations of saltations in behavior be possible.

Procedural description, articulation, and reflexive thought

Because exploring sub-dominant structures requires intervention, an experimenter must have extensive knowledge of the subject's experience and a common repertoire of experiences, ideas, and terms to permit revelation of what is in the subject's mind. For Miriam and me, procedural desciptions, ideas of debugging, theorizing, and even thinking out loud about our own problem solving were central to our study. Such experiences enabled Miriam to articulate what would have been beyond observing otherwise and explain her ability to reflect articulately on thought processes, as witnessed in the following example from the 'Fermi spool' experiment, age 6;5;21.

Two disks, a large pencil, and a piece of string are assembled rather like a spool of thread (see diagrams). When the subject pulls gently on the string, which way will the spool roll?

FRONT   SIDE

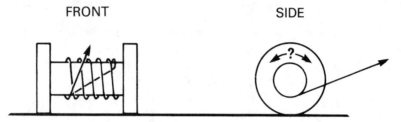

Bob: [Showing the spool to Miriam] What have I got here?
Miriam: It's sort of like a little car. . . . See, this [points to string around axle] will come rolling off. [She translates both hands away in parallel from the axle's location] Roll.
Bob: What is going to happen if I pull on this string?
Miriam: [Cupping her hand around the wheel] This will go rolling off [gesture away from the direction of pulling on the string]. This [pointing to the string end] will come pulling off. This will pull. And this [the string] will give this the pressure [hands on the axle where the string goes around it] to go. [Hand gesture away form pulling direction of the string.]
Bob: Pressure? [Miriam looks uneasy when challenged on the word] . . . . And something's gonna make it roll? That's your best speculation, right?
Miriam: Yeah. [Miriam reaches out her hands] Can I try it?
Bob: I'm not sure that what you said is true.
Miriam: Neither am I.
Bob: I think this a good test. Pull it very gently. Your prediction is that its gonna go this way. [Pointing gesture in sense opposite to the string end.]
Miriam: Hold it. It might come to me, though.
Bob: Oh? What would make it come to you?
Miriam: If I pull this [the string end]. It might go rolling this way. [Rotational gesture at the wheel in a sense indicating motion toward the string end]
Bob: [Rotates the axle as she described it] It might roll this way?
Miriam: Yes. Although that isn't my best speculation. I speculate it's gonna go towards you.

Having been confused myself by this Fermi spool puzzle, I can appreciate Miriam's uncertainty. I consider her clear articulation of alternate outcomes quite surprising for one so young. She does not, of course, express her sensitivity to two views of the problem in terms an adult might employ, thus: one way of seeing the problem focusses on rotation about the axle, a direct consequence of which would be rolling away from the string end; a second views the string as pulling an object which can pivot at the point where the wheel touches the ground, resulting in the spool's rolling towards the end of the string. Miriam's preferred speculation is clearly the former, but she recognizes, at least expresses, an alternative view. From this experiment, I conclude that not only are competing ways of viewing problems simultaneously active, but that also even such a young child as Miriam can give evidence about it. Whatever the causes, Miriam had become sufficiently articulate that she was able to reflect upon her thought.

Miriam on her own

A further question is whether Miriam's sensitivity to procedural description is forward only when she is in the computer laboratory or with me, or whether she has adopted ways of thinking which she carries out to her life beyond my immediate influence. Two other bits of evidence support the latter case. At the beginning of The Intimate Study, Miriam's solution of arithmetic problems indicated she was typically more concerned with getting the right answer than with perfecting procedures. Six months later, her first grade teacher told her mother that Miriam seemed to enjoy solving problems: her focus was not on getting the answer; she seemed to enjoy the process of working out problems, to take pleasure in the process more than in the result. Clearly, the pressure of my influence was potent in this change, but it is not unreasonable to believe that Miriam's satisfying experience of programming and debugging inclined her to focus more on processes and less on results than before.

A final incident bearing on procedural description also touches directly on the issue of reflexive thought, as well as pointing to ways that this experience may be profoundly important to Miriam in a personal way. Miriam's work on this project has developed a perspective on self control which may be quite valuable for her in an entirely separate area of her life — controlling her allergic asthma.

> While we visited kin one evening, the children played tag. I found Miriam outside, sobbing, very much out of breath, and needing a dose of her wheeze-suppression medicine at that time. Inside, my brother sat down with Miriam, who was still wheezing heavily, in an out-of-the-way place. As he subsequently related their conversation to me, Dave told her of his severe childhood asthma, and how he had found that through conscious effort he could bring his breathing and his emotions under sufficient control to stop an impending asthma attack.
>
> Later in the evening, I accosted Miriam outside. She was again breathing heavily, engaged once more in a game of chase with the boys. I pointed out how she was breathing so heavily I feared she would end up wheezing. She explained to me, 'Daddy, I have a very good trick, to stop it when I have trouble breathing'. 'How's that?' I asked. 'I just think about it [pointing to her head], and after five minutes, or maybe even 15, I won't be breathing so hard'. I left Miriam playing tag.

My brother confirmed that his was substantially the advice he had given Miriam and volunteered the judgement that he had never met so young a child so well able to understand the idea of controlling her own processes.

Vignette 107; age: 6;6;14

My brother is not an educator nor a psychologist but an engineer, used to thinking in terms of procedures and control. If his judgment is correct, Miriam's Logo experiences have helped her understand herself in the sense that she can establish a theory of herself as an object. Although we may criticize a culture or subculture for leading people to think mechanistically about themselves, approximate, wrong theories can be a first step toward something better. Those children's theories of mind that will grow out of computer cultures are worthy of respect because they can serve as precursors to mature computational theories of mind which look toward sufficient complexity that they do not demean the person.

CONCLUSIONS

It is clear that even the little Miriam learned about programming and debugging changed her ability to describe activities in analytic, procedural terms. Her engagement in The Intimate Study created between us a language which permitted me to intervene in her problem solving in such a way that she showed systematicity of behavior normally appearing spontaneously only in children twice her age. Such systematicity and articulate reflection of thought as Miriam exhibited are characteristic of the formal stage of thought as described by Inhelder and Piaget (1958) and Piaget (1976a, 1972). Miriam's reflection on her own thoughts and about cognitive questions was seen both within experiments and outside the laboratory. The invigoration of articulate, reflexive thought is not so much an artifact of the experiment as it is a consequence of her immersion in a computer microculture.

The intervention of The Intimate Study, teaching Miriam programming and debugging, has made a difference in her mind, albeit a subliminal one with respect to spontaneous expression in behavior. The detail of Miriam's programming experience and its consequences point to a different way of thinking about stages. Considering her systematic, reflexive, articulate thought as already existing in sub-dominant cognitive structures (microviews amd microview clusters) permits us to imagine the future emergence of formal thought in her mind as a non-mysterious change in the balance of competing, long-existing structures. This version of mind, different as it is from Piaget's, is an equilibration theory and inescapably Piagetian. Finally, the extent and depth of probing necessary to establish the existence and the functioning of sub-dominant cognitive structures — through which alone we can explain stages as saltations emerging in behavior — points to the essential difficulty of studying learning: there is very little learning, and much behavior; as an engineer would put it, the signal to noise ratio is very low.

4

The articulation of complementary roles

Given that the mind is a personal and essentially private construct, understanding learning requires a vision, at least, of how particular experiences from an individual's social life relate to that personal construction of mind. The requirement cannot be avoided when the experiences involve the interaction of one person with another — as in competitive games. What I offer here is a description, not a theory.[1] What I struggle to develop is an *ur-theory* of how social experiences generate the personal construction of the individual mind. I begin through the following example and use it as a guide for interpretation through the body of the chapter.

PRELUDE

Miriam has a long history of joke telling and invention. The following vignette is about her sister Peggy, two years old at the time. Their relation is basically amicable but also more than that.

> Peggy imitates us and her siblings and has begun imitating Miriam's knock-knock jokes. This was Peggy's first form of imitation:
>
>> Peggy: Knock-knock.
>> Bob: Who's there?
>> Peggy: [Broad laughter.]

1 This is not a *mere* description, however, but one with aspirations. One contribution by Winston (1975) was his observation that a particular description, through processes of part and relation emphasis, could come to function as a 'concept'. One could say such a description aspired to be a concept of that class of objects. I call such an aspiring description an *ur*-concept, after the German.

That first night, Peggy plied her joke upon me time and again. It was amusing enough because of her imperfect command. We both enjoyed it. Eventually, the joke became wearing. I tried to begin the joke with her. When I began 'Knock-knock', she did not reply; I would say she could not reply. I tried many times. Even though she sensed something was expected of her, she did not reply.

The next morning I heard Peggy talking to herself in her crib: 'Knock-knock. Who's there? [Laughter]'. Later, when she was brought down to breakfast, I cooked Peggy a muddled egg and we sat down to eat. Her first words were 'Knock-knock', and I responded appropriately. In my turn, I tried again:

Bob: Knock-knock.
Peggy: Who's there? [Laughter].

That same afternoon, Miriam confirmed my observation, 'Dad, Peggy can say "Who's there'. I consider this a very simple and lucid example of the processes of the articulation of complementary roles.

Here is how I describe the elements of the example. Someone, a learner with (most probably) a relatively inferior comprehension, is engaged socially with more comprehending people – in this case focussed around what is literally a script for a joke's telling. The reasons for their common engagement may be of any sort, friendly, helpful, even antagonistic. During the engagement, the social demands push at the boundaries of comprehension of the person with the undeveloped perspective. Peggy was regularly asked 'who's there?' at first, but later she was expected to respond that way herself and could not. Subsequently, in a period when deprived of that social engagement, the learner recalls and recreates that kind of engagement, compensating for the solitude by simulating the role of the other actor. The first type of process I call *homely binding* ('homely' being a contracted form of 'home-like'): the learner attaches herself to uncomprehended 'routines' of engagement (in both the theatrical and programming senses). The process may be friendly or not so – but it is more aptly and generally described by that wide-ranging class of intimate relationships that characterizes the interactions of a small society, the home.

The second type of process, *lonely discovery*, occurs when the learner is deprived of social engagement – left to her own devices – and uses those devices to re-enact the uncomprehended experiences. This simulation of the other actors imposes a real demand for the distinction between roles and their relations which was lacking in the initial engagement. My name for this pervasive and oft-repeated sequence of homely binding and lonely discovery is *the articulation of complementary roles*.

The relation of social experience to personal construction is that more integrated discriminations are required for controlling multi-role enactment of scripts than are required for acting in them. On the stage, an actor may memorize his lines and take cueing from the tag end of a fellow actor's preceding speech. An actor, or a learner, in taking on two roles must do more, must not only cast herself in the second role but must also function as director of the entire scenario. The director's function (a global control of the script's progression as distinct form serial cueing) requires the articulation of roles; executing this function requires reflection and leads to a refined comprehension of the script.

Our example of Peggy's learning knock-knock jokes does not, of itself, distinguish between a better articulation of a serial process and the creation of a control element which functionally has subordinated pre-existing structures. We do so now. Peggy never began 'Farewells' herself, but when someone else initiated an interchange by saying 'Goodbye, Peggy', she would reply 'See you later'. In such a separation protocol, she played rigidly the respondent's role. Two days after her better articulation of the knock-knock joke script, Peggy used this rigid protocol as the content of directed speech, thus:

> We were in the same room, had played for a while, and she decided to leave. At the door, she turned to me and said, 'Say "Goodbye Peggy"'. 'Goodbye, Peggy'. I repeated. 'See you later', she responded as she left the room.

From these incidents I take the following conclusions. The relations Peggy worked out for controlling what is said when playing an alternate role in the joke affected her ability or inclination for the more explicit control of speech. This is true even for other exchanges which might not seem to us so strictly conventional as the more recognizably stereotyped joke script.[2]

These incidents provide a succinct example of how the articulation of complementary roles creates new control structures in the mind. I now offer in detail a much more elaborate case study of the articulation of complementary roles, one spanning several years and interleaving the functioning of highly specific knowledge developed through homely binding and the creation of refined control through lonely discovery.[3]

INTRODUCTION

Tic-tac-toe is generally considered a trivial game and lacks an extensive literature, but I believe its study permits the raising of questions similar to those which have drawn the Artificial Intelligence community to the study of chess: what is the nature of expert knowledge? How does a novice become an expert? If the game is so simple as to be child's play, its study in significant extension can be the foundation for worthwhile appreciation of how learning happens. In comparison with the lifetime of learning chess requires, this simpler game has the right balance for observing the development of knowledge.

---

2 One can not argue coercively that *this* single incident *must have been* the sole generator of such a change. On the other hand, if particular experiences are the foundation for cognitive development, then some one among them must have been the first. This experience clearly exhibits a set of characteristics which seem essential to the process.

3 This study builds slowly, appropriately so, because this reflects the character of the cognitive processes traced. Impatient readers may want initially to skim the section 'Homely binding' to read the more novel discussions of 'Lonely discoveries'. A critical reader will need to read closely the section on 'Homely binding' to follow the later interpretations.

The markers typically used in play, 'noughts and crosses', exhibit the state but not the progress of a game and are thus not adequate for our analyses. To indicate the sequence of both player's moves, I represent Miriam's markers by letters and those of her opponent by digits. The first marker of the initiating player is duplicated at the top of the grid. Game (a) below is reached in this system as game (b).

noughts and crosses				sequenced recording				cell numbers		
X	X	X		C	A D	B		1	2	3
O	X			2	A			4	5	6
O		O		1		3		7	8	9
	(a)				(b)				(c)	

I will refer to specific cells of the game grid by the numbers given in (c) above. Individual games from the corpus will be referenced numerically by sessions and serial number; e.g. '2.3' is game number 3 from the second session played. Where appropriate, the session's date will be specified with age-relative dating; for example, '6;1;5' means the games were played when Miriam was six years, one month and five days old. All Miriam's publicly manifest behavior relevant to tic-tac-toe is captured in the corpus and a significant selection of that behavior is presented here. For the purpose of analysis, I developed the classification of games presented in Fig. 4.1. The game labels, such as M1 and C3, will be used to characterize individual games in the text.

Tic-tac-toe versus addition

This study continues the program of Chapter 2, exploring a vision of learning as changes in the organization of separate and distinct cognitive structures through detailed analysis of case study material. While that chapter described Miriam's learning of addition, this describes her learning about Tic-tac-toe during the same period of time. The primary contrasts derive from the nature of the material, in three specific senses. Addition is a problem-solving process that can go forward in a single mind, whereas tic-tac-toe involves essentially a second person (or a second person's role, at a minimum). Further, learning addition involves an extensive knowledge of numer which children typically construct in different settings over many years. In contrast, tic-tac-toe apparently lacks so long and broad a dimension in personal cognitive history. Finally, criteria for what significant learning might be in respect of tic-tac-toe are not so obvious as they are for addition. The interpretation also differs from that of Chapter 2. In the context of a cyclic series of problem moves (as opposed to problems solved in a single pass), it focusses on the development of interactions between microviews

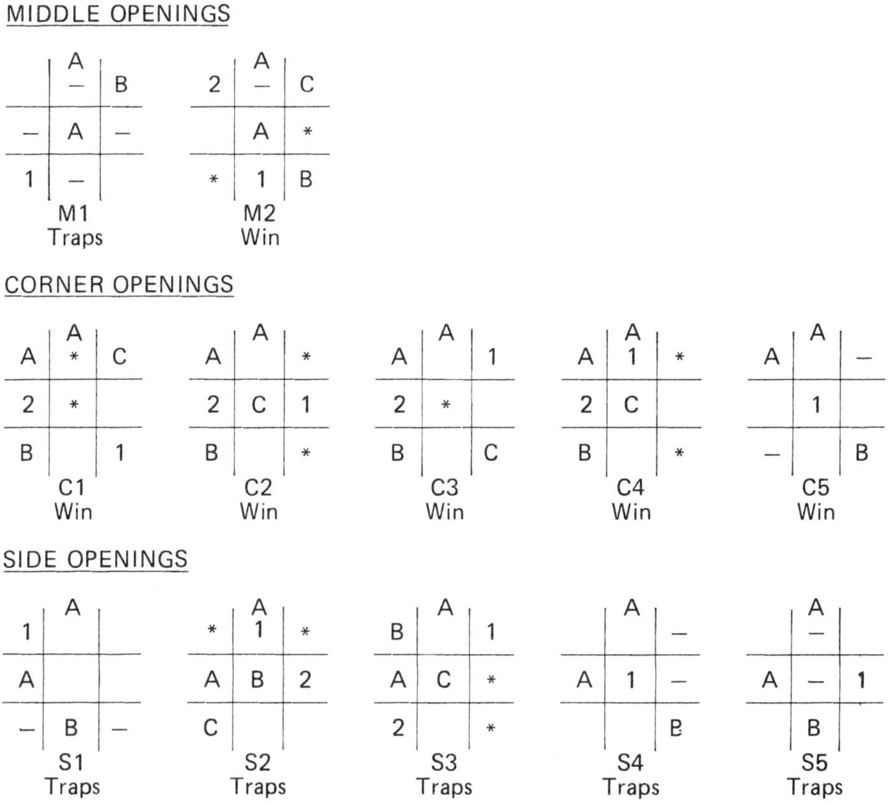

MIDDLE OPENINGS

M1
Traps

M2
Win

CORNER OPENINGS

C1
Win

C2
Win

C3
Win

C4
Win

C5
Win

SIDE OPENINGS

S1
Traps

S2
Traps

S3
Traps

S4
Traps

S5
Traps

Notes:

'–' means the opponent can be forked if he moves here.

'*' means this is a cell where the initiator may win after his opponent's next turn; two such imply a fork.

Different expert wins form those shown are possible. For example, in game C3, move B in cell 9 is a winning move.

The critical move in each game, the *crux* I call it, is the second move of the opening player. In expert play, this move is used both to link the two ways to win of a fork and to force the opponent's second move to an innocuous cell.

Fig. 4.1 – Tic-tac-toe: twelve opening games.

at a slightly 'higher' level of control. The central technical formulation is that a structure which begins as a socially governed convention for a series of inter-actions provides nodes at which later, internally generated decisions can affect behavior. The empirical material provides examples of what this means.

Agreeing that around age six, children first become capable of putting themselves in other's roles, scientists of various paradigms have raised the issue of how another becomes a part of the self; each has provided a characteristic vision. Freud, for example, proposed that the other within the self derives from the introjection of parents. I offer an information processing perspective, in the broad sense, on that question: the ability to imagine the thought of another develops from the splitting apart and subordinating of alternative structures within the self; further, whatever the cause may be for such development, we can trace its occurrence in experiences with problem domains whose particular structure permits essentially different sorts of problem-solving activities to proceed.[4]

Cognitive structures

This study does not present explicit cognitive models, but some of its ideas bear on cognitive modelling and in particular on the explanation of stages.[5] This chapter does not explore further the internal structure of microviews, because the nature of the observational material does not permit doing so. If my descriptions were more precise, they would be less accurate. Consequently, the summarizing to be encountered in this paper will contain many 'empty circles' representing microviews.[6] Although it does not illuminate internal structure, this empirical material does permit us to ask and to answer such questions as: 'What microviews should we ascribe to Miriam?' and 'How does the control structure of inter-view organization develop?' Figures 4.2 through 4.7 summarize the conclusions of our analyses for the convenience of the reader. The topology of the flow-chart-like diagrams is justified through the interpretations of the text, but the diagrams themselves do not deepen the related arguments. They do provide, however, a series of time-sequenced sketches of structure relations underlying a significant movement of cognitive development.

After I trace developing inter-view control structure through the interpretation of the corpus, I will discuss the relation of changes in that control structure to the appearance of stage-like changes in modes of behavior. I use here the term stage in its weakest sense, that of a label for mutually exclusive periods of time with significant commonality in modes of play and imputed comprehension. Based on her answers to such predictive questions as 'Have you won this game already?', I will conclude that Miriam's knowledge of necessary relations between pattern and serial aspects of the game progressed from the first to the third of the four stages of comprehension described below:

(1) naive comprehension — witnessed by complete rule knowledge coupled with an absence of strategic play;

---

4 A reasonable objection may be raised here: having an agent in the mind, such as the super-ego, is not the same thing as being able to imagine oneself in the role of another with that agent's character. Exactly so. How the latter ability derives stepwise from the former is a central theme of this detailed analysis. See especially the sections 'Table turning', 'Two in a row', and 'Playing against herself'.

5 See the discussion of Piaget and Papert and the section 'Equilibration and Stages' in Chapter 3.

6 For the sake of those readers who — like myself — feel uneasy when they see such diagrams, I have attempted to describe the internal structure of microviews in Chapter 7.

(2) fragmentary comprehension – shown by strategic play based on well-known outcomes of specific games;

(3) procedural comprehension – exhibited by the stepwise proof of determinate games and forward play in the tree of possible games;

(4) systematic comprehension – as exemplified in the classification by openings and game analysis of Fig. 4.1.

DESCRIBING THE INITIAL STATE

Tactical play

The first two sessions of games permit characterization of Miriam's play before any didactic interventions.

Two games representing others as well
(age: 6 years; 1 month; 5 days)

```
          A                        A
     C    |    2            B   |  3  | E
          |                     |
1.1  D  | A             1.2  4  | A | D
        |                      |
     B  | 1  | 3           1  | C | 2
          M2                      M1
```

(M1 and M2 are respectively the designations of the middle-and-corner and middle-and-side opening games from the classification of Fig. 4.1.) Whenever Miriam initiated a game with a middle opening and I responded with a side cell, as in game 1.1, she won. She did not refer to these games as involving any sort of 'tricks' (her word for strategy). When I altered my responses to a corner cell, we came inevitably to a draw, neither of us making any mistakes. The games above show Miriam winning a game (1.1), blocking a threat (move 'C' of 1.2), and selecting unforced moves by preference. I do not believe Miriam planned the fork she achieved in game 1.1 but can not prove she did not.) Her performance – based on knowing the rules of play and preferences for center and corner cells – was roughly equivalent to that which would be generated from activation of the production system (abbreviated as PS) offered by Newell and Simon (1972, p. 62) as embodying what 'is generally regarded as a good strategy for the first player'.

Simple tic-tac-toe production system model

side-to-move = opponent → stop
⟨own-winning-side-pattern⟩ (→ blank-cell) → play (blank-cell)
⟨opponent-winning-pattern⟩ (→ blank-cell) → play (blank-cell)
⟨own-forking-pattern⟩ (→ intersection) → play (intersection)
center = blank → play (center)
⟨opponent-on-side⟩ → find corner = blank; play (corner)
⟨opponent-on-corner⟩ → find opposite of corner; play (opposite)

This computer-initiator always opens in the center, sets the M1 traps, and achieves the M2 fork.[7]

How rough was the fit between the Newell–Simon PS and Miriam's play can be clarified by the following four dimensions of contrast. First, although the moves generated by the PS and Miriam were similar, the thought behind them was quite different. Newell and Simon as mature players observe that 'since the game is drawn when viewed from a game-theoretic standpoint, good means here a strategy that will guarantee a draw and that will give the opponent as many opportunities as possible of making a losing mistake'. Miriam did not play with the stability of well-reasoned knowledge nor with the commitment to winning common in older players. To her, it was more important to be engaged in the game than to win it, and it was more important that the engagement be fair in her judgement than to continue playing. Next, even if her dominant play was well represented by the PS, two extrinsic sources of influence on underlying structures, boredom and social suggestion, modified her performance. (Playing the 'same' game too often led to variation. Even given that her dominant micro-views would propose a corner move before a side cell move, a social challenge, such as 'Why do you always move in a corner?', could lead to the rejection of corner move proposals with the resulting side move manifest in behavior.) Further, *how* she played depended on *whom* she played. Finally, the PS does not distinguish between strategic and tactical play, which came to be a major functional distinction in Miriam's play. So that we may better understand how Miriam's later play developed from this irregular beginning, let us enrich the characterization of her initial state, first by presenting a little background and then by recounting a specific incident which directed her thinking about tic-tac-toe in all subsequent play.

Two years before our study began, I brought Miriam's brother, Robby, a Tic-tac-toe game, which I introduced to both children. Miriam, then aged four, learned that one took turns and that winning was getting three counters in a row. I advised the children to look for 'two ways to win'. Robby (then six) was able to absorb the instruction easily enough, but Miriam could not. At most, she learned that there could be such a thing as a fork (any move which creates two ways to win) but did not learn how to create one. They played with different competences: Robby winning with an occasional fork; Miriam winning frequently enough when he made errors to be satisfied. As Robby came to make fewer errors, they played less and the game dropped from their repertoire of favorites.

Corner openings

Combining the objectives of achieving a fork with a specific plan for doing so entered Miriam's game playing through the following adventure. Shortly before the beginning of The Intimate Study, I visited the Boston Children's Museum with Miriam, Robby, and his friend John. One single incident made a tremendous impression on Miriam and markedly influenced all her subsequent play. John

---

7 This simple rule system can be modified for the second player by adding an eighth rule of the following sense; when the opponent has occupied opposite corners, move in any blank corner. Such a program seems to represent well the computer program against which Miriam played, as described in the upcoming section 'Corner openings'.

and Miriam both played tic-tac-toe against the Museum's computer with openings M1 and M2. When they fell in the pitfall of a side response to the computer's invariable middle opening, they were regularly defeated. The computer — which could be accurately described as playing with the Newell and Simon strategy, supplemented by the defensive extension noted earlier — always responded in the corner to their middle openings, so the children's best game was no better than a draw. Eventually Robby got a turn (the others peering over his shoulder) and opened with a corner move. The game unfolded as below, and Robby won.

Three-corner fork

	A	
A	D	C
	1	3
2		B

- letters: Robby

numbers: computer

C5

John and Miriam were astounded. Robby clearly owned some powerful knowledge. Since he was to share that knowledge with them, the three-corner fork entered Miriam's repertoire and exerted a dominant influence in the development of her play. Tic-tac-toe became a game of frequent choice as The Intimate Study began. This incident shows a socially current but uncomprehended slogan ('look for two ways to win') given a personal meaning by the close observation and imitation of another's striking performance. This particular form of the game is my archetypical example of strategic play. It is quintessentially a game length plan for the single player — as contrasted with the single moves, either choices or responses, of tactical play.

The limits of what Miriam learned from imitating Robby are shown by the remaining games of session one, wherein Miriam introduced corner openings. Game 1.3 duplicated the play by which Robby had defeated the Museum's computer. What became increasingly surprising as I probed her play was Miriam's rigidity in this form.

6;1;5

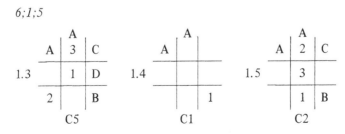

When she confronted an opposite corner response to a corner opening in game 1.4, Miriam did not know how to proceed at all. Her response was primarily social: she complained loud and long. Eventually she moved with no coherent objective. Her inability to counter an opposite corner response in game 1.4 shows the rigidity of her strategy. Game 1.5 shows Miriam continuing with a three-corner fork objective despite move '2' rendering the as-yet-unachieved-fork completely ineffective. Apparently, she did not consider the relation of my moves to hers at all. Further, her not recognizing her own winning move ('C' in the middle, cell 5) establishes how disparate are the microviews of this strategic play and the microviews of her pre-strategic play. If we conceive of the strategy as a specific, three-move plan, the strategic microview can be seen as quite different from other microviews which recognize and seize opportunities based only on the current state of the game.

Turns at winning

In games 1.4 and 1.5 (played against me), Miriam met two impediments to her three-corner objectives. In the games of session two against Robby, she did not adopt either of those specific moves as defenses. In surprising contrast, she attempted victory by negotiation. Game 2.1 below shows Miriam falling into the trap (move B) of opening form C5. Either she could not defend against that opening or did not choose to do so. I believe she initially accepted that loss, hoping to be allowed to win in her turn. But Miriam had come to doubt that Robby would play 'fair' by her standards; thus in games 2.2 she tried to avoid going first (in her turn) because she believed Robby would block her attempt to occupy three corners: 'I'm afraid he will take the place I want to go. I won't get two ways to win'. Whom she played controlled whether or not she played with a game length stretegy.

6;1;14

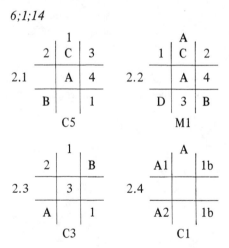

The extreme of this opponent-specific tension — in relation to her expectation that she should be allowed to win games in her turn — surfaced in the play of game 2.4. Miriam's fear that her corner opening stategy would be blocked resulted in her attempt to negotiate a victory:

Miriam: Are you going to block me?
Robby: No.
Miriam: [Puts marker in upper left corner — A1.]
Robby: [Puts marker in lower right corner — 1a.]

Miriam: [Shifts her marker to lower left corner – A2.]
Robby: You took your hand off it! [outraged gripe].

Miriam's concern was that Robby should not block her diagonal way to win (by occupying cell 9). Her switching to the adjacent corner was an attempt to avoid his blocking of her second step. When her functional resources were exhausted, she negotiated and cheated. (Of course, he lied.) The explosive disagreement which concluded game 2.4 ended their play for the day and up through session 14 (five months). Beyond noting the influence of the opponent on the choice between strategic and tactical play, we may conclude that Miriam judged winning as subject to a turn taking convention whose failure to be respected justified abandoning play altogether. (This was not unreasonable of her, for the game is played in alternating moves and alternating the first move is common.)

An initial sketch
On the basis of this characterization of her initial play and thought, let us ascribe microviews to Miriam covering the main points of the verbal description. Fig. 4.2 is a sketch of the tic-tac-toe microviews I ascribe to Miriam at the beginning of The Intimate Study. Because we can clearly identify the incident through which strategic play first entered Miriam's tic-tac-toe repertoire, we can confidently assert that her play was of two major kinds, strategic and what I call 'tactical', implying by this latter term a shorter planning scope. More simply put, strategic play has a game length objective; tactical play only focusses on one move at a time. Once she learned about the three-corner fork – the knowledge effecting which is the content of the *Corners* microview – Miriam's failure to block the threat of game 1.5 argues that when the Corners view was active in a specific game, tactical play did not operate. That is, strategic and tactical are alternate modes of play. Miriam regularly preferred strategic to tactical play. Nonetheless after the beginning of strategic play, Miriam's tactical play remained operative, functioning in a default capacity when she did not move first (and thus could not get enough corners for her fork) or when she consciously avoided the only strategy she knew.

Even a rough sketch should respect the need for a system of such structures to function in playing the game. They should be able to propose a reasonable move at any time and to inhibit moves at the 'wrong' time, i.e. one should not move out of turn but should respect the basic rules of play. The flow of information follows an 'input/output' cycle; because we assume microviews are fundamentally active, we describe this as an *acquisition/proposition* cycle. Somehow is presented *query*, a question, 'What move next?', and information (the markers already in place in the external grid). Upon acquisition of input, the microviews propose moves. Miriam did not attempt to make every move she thought of, only those possible in her turn. The game *issues* represent such contextual control as the rules of the game require. For example, within each game, one must not play in the opponent's turn. Further, one must decide who should move first in a given game. Miriam's play showed numerous times that she was inclined to move out-of-turn, knew what specific move she would make

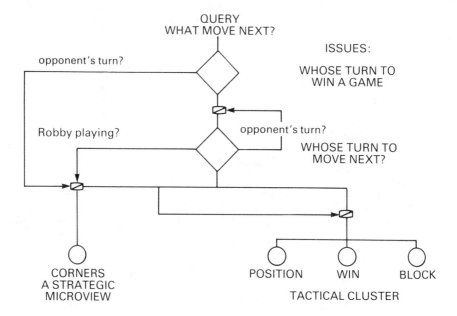

QUERY
WHAT MOVE NEXT?

ISSUES:

opponent's turn?

WHOSE TURN TO
WIN A GAME

Robby playing?

opponent's turn?

WHOSE TURN TO
MOVE NEXT?

CORNERS
A STRATEGIC
MICROVIEW

POSITION   WIN   BLOCK

TACTICAL CLUSTER

Circles are microviews.
Diamonds are issues for decision.
Box switches are opened on output when arrow lines are active.

I ascribe to Miriam a cluster of three competing tactical microviews. WIN recognizes ways to win in any orientation. BLOCK
recognizes opponent's threats. POSITION directs the next move
preferentially to the center, a corner cell, or a side cell when
neither an immediate win nor a threat is recognized. Observational material in the upcoming section 'Forced moves' supports
the ascription. Two other points bear on the triple-view ascription,
albeit in a permissive more than a constraining way. The corpus
does not permit us to justify either the one-view or three-view
ascription because there is not a detailed record of behavior
before the advent of strategic play. Further, at the level of performance, it doesn't really matter much whether there is a single
tactical microview or a cluster of three. The facts of how the
moves of the game develop prevent the microviews from coming
into regular competition except in mid-game moves. One can't
win until the third move nor block a threat until the second, at
the earliest. Finally, after four moves, significant choice of
positions is limited severely by the cells already occupied.

Fig. 4.2 – Microview clusters for strategic and tactical play.

if it were her turn. *She inhibited her action, not her thought.* I show the impact of these issues on play as inhibitions of microview output. One major issue is 'how to play this turn?' A second set of issues, quasi-contractual, addresses the question of whether or not one should be playing tic-tac-toe at all. For Miriam at the age of six, her criterion of a fair game contract was that she be allowed to win in her turn, which we indicate with the question, 'whose turn to win a game'? The issues' potential for inhibiting output is indicated by a normally-closed switch on the output data path.[8]

HOMELY BINDING

Forced moves

In the preceding section, I chose to describe Miriam's tactical play as a cluster of three competing microviews. One of the reasons for that choice derives from the specific changes in her behavior after I taught her to make forced moves. The sessions represented by game sets three through nine where didactic but in no way formal. Typically, Miriam sat in my lap and asked to play tic-tac-toe after we finished 'doing some adding'. My instruction was at first no more than a response to and a reflection upon some immediately preceding action of Miriam's, to help her understand and fix mis-steps of her play. Early on, I introduced a 'loud thinking' style of play focussed on making forced moves and explicitly considering what the opponent would do in turn. When Miriam failed to establish an attempted three-corner fork in game 3.1 (not shown) because she pursued that objective instead of blocking a threat, I emphasized verbally the role of forced moves in play, thus in game 3.3:

> Bob: Now you have one way to win there [A−/−B]. I am forced to move here [moves 2 in middle].
> Miriam: I am [i.e. forced to move; moves C, blocking 1−2−/].
> Bob: Yes. You are forced to move there. Now you have one way to win there [B−C−/]. I am forced to move here [moves 3, blocking B−C threat].
> Miriam: [tooting noises].
> Bob: Do I have one way to win? Yes. You are forced to move down there.
> Miriam: [Moves D, thereby blocking 3−2−/].
> Bob: You have one way to win there [B−D−/]. I am forced to move there [moves 4, blocking B−D].
> Miriam: X ! [moves E, blocking 4−2−/].
> Bob: So that's a tie.

8 Information always flows in. They open only during the output phase of the move cycle. Behavior is selectively inhibited. Similarly, the preference for strategic over tactical play is shown by the output of the Corners view inhibiting the output of the tactical cluster.

6;1;16

```
           A                       A                      A
     B │ C │ 3             A │ C │ 3            B │ 1 │
3.3  ──┼───┼──        3.5  ──┼───┼──       3.8  ──┼───┼───
   4 │ 2 │ E             4 │ 1 │              C │ A │ D2
     ──┼───┼──               ──┼───┼──             ──┼───┼──
     D │ 1 │ A             D │ 2 │ B            3 │ D1 │ 2
        C4                    C5                    M2
```

With this external verbal support, Miriam for the first time subordinated her three-corner fork plan to blocking a threat. In game 3.5, she made forced moves C and D without specific direction to do so. That is, as we played in this cooperative mode of talking about our reasonings, Miriam was able to subordinate her Corners objective to the threat-blocking requirement of standard play. Miriam's learning to block threats is an example of homely binding.

Her success at taking advice on blocking makes even more interesting Miriam's inability to take the next step. In game 3.8, she preferred blocking the threat $(3-/-2)$ with D1 to winning with move D2. (The occurrence of her fork is not the result of a strategic plan. I consider it most unlikely that she intended to achieve this fork yet failed to recognize it.) Because she preferred blocking to winning directly in this game, I codified for Miriam a list of ordered rules for playing Tic-tac-toe:

> Bob: The number one thing you look for [writing a list], you say 'Can I win?'
> Miriam: Can we stop for a while?
> Bob: Yeah. The second thing is: forced moves. And the third thing is what?. . . Two ways to win.

She was not able to take the advice of controlling play as a list of ordered rules. In this particular game and set of games, my emphasis on making forced moves might have biased Miriam to look only for those and react by immediately blocking the threat. However, even two years later, she remained strongly inclined to make a forced move instead of winning. I represent this state with the graphic sketch of Fig. 4.3.

Let's ask why Miriam could assimilate the advice about blocking but not the list of rules. Notice first that the latter ignored the Corners view — which became an increasingly central structure in Miriam's play. A further answer comes from the sketch of Fig. 4.3 by analogy, that the blocking advice required only a single change in control structure to implement, whereas accommodating the list of rules would have required more extensive reorganization. Thus, in a comparable 'list of rules' structure (not shown) one would see not only removal of the Tactical organization as such, but also (and consequently) removal of the inhibiting link from the Corners view to Tactical cluster and the insertion of *two* new control elements. I do not claim forcefully that what we find easy to describe must be real. And yet, if the control of information is the quintessence of mental function, one should consider descriptive parsimony in ascribed structures worth noting even if it is not taken as serious support.

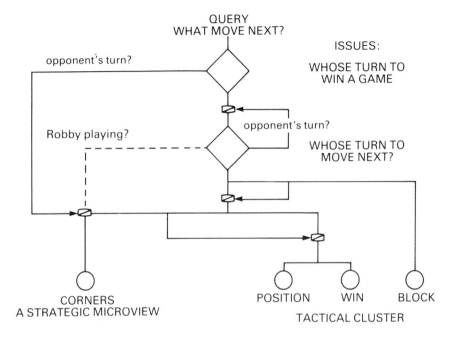

QUERY
WHAT MOVE NEXT?

ISSUES:

opponent's turn?

WHOSE TURN TO
WIN A GAME

Robby playing?

opponent's turn?

WHOSE TURN TO
MOVE NEXT?

CORNERS
A STRATEGIC MICROVIEW

POSITION   WIN   BLOCK

TACTICAL CLUSTER

Circles are microviews.
Diamonds are issues for decision.
Box switches are opened on output when arrow lines are active.

To represent the interruption of strategic play by blocking, I propose the partial separation of the BLOCK view from the TACTICAL CLUSTER by shutting off all other output with substitution of its own proposal for any other. This functions as the insertion of a new control element in the data path in response to an intrusive focussing of her behavior on choices she could understand as obvious: block or lose. The behavior represented by this change remained in effect for years. (This significant and long-lasting change further justifies the earlier choice to WIN, BLOCK, and POSITION as disparate microviews.) Whereas such a change in a PS (production system) could be effected by advancing a specific production to a prior place in a list of productions (or duplicating it and inserting it earlier in the list), I sketch the change as output-inhibition with substitution. I prefer this 'inhibition with substitution' alternative because it permits the description of this specific development to be coherent with a major feature common to later developments: new control elements enter the structure as inhibitions or earlier outputs at 'sites' of old issues.

Fig. 4.3 – The effect of instruction on the tactical cluster.

TABLE TURNING

During Miriam's apprenticeship, my own appreciation of tic-tac-toe developed from a procedural comprehension to the systematic views presented in Fig. 4.1. Despite this varying perspective on the content of instruction, the method continually revolved around turning the tables on an opponent. By *Table turning*, I mean this sequence of events:

(1) Whenever Miriam lost a game or found a strategy frustrated,
(2) we replayed that game with the roles of initiator and opponent reversed,
(3) so that she could copy and actively execute the winning procedure,
(4) during which re-execution we could (but did not always) discuss each move and verify that she was copying it accurately.

The alternation of first turns, the disparaity of our skills, and Miriam's proclivity for a negotiated settlement all joined to favor turning the tables as a technique of instruction. Her strong distaste for permitting others to copy her ideas and her desire to really outwit me instead of accepting my tolerance of her copying both weighed against the method. Despite initial reluctance and despite her not turning the tables of her own initiative during this apprenticeship, Miriam came to accept the method and use it effectively. Because of its influence on subsequent play, I present that introduction in detail:

After defeating her in game 3.6, I introduced Miriam to table turning:

6;1;16

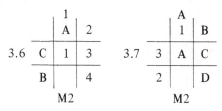

Dialogue of game 3.7

> Bob: You move first. You're starting with an X. I'm going to go right where you went. Let's see if you can beat me just the same way I beat you.
> Miriam: Wish.
> Bob: Is that the same way?
> Miriam: Did you go here? [Cell 3]
> Bob: Yes. So you're going in the corner now.
> [Miriam moves B]. Now, this [2] is a forced move, because you have one way to win, so I have to go here.
> Miriam: [Placing C] Two ways to win!
> Bob: Yes, you do. And you went over here [C of prior game] so I will too [move 3], and you beat me [as M. moves D].
> Miriam: [Cheering herself] Yaaaaah! I won for the first time. Hooray!

From Miriam's penultimate comment ('Two ways to win') it is clear she recognized the fork when she achieved it through table turning. I tend to doubt she had the fork in mind as one capable of being a strategic objective. (By contrast, the three-corner fork was surely a strategic objective.)

Results of early instruction

What, precisely, did Miriam learn from table turning? The games and dialogue of this period witness her effective play — and also the limitations of her understanding. Table turning helped to fix, at least temporarily, specific game results in Miriam's mind. That is, Miriam believed she could win games with openings C1, C2, C3, C5 and often did so. Her learning to apply specific expert playing patterns through table turning is a second example of homely binding. I think of Miriam's judgment that specific openings lead to victories as associated properties of multi-move patterns raised to salience by the very emphasis of my asking questions about them. Further, as witnessed by her not distinguishing between games permitting common forks, it is clear that what was most important to her in the definition of a game was her own pattern of action; for Miriam, tic-tac-toe at this time was an active game but not yet an interactive game.[9] Finally, Miriam's ability to predict victories with games of specific opening patterns raises the issue of how her playing knowledge was related to knowledge about the outcomes of play. This is an important question; the later section 'A stage change' will be dedicated to it. A preview of our conclusion there is that at this point in time (around age six and a half), Miriam's predictions of victory were known as associated properties of opening patterns and not as game-length deductions from playing knowledge.

The idea of table turning — as contrasted with ordered rule — was easy for Miriam to assimilate for at least two reasons. First, table turning was a socially approved method for alternative winning which could displace the unacceptable method of public negotiation. (Two years later, when Miriam could no longer remember how to turn the tables, she still remembered that it was a method for her to win in her turn.) Second, the procedure was based on copying. Our markers were usually written in different colors of ink and the sequence of markers was always preserved (we typically used either letters or numbers as markers). Copying is a very primitive activity, and one unrelated to prior game knowledge. The moves of table turning were substituted for the normal outputs of Miriam's microviews. I indicate Copying in Fig. 4.4 as both switching off the output of the tic-tac-toe microviews and proposing its own moves. In effect, I describe it as the insertion of a choice point for the invocation of another disparate microview, attached to the issue 'whose turn to win a game?'

9 Her one-sided play is thus reminiscent of the egocentric speech Piaget documented in his early study, *The Language and Thought of the Child*, 1926.

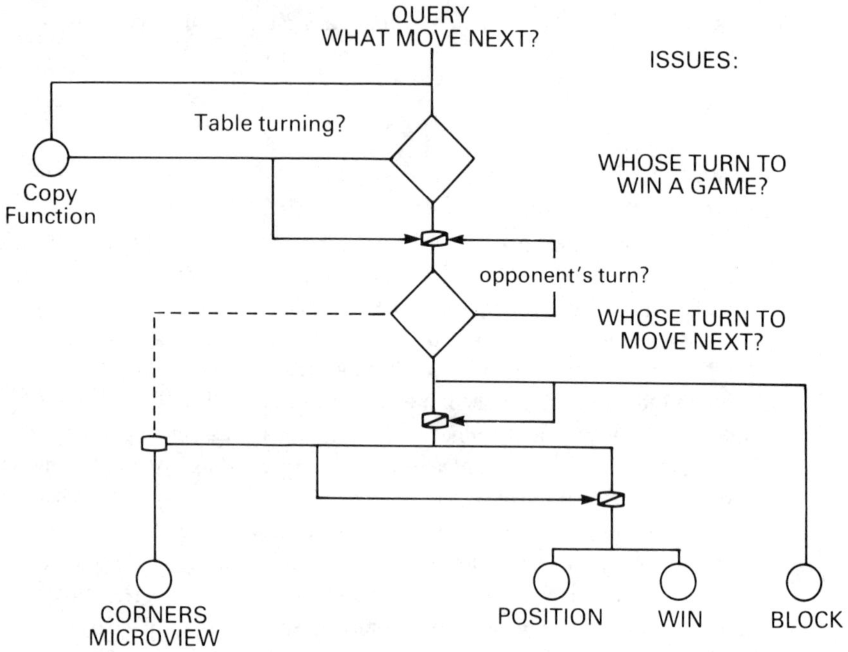

QUERY
WHAT MOVE NEXT?

ISSUES:

Table turning?

WHOSE TURN TO
WIN A GAME?

Copy
Function

opponent's turn?

WHOSE TURN TO
MOVE NEXT?

CORNERS
MICROVIEW

POSITION   WIN   BLOCK

Circles are microviews.
Diamonds are issues for decision.
Box switches are opened on output when arrow lines are active.

Combining 'inhibition and substitution' has the flavor of 'patching'
an invocation of a different cognitive structure into a malfunctioning system. The appearance of developing a better organized
and more complex structure derives from the changes being
identified with the site of a long-existing issue for the child, 'whose
turn to win?' That is, the structure has actually been there all
along in the issues and hierarchies of inhibitions. The second
major characteristic of this choice point is that the insertion short-
circuits knowledge application of the tic-tac-toe microviews but
not their activation nor their output. The implication here is
that output of those views, though not effective, could be contrasted with the Copy proposals. Such would permit the kind of
learning to take place described in Chapter 2, 'The progressive
construction of mind', as the generation of specific inter-view
relations through the accidental confluence of proposals.

Fig. 4.4 – Turning table.

OPENING ADVANTAGE

Miriam propelled herself to independence, as the analysis of this section shows in detail. She had been my captive antagonist at tic-tac-toe for some months when, while I was distracted otherwise, she engaged Glenn, a Logo project colleague, in play. I decided thereafter to terminate instruction as such and attempted merely to evaluate what Miriam had been able to learn. (My intentions as her opponent in sessions 11 through 16 were not purposefully didactic – though it's hard to keep the doctor down.) Miriam at six-and-a-half held her own with a brother two years her senior and with our games-knowledgeable colleague Glenn (some mere twenty years her senior). The most surprising observation of this period is that Miriam did not appreciate opening advantage at all.

On her own

At the end of session 7, Miriam refused to initiate a game out-of-turn and required my going first. With no specific objective on my part, I played out a game of form C2 in game 7.7 below. After her defeat, Miriam confided to me that when next they played, 'I'll try to get Robby to move here [pointing to cell 6], then I'll move my B here [cell 7], then I'll try this trick on 'im'.

Miriam did not play against her brother till much later, but in session 10 she seized upon Glenn at Logo as a likely victim. In the interim, she had received table turning instruction in the gambit (of game 7.7) and attempted to apply it against me. Contrast these three games:

Miriam played Glenn with the obvious intention of defeating him by the C2 expert play. And she got it all wrong! Glenn informed me that Miriam had asked him to open in cell 6 (game 10.4); this is the responding move of the C2 opening game. He moved first then Miriam in her turn made the initiator's 'opening' move (A in cell 1). This combination is the opening for the side game S3, which Glenn had the knowledge to win. After her defeat, Miriam and Glenn replayed the opening configuration but with her having the opening advantage, and she defeated him. (His moving in a symetrical variant of his opening counter's position in the prior game suggests the choice was his. Miriam would have asked him to move in the same location as move 1 of game 10.4.) This senquence of games is striking evidence tht Miriam had no idea at that time of the significance of opening advantage.

Miriam's insensitivity to opening advantage was shortly confirmed by her loud thinking. The following dialog (recorded with game 12.3) exhibits this essential difficulty of her play. In addition, it argues that any representation of her tic-tac-toe knowledge at this age must *not* depend on her attending to or representing her opponent's possible moves.

6;5;26

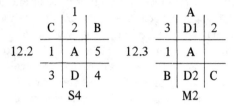

Dialog of game 12.3

Miriam: My turn to go first?
Bob: Yeah.
Miriam: [Moves A in middle.]
Bob: Let me ask you a question. [Placing counter 1 at side cell]. If I move here, can you beat me?
Miriam: It will probably be like the same game.
Bob: The same game as what?
Miriam: The last game.
Bob: You think it will?
Miriam: Yeah.

Miriam's comment that the two games will be the same is unforced confirmation that she had not yet made a distinction which nearly any other person would see as implicit in tic-tac-toe. It does matter whether one goes first or second; Miriam apparently did not appreciate that fact. With the profoundly non-standard perspective, one which does not recognize the opening advantage of the first player, with her failure to make a distinction which adults assume, her representation was more different from the casual player's than any casual observer would guess.

Two in a row

Playing with variations of standard games was a common activity in Miriam's experience. For example, I sometimes played 'half a game' of checkers with her (each player had six checkers) and at the end of session 10, I interrupted Glenn as he was introducing Miriam to tic-tac-toe played on a four-by-four grid. Thus, I see Miriam's following discovery as not too surprising.

Very early one morning (6;8;24), Miriam popped into bed between my wife and me, and by her chatter and playing kept me drowsily awake. She asked first if I wanted to play 'Tic-tac-toe — Four in a Row'. I responded that the game was too complicated for me, even before I realized her mode of play was to be marking moves by gestures in the air. When I asked how she could possibly do that, Miriam explained she was envisioning the grid as lines through a series of nail heads visible in the wallboard of the ceiling. 'Then all you have to do is make the marks there.' I still refused to play, even 'Tic-tac-toe – Three in a Row.'

Miriam continued, 'Hey, Daddy, if you play 'Tic-tac-toe – Two in a Row', the first guy always wins'. I asked what she meant. Miriam explained, 'If the X goes first, say in one corner, and the O goes in the opposite corner, the X still has two ways to win, every time'. I asked if she thought anything like that could be true for 'Tic-tac-toe – Three in a Row'. 'No, it couldn't', she concluded.

The next day Miriam agreed to a videotaped session about tic-tac-toe in our home, during which she passed from believing that no such thing as opening advantage existed in tic-tac-toe to producing a crisp formulation of what opening advantage means as it applies to that game: 'whoever goes first who knows a good strategy can win'. (Miriam's formulation of 'good strategy' in opening advantage was confirmed subsequently as meaning 'a strategy which leads to a fork'.) She did not apparently see the good strategy as one relating an opening pattern and the fork achievement. This crisp formulation is clear evidence that, in one sense, Miriam 'knew' what opening advantage means. Her subsequent play is likewise clear evidence that this verbally formulated knowledge had no discernible impact.[10] Miriam's formulation may have had an impact on her play, but there is no way of telling. In games played against herself subsequently, 'she' always goes first, but I can claim no obvious effect from the fact observed. An appreciation of opening advantage would incline a person to prefer going first whenever possible, but such a preference is one Miriam owned since first she began the game.

Does Miriam's description of opening advantage indicate the occurrence of a lonely discovery or is this an instance of homely binding? I judge Miriam's description of opening advantage as an example of homely binding through contrasting it with the 'two in a row' insight. In the latter circumstance, literally in the midst of her family, Miriam was intellectually isolated; she could get no one to play the opponent and did so herself. By an accident of elaborating her attempt to make the game simple enough for me to play, Miriam stumbled into a degenerate game where her single opponent's-move look-ahead was adequate to take her to game end. Her discovery of a determinate win made sense in terms of her understanding of what's what. That was a 'lonely discovery'. In contrast, during the 'opening advantage' session, I focussed Miriam's attention on pairs of games permitting expert wins, the order-free patterns of whose moves are identical, e.g. C2 and S3. Miriam's verbal formulation of opening advantage seems an observation and thus a consequence of the problem-solving situation in which she agreed to be placed. Such an observation should be distinguished from an insight based on her working through a specific problem from her understanding of what's what. (An explicit and extensive example of such behavior appears in the section 'A new strategy'.)

10 Classifying the knowledge as 'merely verbal', would beg an important question, the relation of verbally formulated knowledge to problem solving. That question is quite beyond the scope of this study.

Speculations

Miriam's early understanding of tic-tac-toe didn't distinguish between games where she or her opponent was the initiator. I say she had then a *syngnostic* perspective, one which recognizes without discrimination what others can see as distinct. Recognition that something so central as order of moves is relevant to play raises a question: is this change so profound as to render obsolete whatever prior knowledge Miriam owned? A negative answer to this question would bear on the importance of the young child's egocentricity, noted long ago by Piaget (1926). If the knowledge embodied in microviews is internally represented in terms of one's own actions (these can be known and controlled stepwise), discriminations based on interaction (appearing to the syngnostic perspective as random) come into being as incremental refinements of already established knowledge. Such would help to account for the stability of knowledge based on ego-active, syngnostic perspectives, the progressive refinement of that knowledge, and the adaptiveness of the child's egocentricity.

LONELY DISCOVERIES

The inception of multi-role play

Table turning was effective initially as an instructional mode of play. It became more than that, for Miriam turned the tables spontaneously. After being defeated by Glenn at MIT, Miriam first asked me to replay the specific game and then turned the tables on me. In later games, Miriam went further and incorporated her opponent's play with her own. It is this skill, simulating another person as an opponent, that is required first, to perform the analysis which leads to an explicit understanding of specific games, second, to transfer knowledge from aggressive to defensive play, and ultimately perhaps, to develop an articulate and well-organized understanding of the micro-domain of playing tic-tac-toe.

Playing Robby

Miriam played most games of session 14 against her brother. After an initial tie and a loss to Robby in a corner opening (from C5), Miriam began game 14.3 (below) in a corner. Robby's opposite corner response (he had successfully blocked her three-corner fork there in all previous play) led first to her noisy complaint ... and then this comment, 'Robby, you're gonna kill me for this'. She made an effective crux (defined in Fig. 4.1) for game C1 and continued with a 'million dollar promise' that she would not move in cell 4. (I believe she was drawing his attention to cell 4 and egging him on to move there.) After Robby made his forced move in cell 4, Miriam informed him she wasn't going there anyway. At my question of whether or not she would beat him, Miriam replied, 'Yeah, I think so', and linked her two chances to win into a fork. Miriam honestly beat Robby at a game at which he had been master in all their previous play.

6;6;22

```
            A                          1
        A | D | C              C  |      | A
14.3    2 | 3 |        14.4    4  |  1   | 3
        ---------              ---------
        B  |    | 1            2  |      | B
           C1                        M1
```

In the next game, Miriam invited Robby to turn the tables on her. Robby, not privy to our experiments with tic-tac-toe at that phase, did not share with Miriam the specific meaning she assigned to that procedure. Does game 14.4 show Miriam pursuing a three-corner fork despite the intrusion of Robby's 3 where a hole should be? Or was it a gift to him? I prefer the latter interpretation because Miriam mentioned to me her surprise that he didn't know how to turn tables. Such a gift would be another way of alternate winning when your opponent can't turn the tables.

Playing against herself

In the midst of this interesting situation, I was called away for a few minutes. I asked the children not to play together till I returned. Coming back, I found Miriam had been playing tic-tac-toe against herself, in her words, 'making smart moves for me and the other guy'. She showed me her play of game 14.5, where the first player wins after the second falls into a trap of opening C5.

6;6;22   *6;7;3*

```
            A                          1
        A | D | C              1  | d  | c
14.5       | 1 | 3     15.1    B  | C  |
        ---------              ---------
        2  |    | B            b  |    | A
           C5                        C1
```

Attempting later to probe Miriam's ability to play defensively against a corner opening, I asked her to play as opponent a C1 game (15.1 above). I opened with corner 1. Miriam took over once the chalk was in her hand. (Her subsequent 'non-self' moves are shown in lower-case letters.) After move B, she paused and wavered, 'No. He wouldn't move there'. I laughed at her attempted cheat and said, 'Oh yes, he would', Miriam made the smart move (c) for her opponent and concluded, 'I block him in the center and he wins'. Thus we have a second example of Miriam's playing both sides of a single game.

The specific game knowledge with which Miriam defeated Robby in game 14.3 was forgotten; that satisfying victory did not permanently affect cognitive structures. In direct contrast, multi-role play (first beginning in game 14.5 at age 6;6;22 and reappearing in the 'two in a row' incident at 6;8;24) became a permanent feature of Miriam's play and one which enabled later significant development. Almost by definition, in the inception of multi-role play we observe that characteristic of lonely discovery, simulation of the role of another, as primary. More importantly, we can see in game 14.5 that Miriam played with her Corners strategy, while 'the smart moves' of 'the other guy' were precisely the proposals of her own tactical microviews. The *ego plays strategically*, the *alter-ego tactically* (game 15.1, initiated by me is the single exception to this pattern in the corpus). The multi-role play appears to be achieved by the splitting apart of two sometimes competing sub-structures under control of a new decision on an old issue, 'how do I play this move?' This control element insertion can be seen as effecting significant changes in behavior with minimal changes in structure. The appearance of creating new structure from nothing can be avoided if this new control element insertion is seen as a patch of peculiar power — because it substitutes a particular decision for what had been merely an inhibition in pre-existing structure.

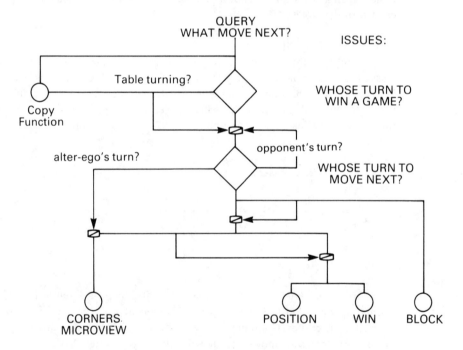

Circles are microviews.
Diamonds are issues for decision.
Box switches are opened on output when arrow lines are active.

In the sketch of Fig. 4.5, *whom* she plays determines *how* Miriam plays; her strategic microview is inhibited during the opponent's turn. This change is similar to a return to the structure through which Miriam inhibited strategic play against her brother. The opponent is now internalized, is her alter-ego or other self.

Fig. 4.5 — Using separable sub-structures for multi-role play.

A NEW STRATEGY

In the years following the core period of The Intimate Study, playing tic-tac-toe lost social currency with Miriam and me. My energies were much absorbed by the analyses and composition of *One Child's Learning* (Lawler, 1979). Peggy was born to our family. Miriam couldn't find a tolerable partner for the game, but this was not a major concern to her for she, as well as I, had other preoccupations. Two sorts of play occurred during this period of relative inactivity: first were the few games we did play (sessions 18 through 21), second was Miriam's solitary play and her reflection upon it. From these two sorts of play, two new developments arose: Miriam discovered a strategy different from the three-corner fork; she also became capable of game length prediction (an issue I will address in 'A stage change').

Announcing her discovery

Reviewing her play of the intervening years, Miriam stated that she played rarely and mostly against herself (30 games in two years was her estimate). As I introduced my objective, Miriam proposed one of her own: to apply a newly discovered strategy against me. When I asked her to discuss it with me, she responded, 'No way! Then whenever I play you'll know my tactics'. This more independent stance of hers undercut the loud-thinking openness of our earlier play, but Miriam's new strategy, which I name the Middle and Corners Fork, is nonetheless clear from her play on the games below and commentary on 22.2:

8;9;21

```
                 A                        A
           A |  1  |  *              A |     |  *
  22.1     * |  B  |         22.2    * |  B  |
           C |     |  2              C |  1  |  2
                C4                       C2
```

Bob: [After move C of 22.1] We don't have to play that out. You've clearly defeated me. Masterful. Let's play another one here. You go back in that corner. That's where you went the first time.... And I want to try some other places and see if I can get away from you and your new tactic. I'm going to go down here (cell 8). That's on the side away.

Miriam: [Moves B in cell 5.]

Bob: Arrgh! [Moves 2 in cell 9]. This is a different game. See, I've got a way to win....

Miriam: [Moves C in cell 7.]

Bob: Oh no!

Miriam: Careful of your moves, Buster.

Bob: So you've got two ways to win now. Let me ask you something. When did you invent this trick?

Miriam: Oh, I was playing with myself.

Bob: Well.... That's another one for Miriam.... When did you do this? Was it recently or years ago?

Miriam: Recently.... See, what I happened to do. [Here Miriam moves to her desk and returns with a copy of Richard Scarry's *Rainy Day Book*]... What I did is I went X. He went O. I went. He went O.

In a final comment on the discovery of this new strategy, Miriam added that she had played the game and only days later noticed the fork created with her third move. (This comment is born out by the appearance of the original game, where the first six markers are made in brown crayon and the last, the winning move (D) is marked in ball pen.)

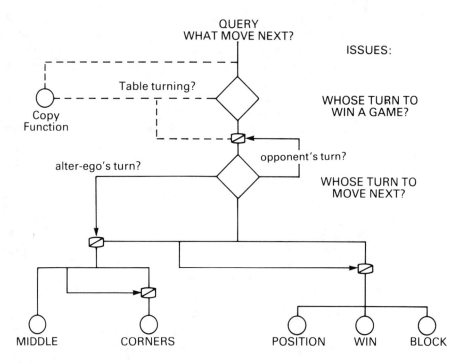

Circles are microviews.
Diamonds are issues for decision.
Box switches are opened on output when arrow lines are active.

A new strategic microview added to the structure. Abandoning a game as a draw, Miriam later noticed an overlooked way to win. In working through the moves of the prior game, she discovered a new strategy. Since that strategy is known to be effective when it applies, it is preferred to the play of the CORNERS view which is vulnerable to a defensive response.

Fig. 4.6 – A new strategic microview added to the structure.

Once Miriam discovered this new strategy, its pattern played a role as a strategic objective, analogous to that of the three-corner fork. I indicate this new strategy as the creation of a new microview in Fig. 4.6, where the Middle microview joins the Corners view to form a Strategic Cluster. A striking quality of Miriam's Middle view play was her certainty of its power. She knew she could win games of C2 and C4 opening forms. This was not so for the Corners view, where the C5 game is indeterminate and (as we shall see) the C1 game had been forgotten and was not mastered. This difference in certitude is indicated by the Middle view's switching off the output of the Corners view in any competition.

No development for two years

Tracing through all the games of the corpus, I find Miriam first showed sensitivity to the 'middle and corners' fork as an objective comparable to 'three corners' (in game 5.3), two years before she was able to use it with power. Miriam could have owned an objective to win games using the 'middle and corners' fork. It is an empirical observation that no such objective asserted itself with vigor. All earlier middle fork victories can be explained away as no more than recall of game-specific, fragmentary knowledge. One should conceive then of the structure behind Miriam's early noticing of the middle and corners fork and subsequent ability to recognize forks once achieved as a kind of nonfunctional proto-view. The earlier frequent injunction to 'look for two ways to win' sensitized Miriam so that she could appreciate the specific victory by which Robby vanquished the Museum's computer. Thus we can similarly describe the formation of the Corners view as a significant further specification of an earlier Corners proto-view created by homely binding.

DISCOVERY RECONSTRUCTION

The transformation of this proto-view into the Middle microview occurred during the incident wherein Miriam reviewed and reflected upon the game recorded in Richard Scarry's *Best Rainy Day Book Ever.* Let us try to reconstruct the sequence of moves:

circa 8;9

original			one reconstruction	A		another		
X	O	O	A	1	3	C	1	2
*	X		*	B		*	A	
X		O	C		2	B		3
				C4			M2	

(The * represents the way to win Miriam discovered on reflection days after the initial game.) Miriam's markers do not preserve enough information for a decision as to which game (C4 or M2) she actually executed in her original play. Her testimony is that she played game labelled C4 above. On reflection she recognized the fork and interpreted her prior play as the C4 game. After recognizing a way to win she had not taken advantage of, Miriam tried to figure out how she had achieved it. Let us suppose that she attempted replaying in her mind the games below:

circa 8;9

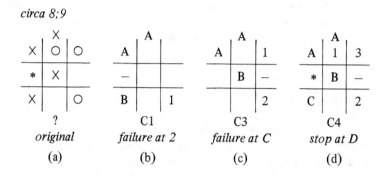

original	failure at 2	failure at C
(a)	(b)	(c)

Miriam knew she was on the trail of a good strategy that must fit the constraints of moves of the original recorded game. How could her prior knowledge have helped her discover it? The only other good strategy she knew began in cell 1 and most likely so did her prior play. If in her second turn she selected cell 7, as in (b) above, the Corners preferred cell 9 being occupied, she would have twice missed a forced move (during Alter's second and third turns); surely she would have thought this unlikely. If Alter's first move were to cell 3, as in (c), and Miriam's crux in the center, his response would have been 9. Placing the remaining markers (C in cell 7 and 3 in cell 2) would have required her missing a forced move (to cell 6) and his preferring a pointless cell 2 move to winning. Most unlikely. This second possible game, although beginning in the corner, specifically lacks a three-corner objective. Play for both Alter and Ego goes forward by the functions of the Tactical Cluster.

The third reconstructed game (d) also goes forward with play of the Tactical Cluster. Given the opening move in cell 1 and Alter's response in cell 2, the Ego's next choice of move, proposed by the Position view, was to the center; Alter moved to cell 9 as required. Because the opening response was to cell 2, there was no threat to be blocked; move C is a corner choice such as the Position microview would propose. Move 3 could be explained as Alter's second forced move. Even if she noticed Alter's way to win (3–/–2) – which a move D, not made, could have blocked – Miriam's Ego would not have felt compelled to complete a drawn game. With this last game played out stepwise, with the fork before her, all Miriam needed to appreciate fully her good strategy was to notice that Alter's moves 2 and 3 were both forced. With such an insight, Miriam could have become master of a fully determined strategy for a specific opening game. She did show such mastery.

In the working out of this specific game as reconstructed, playing both sides according to her documented tactical and game-specific knowledge, Miriam could very plausibly have discovered her new strategy. If so, then her awareness ,——

of the individual steps of her own play, in the roles of Ego and Alter, permitted her analysis of a situation most probably noticed 'accidentally' by the views of her Tactical Cluster. What is most striking about such a situation of thought is that the process (reconstructing the achievement of an objective) not only created a new strategic microview, it also promoted the integration of pattern and serial aspects of play whose long separation I have noted. Now focus on the role of this particular experience in advancing Miriam's ability to integrate serial and pattern aspects of play.

A STAGE CHANGE

Miriam's play at age six showed she did not own an integrated understanding of pattern and serial aspects of play. In striking contrast, the final review (age 8;10) of Miriam's play establishes her ability to work out games in her mind. Multi-role play — originally a social convenience — became a significant cognitive development because it fitted a fundamental aspect of tic-tac-toe[11]. My proposal is that Miriam discovered offensive forcing through multi-role play, experiencing 'being forced' as Alter while simultaneously, as Ego, experiencing the offensive use of forcing. Where is the evidence that her very processes of thought changed in quality? If there be such evidence, what light does it shed upon the transition from one mode of thought to another?

Addressing these questions requires we distinguish between exposure to some formulation and the internal processes by which the individual makes sense of what he may have already 'known' in a more limited way — no easy task. I address these questions through explorations that revolve around the necessary truth of a conclusion. This focus reflects a central theme running through Piagetian psychology; first, belief rooted in logical deduction is different in kind from belief based on the probabilities of experience; next, when justification by appeal to logic replaces an appeal to experience, a new stage of thought is achieved.

Necessity as a criterion
The central issue of tic-tac-toe session 23 was forecasting victory. Miriam did predict her victory from opening configurations of markers (and prove her judgment correct).Typically, after my opening response, I asked Miriam whether or not she would defeat me and if so, how, as with game 23.5:

> Bob: Will you beat me?
> Miriam: Yes, I think so.
> Bob: How?
> Miriam: I'll move here [cell 9], then you move here [cell 5, forced], then I
> move here [cell 7] and get two ways to win.

11 Recall from Fig. 4.1 that Expert play requires offensive forcing at the initiator's second move.

8;10;29

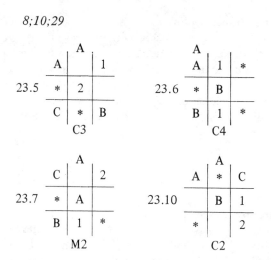

Game 23.5 joins together in Miriam's link placement a 'forced move' and the three-corner fork. In game 23.6, Miriam predicted victory also:

Bob: Will you beat me [after move 1]?

Miriam: [A long pause — we may assume she was working out the game in her mind.] Yes. I'll move here [cell 5]. You'll move here [cell 9, forced], and I'll use my new tactic [link the middle and corners fork].

In game 23.7, Miriam responded 'yes' to my prediction question as she wrote move B, and continued, 'You're forced to move here (cell 3) and I get two ways to win'. She was uncertain about whether or not she would win the indeterminate games of form M1 and C5. Miriam paused long before answering that she would win game 23.10 and objected to my even asking her the question because she was 'trying to think'. Once she did give her judgment about victory, Miriam admitted she had the complete game worked out in her mind.

At the end of the study, Miriam had achieved that phase of procedural comprehension mentioned earlier and exemplified most fully here. Notice that her uncertainty in the indeterminate games is both appropriate and supported by her fragmentary comprehension of the specific game C5. In game 23.10, when she said I would move 2 in cell 9, I objected. Miriam countered that I had to move there or she would win directly. There can be no clearer indication that she was using offensive forced moves both in mental play and in the justification of a victory claim. (This does not imply she had crisply formulated and used for guidance a general principle that the crux must force the opponent's second move out of the way of the planned fork.)

We have used the stage change criterion of a qualitative difference in thought to support the claim that Miriam exhibited some significant learning, but that does not necessarily commit me to adopt, ultimately, a stage theory. This is especially the case when one aspect of my endeavor is to explain stage changes as emergent saltations on behavior from incremental changes at the micro-structural level.

How did Miriam learn about the use of offensive forcing? There are at least three obvious candidate answers to the question. First, it is possible that someone told Miriam everything she knew. Alternatively, she may have figured out everything herself (regardless of whatever cultural presses existed). An intermediate position is that someone told Miriam what's what (which objects or categories of things are important) and that subsequently she was able to figure out what follows (what categorical and functional relations obtain between those highlighted elements).12 Miriam's corners strategy was long preceded by the slogan 'look for two ways to win', and the earliest sign of her sensitivity to other forks and attempting to achieve them occurred two years prior to her working out of the middle and corners strategy. We should not be surprised if Miriam took from my instruction the notion that there might be such a thing as offensive forcing and later, alone, discovered situations in which the relation applied with power.

We cannot exclude any of these three possible interpretations of this incident. Miriam could learn both by instruction and by creative problem solving. As in the incident of her introduction to the three corners strategy by Robby, it is clear that instruction was best absorbed when it was a response to questions she herself posed. I explicitly told Miriam, in discussing game 20.4, that what was required for expert play was 'forcing the other guy's next move out of the way so you could get your two ways to win'. Even though, consequently, she *might* have learned offensive forcing from me, that instruction was *my* lesson and not one she provoked with her own questions. In the earlier 'Discovery reconstruction', I traced in detail a plausible sequence of problem-solving moves as a result of which Miriam could have not only discovered her new strategy but also experienced 'being forced' as Alter while working out a win for herself as Ego.

I choose to believe that Miriam learned as described in 'Discovery reconstruction', even though my family and my experiments functioned as an intrusive didactic system. The interpretation is not established, but the possibility of such learning, in a nearly computational description, is established by the analysis in this particular case. Maybe that's enough. No one need be ashamed to admit that people can learn through being taught (how, precisely, those lessons might be internalized is a major technical problem once one admits *any* complexity to the structure of the human mind), nor to admit that some people learn this or that, according to their own objectives, from what other people do and say (technically a more tractable problem than the former) so long as all recognize that all people can learn from what they do (once we admit that control of learning is within the mind of the learner, this may be the easiest, technically, of the three problems to describe and model).

The functional lability of cognitive structures

The criterion for the qualitative change in Miriam's thinking is that she showed herself newly able to predict and prove claims of victory by forward mental play in the tree of possible games. If Miriam discovered the use of offensive forcing

12 But such a position raises immediately the question of how one explains how a particular bit of advice comes to function with power in thought.

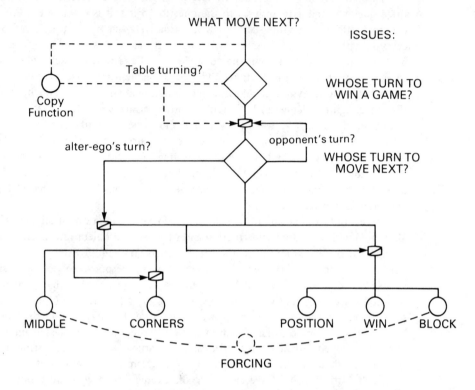

In this sketch of the organization of Miriam's tic-tac-toe knowledge at the end of two years' development, there is nowhere added any special structure to represent offensive forcing. None is needed unless one claims she could relate strategic to tactical play in a descriptive more than functional manner. What is required for game-length mental play is the computational simplification of the standard game by the use of offensive forced moves. It was quite explicit in the 'Two in a Row' incident that Miriam could play in her mind and suppress the output if the possibilities were not computationally explosive. Here, the structure capable of forward play in the game tree is not new; it merely recognizes what had been there before and was not represented in previous diagrams. What is new in the sketch is the microview FORCING, shown as the dotted circle because it did not exist as a completely articulated structure in Miriam's mind. Let us call the FORCING view a proto-view. The content of this assertion is imputing to Miriam a vague sense of the relatedness of strategic and tactical play without abscribing any precise and detailed description. Notice. that the FORCING microview does not enter into play. Its knowledge is more descriptive than functional. Such is knowledge about knowledge (named the correlation of perspectives in Chapter 2 and exemplified there by the Conformal microview).

Fig. 4.7 – A structure capable of forward play in the game tree.

as portrayed in 'Discovery reconstruction', this stage change which her ability to prove game outcomes implies must be seen in a new light, as no more than (and no less than) the application of structure developed in one task to a second related but different task.

The task is different because the balance in use of the structures is different. Proposing a move permits reactions as well as reflection. In contrast, proving a victory begins from limited input, has a different output, and requires thought in a more deductive mode. Miriam confronted this new task only because it was presented forcefully to her by her society in the person of me, her father, functioning as psychologist. We should not be surprised that a small change in a system of cognitive structures permits it to cover a new class of related but distinct problems if we take seriously the idea (presented crisply in a limited context by Sussman (1975) that the mind functions as a closed system, doing the best it can on problems beyond its capability by deforming its interpretations of the problems into little more than minor variations of others it has solved before. Miriam's working through the puzzle of how she achieved the fork in the discovery incident gave game-length mental play a significance she could appreciate. Once this major extension to game-length mental play had been established, the next stop, to answering predictive questions, was a small one to make. The incident wherein this new capability emerged was essentially private and different in character from its first public manifestation. Such functional lability is the hidden power which gives effect to lonely discoveries made through the accidents of application of already existing ideas to new problems. Is learning, then, any more or less amazing than the evolution of flight or the invention of writing?

CONCLUSIONS

I have applied a vision of the interaction of social experience and the personal construction of knowledge in the interpretation of a corpus which spans a period of significant cognitive development in one child's learning about a single task environment. This chapter presents in considerable detail a particular path of experience and structural change which constitutes a worked example of how a 'stage change' in task-domain performance could emerge from the incremental elaboration of local clusters of knowledge. One striking result is that simulating an opponent with pattern-driven, ego-activity-focussed microviews can lead in simple steps to that mature mental play described as 'forward search in the game tree of possibilities'. The separability of the tactical and strategic modes of playing tic-tac-toe, reflected in cognitive structures, permits the simulation of an opponent to develop for interactive mental play. The wealth of fragmentary knowledge acquired in situations of homely binding permitted Miriam to work out in private a new strategy — itself a creative application of imperfectly comprehended experience. I have proposed, with reasoned though not coercive argument, that the working through of this new strategy also entailed development of that progressive mental play which permits prediction and proof of outcomes from openings — an advance in behavior which could be seen as so significant as to mark a 'stage change'.

I began by admitting that tic-tac-toe is generally considered a trivial game. Now it seems more appropriate to ask and answer a deeper question: 'Given the simplicity of information processing descriptions of mind, how is it possible that one could learn so complicated a thing as tic-tac-toe at all?' The first answer is of a computational sort, in the sense that fragmentary specific game knowledge enables insights which simplify the exploration of possible paths of play. Further, we have been that the structure of the game permits the separate development of different ways of playing, each embodied in a relatively self-contained sub-structure (microview or microview cluster). The separability of these sub-structures, which once separated, could be assigned roles in the turn-taking structures of behavior that we have all practiced since infancy, permits ego-active knowledge (as in Miriam's first strategy) to be extended first, to ego-with-controlled-alter knowledge (witnessed in her multi-role play), and finally, as we may imagine, to knowledge of interaction as such. The answer is, in short, neither purely psychological (depending on the developmental processes and structures of information in the mind) nor entirely epistemological (dependent on the structure of the game), but rather it resides in the synthesis which is that of the mind interacting with things of the world.

Tic-tac-toe stages

I earlier discriminated four stages of tic-tac-toe comprehension. *Naive comprehension* characterizes Miriam's play at the beginning of the study, where her play was guided by propensities or by the three-corner objective when devoid of any sense of how to achieve it regularly. *Fragmentary comprehension* is quite clearly exemplified in Miriam's highly specific knowledge of the two outcomes of game C5 (corner-middle opening). *Procedural comprehension* is exhibited by Miriam's later proof of victory predictions. A *systematic comprehension* is witnessed by the view of tic-tac-toe presented in Fig. 4.1. Miriam never got this far. Let us now step back from the detail of the study to observe how transitions between these four stages of play relate to the articulation of complementary roles and to the processes of homely binding and lonely discovery.

Miriam's inventing of her middle and corners strategy, a central event in her transition to procedural comprehension, is a case of lonely discovery. The sense of a casual mulling-over of previous activity in our reconstruction of the discovery incident recalls William Wordsworth's observation that poetry is passion, 'recollected in tranquillity'. My formulation echoes his:

Understanding is a description of experience articulated through reflection.

We may choose to say that both systematic and procedural comprehension are forms of understanding without doing violence to the common sense of the terms — but it would stretch that use unacceptably and with little purpose to include under that term Miriam's initial propensities and her fragmentary comprehension, as of specific games. Thus we get the watershed of understanding between fragmentary and procedural comprehension.

The major transition

The main question to ask, then, is how the transition from a fragmentary to a procedural comprehension occurred. If the essential insight in Miriam's middle and corners strategy is the necessary relationship of the crux and the fork, what is implicated is a revision of the idea of forced moves so that they are seen as offensive tools as well as being threats to which a defensive response must be made. What was behind this discovery? I believe the transition came in multi-role play where Miriam could feel herself 'being forced' as simulated opponent by the crux she herself placed as initiator. This insight occurred as a lonely discovery, but its social underpinnings were both pervasive and manifest. Multi-role play grew out of table turning and a second practice: my permitting Miriam to specify what moves I should make. The question of predicting victory was very much a research question; but it also was more, with a significant personal and social component: I don't like condescending. This salient question in our play must have sensitized Miriam to the issue of necessary connection between crux and fork. Even if the transition to the progressive level of comprehension was a lonely discovery, Miriam's fragmentary knowledge was very much the fruit of extensive social engagement — beginning with Robby's introduction of the three-corner fork through that multitude of games from which C5 emerged as one opening of well-known outcomes.

The first transition

We can also ask how Miriam moved from the propensities of naive comprehension to fragmentary comprehension. With her first uses of the C5 opening ploy, initially there was no sense of the opponent's role at all. The distinction between the winning and tieing outcomes was socially driven. Without her attending to forced moves, 'tolerable' mature play would have been impossible. The idea of defensive forced moves is the socially determined *sine* qua non for initiation and play as an independent player. Without command of forced moves, the game is random and unacceptable to an opponent such as me; thus, to play with me, Miriam had to endure instruction. The squabble between Miriam and Robby in session 2 is more evidence of the social pressure behind this original transition.

The final transition

Since Miriam did not develop a systematic comprehension of tic-tac-toe, one cannot ask of this study how such a transition happened — unless he is willing to admit as relevant how it happened for me, to take as admissible evidence my reflection upon the entries of a journal I kept during The Intimate Study. Let me sketch my conclusions from reviewing that material. My comprehension was first, at best, procedural. As we two played, I was uneasy with my own ignorance. How could I understand Miriam's play without a solid grasp of the material? I found it too hard to comprehend an ongoing game and its possibilities in terms of thinking of some set of simple rules. Privately, I began tracing out 'chances to win' to improve ny grasp of the game — and found this a dead-end. I began playing against myself.[13] First I played a C3 game to a tie – then found that with the crux in cell 9 I could have an expert win. Next a C1 game followed the same pattern; first I played to a tie, then, doing something different, I discovered an expert win. With games C2 and C4, I went immediately to expert wins. I also found one for the S3 game (but not S2). Now aware that there were so many expert wins, I decided it would be useful to classify them to support my recall and to suppress confusion. Here I realized that a classification by the two opening moves was adequate. A further note, supporting the arguments advanced in the discussion of session 22, is that the forms of winning games I initially developed were the same as Miriam's middle and corners strategy. I later abandoned the initial 'hard' solution for the 'harder' expert wins of Fig. 4.1 because this permitted the use of a common crux for the four games C1–C4. My concern with this 'trivial game' was for me unusual, and driven by my social engagement with Miriam. Because I owned a higher standard of performance for myself (and had a need to achieve it) than was possible with my initially syngnostic perspective on the game, I constructed a richer and more controllable perspective through a process of lonely discovery based upon articulating the complementary roles of the game.

Our final formulation then is that:

Understanding is a description of experience articulated through reflection.

You may ask 'Is that worth the effort?' I respond with the rhetorical question, 'Is understanding worthwhile?', and conclude that if we understand better what we 'knew' before, that is significant learning.

---

13 These games and notes about my formulations were kept in a private journal, separately from The Intimate Study.

5

Cognitive organization

THE CENTRAL PROPOSAL

The explanatory dimension of cognitive organization is the path of genetic descent of specific cognitive structures. Were it possible to represent both sensorimotor schemata and late developed structures explicitly and completely, tracing in detail the descent of the latter from the former and identifying the timing and context of ascribable structural changes would be the ideal method to probe the character, the contingencies, and the causes of natural learning. Even some local successes at tracing cognitive structures to their immediate antecedents in experience and in the mind, as has been achieved in previous chapters, is worthwhile. But what is really needed is a more ambitious attempt to specify how local clusters of cognitive structures interconnect among themselves and with their most fundamental antecedents in development. The preceding studies have not asked why, in principle, some links occur between late developing structures and others do not. To deal with such a problem is the purpose of this chapter.

The central proposal is to discriminate among the major components of the sensorimotor system and their cognitive descendents, even while assuming the pre-eminence of that system as the basis of mind. Imagine the entire sensorimotor system of the body as made up of a few large, related, but distinct subsystems, each characterized by the special states and motions of the major body parts, thus:

Body parts	Sensorimotor subsystem	Major operations
Trunk	Somatic	Being here
Legs	Locomotive	Moving from here to there
Head—eyes	Capital/visual	Looking at that there
Arms—hands	Manipulative	Changing that there
Tongue, etc.	Linguistic	Saying whatever

Granting the distinctness of these five major sensorimotor sub-systems, notice that much of the activity of early infancy specifically involves developing coordinates between them: between hand and eye, between legs and body, between the sound expression system and what is felt, seen, or desired. If the sensorimotor system is fundamental in the development of the mind, one might assume that my significant structure at its base — such as the body-parts model here — should ramify through all descendent cognitive structures developed from interacting with the experiences of later life. I apply this assumption in the following analyses and interpretations of material from this empirical study. The objective of this analysis is ascribing cognitive structures over time and tracing the filiations of those ascribed structures and the interactions of those filiations as a developing cognitive organization.

Cognitive organization

The discussion of 'organization' requires that one describe things that are disparate from one another and then specify how these different things are related. The body-parts mind proposal serves the function here of separating groups of cognitive structures on a large scale. Thus I will argue that some cognitive structures are descended from ancestors in the locomotive subsystem and others from ancestors in the visual subsystem. There remains then the question of the extent to which such structures become related to each other and under what circumstances. If there is body-based disparateness, what is there that ever leads to subsequent integration? Most importantly, and obviously, the achievement of functional goals requires the cooperation of disparate cognitive structures and subsystems of such structures, e.g. crawling to get some desired object requires the use of arms and legs. Thus the progressive organization of disparate structures and subsystems proceeds from the needs of the individual as a complete being. In this study of a child's encounters with geometry, because she had no pressing need to integrate her knowledge, we may hope to see in slow motion the disparateness of knowledge and the processes of its integration more clearly than we would in domains where one might be more directly driven to unification.

The body-parts mind proposal is an obvious one but not a common one. Most scientists follow that sort of uniformitarian commitment witnessed so clearly in the formulations of Piaget or Newell and Simon. Those who do concern themselves with the synchronic organization of mind — and thus follow a 'divide and relate' strategy — usually focus on sensory-dominated divisions of mind. (The work of Hunt, 1973, is an example.) Focussing as it does on the descent of cognitive structures from ancestors in the motor subsystems, the body-parts mind proposal is implicitly committed to favoring the activity of the subject in the creation of cognitive structures over the impression of sensations on the mind. In this specific sense, the proposal shows the influence of Piaget.

Even if the mind is a network of information structures comprised of the same types of elements, one need not conclude that it is uniform. Microviews are shaped both by their specific descent from body-defined subsystems and by their interconnection possibilities in terms of those subsystems. That is, one may see a square and recognize similarity in moving through the pattern of a square, but it would be an unusual mind that asked 'what is the sound of a square?' In sum, the connections between late-developed cognitive structures mirror – and are guided by – the interconnection possibilities of the sensori-motor system which are first explored and described in the motor programs developed during the sensorimotor period of infancy. This idea, which I name the 'channelled description conjectures', is not an hypothesis which was posed for experimental confirmation; rather, it is a ground of explanation which I find useful in making sense of knowledge Miriam developed and failed to develop during her many encounters with 'geometry' during The Intimate Study. Any critical reader will note my interpretations cannot be coercive; the evidence is just not good enough. The arguments here must be seen then as explorations is considerable detail of how a distributed model of the sensorimotor system can help in understanding the developmental path of a mind. Because the idea I present here as the body-parts mind is focussed on the individual body and is entirely asocial, it can at best help us understand some significant part of cogni-tive development.[1]

The domain

In preceding chapters, I described the development of interrelations among Miriam's microviews of common ancestry. Here we are confronted with how to understand the genesis of relations among microviews of arguably different lines of descent. The working out of this process, in detail, is the burden of the following analysis and interpretation of Miriam's learning about essentially different kinds of geometries ('essentially different' in that they connect naturally to different kinesthetic subsystems). My application of the term 'geometry' to our work, as much as that work was very limited in scope, is justified by Miriam's having dealt with the primitive space descriptions of turtle geometry and co-ordinate geometry.[2]

---

1 Chapters 3 and 4 bear on how individual learning is situated in a social context.
2 In turtle geometry, the primitive terms of description are actions, that is, executed com-mands to move forward or back some distance or to turn right or left through some angle. The commands are implicitly directed to an agent, the turtle, and are state centered, i.e. go forward so far from wherever-you-are and turn right so much from wherever-you-are-heading. These are the basic geometric concepts Miriam was to deal with during our project. In coordinate geometry, any point in a plane is represented as an ordered pair of numbers which measure distance along a perpendicular set of axes. Miriam's use of coordinates involved specifying that some object should appear at a destination described by this ordered pair of numbers.

One of the practical challenges of turtle geometry is the child's achieving a bridge between the world of mathematical design on a video display and the everyday world of going forward and turning right, 'navigation' if you will. In the world of body geometry, a right turn would be well served by anything between 80 and 100 degrees. In designs, the difference one degree makes may be profound. Such a difference in quantification sensitivity suggests that the experience of these phenomena must result in disparate structures in the mind. Further, how different for a child must appear an 'angle' when it is first, how much a person turns and second, an abstract number on which some imcomprehensible computer procedure operates to create a mysterious product. Although the labelling of our language, an implict form of instruction, promises connection between disparate realms od ideas, it must be through the individual's experience and intellectual labor that bridges between these disparate realms are constructed. For the two task domains of child or turtle navigation through space and computer-generated design, the ultimate relation is through iteration. In the later section 'Computer-generated designs', I follow Miriam's progress toward understanding such a relation. Tracing the development of a bridge between the microviews of navigating in turtle geometry and creating computer-generated designs is the concrete problem through which I pursue the central theme, the developing organization of disparate cognitive structures.

TWO GEOMETRIES

Over many years at the MIT Logo Project, I have seen that turtle geometry is easily accessible to many children, even pre-schoolers, when introduced with the mechanical 'floor turtle'. This access derives from the connectibility of knowledge about the turtle's actions to the child's own personal geometry, that egocentric knowledge of space we all develop in our earliest years. Turtle geometry is so natural in this specific sense that it is somewhat perplexing to define what a child learns from experience with it. One could almost claim that even an infant knows turtle geometry in a practical form. I have seen a baby at six months turn on her belly to reach a toy initially beyond her grasp and at seven months crawl forward to reach another toy. The states before and after her action were obviously meaningful to the infant and their changes were effected by intended actions. These states of the infant's geometry are specifiable either by naming ('I am here and the toy is there'), or by operations, ('if I turn this much and go that far I will get from here to there'). The origin of the geometry is progressive; it resides at the body and moves with it. It would be absurd to argue that Miriam didn't learn such things until she was six.

To approach the question of what it means to learn something which is natural, one needs a very specific way of describing how new knowledge relates to old knowledge and what constitutes a significant difference between one state of knowledge and another. Let me play the Devil's Advocate: the child's actions and the operations of turtle geometry are sufficiently congruent that those operations are not learned in early encounters with turtle geometry; all that can be said to be learned is the application of those actions to a new domain — the floor plane of the mechanical turtle or the video display domain. Couched in such terms, this conclusion demeans the importance of applying knowledge. It is especially misleading if, as I believe, knowledge is augmented and refined primarily through the application of old knowledge to new problems for which it is not yet perfectly suited.

Turtle geometry

What is novel in the turtle geometry context is the presistent, explicit quantification of actions. I now pursue in detail the growth of Miriam's knowledge about angles, and even more specifically, about turning 90 degrees, since this limited topic provides the clearest example of how her prior knowledge connected with quantification in turtle geometry.

Does a child think of turning as a stepped action or as a continuous one, such as the turning of a wheel around its axle or of a clock's hands? Miriam did not conceive of turning as continuous. If turning is a stepped action, quantification reduces primarily to problems of scale. What is a good default number to try when you can make no well-motivated guess about what's appropriate? What is the smallest increment that makes an interesting change? Miriam appears to have recalled from experience with turtle geometry several months earlier that you need big numbers as operands to generate significant actions. During a review session (age 6;0;23) where she played with SHOOT, a game of locating the video cursor in a circular target, her first angle operand was 50 degrees, and she repeated her 'right 50' three times till the turtle was nearly pointed at a target. Her first distance was 20 turtle steps. It was increased by increments of 10 for successive trials in shooting the target. In Logo Session 3 (age 6;0;28), Miriam revealed the limits to the connectedness of her thinking about turtle geometry and her personal geometry while 'playing turtle', that is, simulating with her own body the responses of the robot turtle to Logo commands:

> Bob: There's another way we could play SHOOT, if we didn't want to use the computer; I made this hoop [a three-foot diameter plastic circle]. We could play SHOOT [dropping the hoop onto the floor].
> Miriam: You direct me how far to go and then I'll do it.
> Robby: [Assuming control] Right 90.
> Bob: [To Miriam] Right 90. . . . Do you know what to do?
> Miriam: Yeah [She turns right a little, about 30 degrees, counts 1, and continues counting one for every 30 degree turn up to 15; that is, more than one full turn].
> Robby: [Laughing]
> Bob: We've got a bug here, don't we.
> Miriam: [Continues and counts] 24, 25, 26, 27 . . . [laughing, she continues] 30, 31, 32, 33, 34, 35, 36 —
> Bob: [Interrupting] *Stop!* We've got a turning bug of some kind here. What does it mean when we say 'RIGHT' then a number?
> Miriam: I'm the turtle, see. You go right, this [again turning right about 30 degrees].

Robby: Suppose I told you 'left 90'. You do that. [Robby demonstrates.]
Miriam: O.K.
Bob: What was that, again, Rob?
Miriam: If you're facing like this, he said turn like that. [Miriam lifts her
arm at her side, then 'jumps' her feet around under it.]

Because Miriam had no strong theory of how '90', the operand of Robby's command, was to be interpreted, in her simulation of the turtle she fell back on the personal geometry's interpretation of what 'right 90' might mean, that is, turn to the right a little bit, 90 times. Such is a sensible and sound tactic. By an accident of history, however, the degree-numbers of the Babylonian scale by which we commonly quantify turning do not fit transparently with the terms of turning in personal geometry, that is, right or left (90), halfway (180), and all the way (360).

Playing turtle is not merely a form of instruction by adults within the Logo community. As Robby showed above, it is also a child-accessible form of explanation. Robby and Miriam simulated the game SHOOT, usually played on the vertical video-display screen, with their body motions in the horizontal plane.[3] To communicate an idea of quantification, the most effective instruction was, in this case, a body-based simulation of what the number meant in the domain. This kind of observation is one that should be recognized as telling us how important to a child's cognitive development is relating current problems to past experiences.

In two subsequent sessions, Miriam came to appreciate and verify the correspondence of the degree scale and her personal geometry. In Logo Session 6 (age 6;1;3), we worked through a short series of speculations about how turns of 90 degree multiples affect the turtle's heading. Typically, Miriam attempted to recall the number value of an earlier observed heading while Robby attempted to deduce the result from remembered turning actions. Her method exhibited the fixed frame of reference in which she saw 180 as related to heading more than to turning. A few days later (in Logo Session 9 [age 6;1;9]) Miriam made the explicit connection between 90-degree multiples and turning around. She was making a simple picture of a mouse face (see Fig. 5.1). The head was an equilateral triangle with circular ears and a small blob for a nose. Miriam assembled these components in the sequence suggested by Ed Emberley's book *Animal Faces*.

Miriam planned to draw the head by invoking TRI.[4] After she cleared the screen, I advised her to turn the turtle before drawing the head by invoking TRI. My candidate turn was 60 degrees, which would have been the smallest turn leading to a horizontal side above an opposite vertex, the nose. This projection of mine interfered at first with my understanding Miriam's better idea:

3 This argues one must not conclude simply that because an experience is *seen* the micro-views relating to it in the mind are connected to the visual subsystem. A more precise way of thinking about this discrimination will be introduced in the later section 'Reflections: movement and the eye'.

4 This procedure draws a triangle with base perpendicular to the turtle's heading and the opposite vertex along the line of the initial heading.

Bob: If the triangle should be turned, we should sort of turn the turtle —
Miriam: How?
Bob: You know how to turn it? You go right or left turn.
Miriam: [As she keys] R, T, space . . .
Bob: What's a good number?
Miriam: 70. . . . What would that big number be? 90 plus 90? What's 90 plus 90?
Bob: A hundred and eighty. I don't think that — that would just make it — oh, that's a brilliant idea!
Miriam: [Keys RT 100 then corrects it to RT 180.]
Bob: Gee, that's really a good idea. Is that what you knew would happen?
Miriam: Robby was right. One turn like that would be 90 and . . .
Bob: Then all the way around is —
Miriam: [Interrupting] Halfway.
Bob: And halfway round's 180.

When once she caught on to the specialness of 90 and 180 degrees, Miriam became able to navigate the turtle in its space quite skillfully and with good comprehension. This is later witnessed by her careful placement of features in 'Football Fred' (see Fig. 5.1) and other drawings. From Miriam's explicitly witnessing Robby's correctness, we may infer she was following his implicit advice to interpret what she saw on the video terminal in terms of her personal geometry.

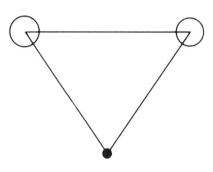

A mouse face

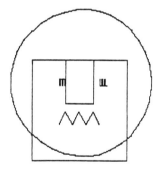
Football Fred

Fig. 5.1

Coordinate geometry

Getting around in a system of absolute coordinates requires learning a description of space with which Miriam was not previously familar. She was introduced to X, Y coordinates with the game READY, AIM, FIRE (RAF), which was written at Robby's suggestion. The game player is a tail-gunner protecting his bomber from attacking fighters. The gunner's canopy provides a gridwork for orienting his gunsight while the attacking airplane appears in a second, remote space. The

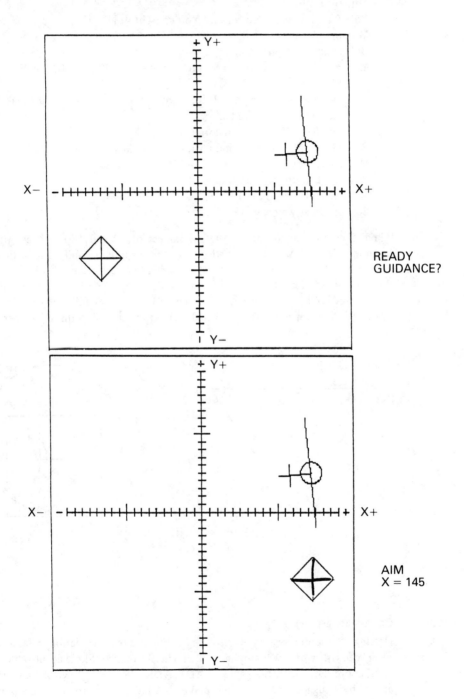

READY
GUIDANCE?

AIM
X = 145

Fig. 5.2 – Ready, aim, fire or RAF.

command READY draws an attacking airplane at a random locus and orientation (see Fig. 5.2). The gunsight appears where the last airplane was shot down and is not re-set after the command FIRE. The gunner now attempts to locate his gunsight on target through one or more AIM commands. The AIM command requests inputs, first X then Y coordinates of the place to which the gunsight will move. The gunsight moves horizontally or vertically from its former locus in response to each input value. When the gunner judges he is on target, he commands FIRE. If the cross-hairs of the gunsight are located within the area of the fuselage, the airplane explodes, 'KA-BOOM!'

Robby showed an immediate, easy grasp of the game; it was not itself inaccessible. His engagement was intense and his understanding sound, as is shown by his immediate and spontaneous retro-fitting of this new space description onto the familiar problems of his SHOOT experiences when first introduced to RAF:

> Bob: [With the airplane and gunsight on the screen] This is X, along this way. If it's over here, those are numbers of X greater than zero. If you're over here (on the left), it's numbers of X smaller than zero.
>
> Robby: Hey, Dad. You know what I would do if we were playing SHOOT? I'd say 'SHOOT X 120' so it would be even with the target, then 'RIGHT TURN 90, SHOOT Y' so it would go in.
>
> Bob: I don't understand.
>
> Robby: What I would do is get him lined up with the target, then right or left turn it, then I'd say SHOOT the other number to get it in because of the X's and Y's and get it in.5

Robby's easy comprehension of this task domain renders the process of his learning impossible to study. In contrast, Miriam's painful struggle with coordinate geometry is more open to examination.

The two children were introduced to RAF together (Logo Session 11, age 6;1;12). My objective was to find out how easily Miriam could understand the space description of coordinate geometry. The best advice is the extent to which she was capable or not of taking advice. My consistent direction was that Miriam should think of the X, Y couple as a name and that all points on the screen had a first and last name, just as she did. Miriam's initial conception was not conformable to my advice, and between us we generated the confusion cited here from Logo Session 12 (age 6;1;15):

> Bob: You had Y as minus 60. Maybe you want to make it −
>
> Miriam: [Keys a positive number.]
>
> Bob: No. Minus.
>
> Miriam: That will make it go up? ... Rub out, minus. Minus.... [keying. As the gunsight rises from $Y = -60$ to $Y = -11$] ... Minus goes up.

---

5 A reasonable translation of Robby's excited expression would be this: I would move the turtle along the x-axis until I got it lined up with the target then I would turn it vertical and shoot in it (determining the distance by reading it off the scales of the y-axis).

What this witnesses is Miriam's partitioning of input values focussed on state change, with the *quantity* assigned to *how far* the gunsight should move and the *sign* determining the *direction* of movement; X = −10 means move left ten units. This is an error with respect to how RAF works. Session 14 (6;1;17) marked the end of our early use of READY, AIM, FIRE. My conclusion from these sessions was that Miriam's focus on two objects, the gunsight and the target, reinforced the disposition she had (from her recent play with SHOOT and other turtle geometry sources) to conceive of the task in terms of differences and state changes produced by corresponding actions. I resolved to make a game of XY values which would not promote this specific confusion.

An intervention

Miriam had long enjoyed making pictures by connecting serially numbered dots in 'dot-to-dot' drawings when I introduced her to MAKEDOTS in Logo Session 50 (age 6;4;7). This very simple system executes through two subprocedures, MAKEDOTS and DODOTS. The first procedure requests X and Y coordinates; when both are input, a small square is drawn at the point they define and the location is entered in a list of places. During execution of this procedure the turtle is hidden. Nothing moves anywhere. DODOTS draws lines from the locus of each member in the place list to the next one. Miriam enjoyed playing with MAKEDOTS. The typical execution of the procedures saw alternately our making dots with my interjecting requests that Miriam speculate about where each would appear. The following from Logo Session 54 (age 6;4;13) is typical. It also shows her making an experiment and linking domains of positive and negative numbers at the origin.

> Bob: I'm gonna make X zero. And I'm gonna make Y zero. Where's it gonna
>   go?
> Miriam: [With no hesitation] Middle.
> Bob: [Keying] Absolutely right.
> Miriam: I'm gonna make ... ah ... minus zero and minus zero.
> Bob: Where's it gonna go?
> Miriam: [Keying new line.]
> Bob: Same place. Hah! I guess plus and minus zero are just the same.
> Miriam: O.K.

Catching on

In the same session as the work cited above (Logo Session 54, age 6;4;13), Miriam rapidly 'caught on' to the significance of numbers in the absolute co-ordinate description of space. What Miriam learned and the genetic path of her learning can be seen clearly in citations from these executions of an RAF variant (with the airplane replaced by an aircraft carrier to be bombed).

The three confusions Miriam grappled with in the following are:

- not relating consistently the X symbol for quantity to the horizontal axis and the Y to the vertical axis on the display screen;

   — conceiving the X and Y quantities as state changers and not as partial point names;

   — confusing which segments of the axes plus and minus numbers apply to.

These confusions all appear early in Logo Session 54. After she succeeded in bombing her first target at (120, −120), a second target appeared in the third quadrant, approximately at (−120, −120). This quirk of the random number generator, producing two sets of coordinates identical in magnitude, simplified the understanding of how selected inputs produce results. To aim the gunsight at the new target, X had to be changed from +120 to −120. Let us trace in detail Miriam's solving this problem, since it represents a breakthrough in her use of X, Y coordinates. Focus your attention in the following dialog on two points: first, how does Miriam keep the gunsight where it is, despite being required to enter an input variable; second, how does she adjust the value (X = −100) to get the gunsight over the target at (X = −120):

> Miriam: Wasn't a hundred twenty, a hundred twenty a good idea?
>
> Bob: Yes. That was very good when the carrier was here [at prior location], but now the carrier is in a different place [pointing to the X-axis]. These are minus numbers on this side, and that's a hundred [a large-scale marking].
>
> Miriam: Think I'll go minus a hundred.
>
> Bob: [Pointing to the 100 maker] But that will get it where the big line is. Is that where you want it?
>
> Miriam: Yeah. [Miriam assumes the gunsight will go onto the X axis where I had pointed] And then what I'll do is get it down. [Keys X = −100; the gunsight moves over.]
>
> Bob: Oh boy. If you can keep the Y just where it is, you'll be in great shape.
>
> Miriam: Y zero?
>
> Bob: No. Y was what? It was minus . . . a hundred twenty.
>
> Miriam: Yeah. [Keys −120] A hundred twenty [no movement].

Here Miriam's first idea was that what she keyed was a state-change operand. When I prevented her from using Y = 0, she accepted my specific direction Y = −120. We now continue in this same dialogue to a critical juncture.

> Bob: All you have to do is get your X over here to the center of the carrier.
>
> Miriam: [Keys AIM and enter] Here I go. X will be . . .
>
> Bob: Plus or minus?
>
> Miriam: Plus? No, minus. Minus 20. [Keys −20; the gunsight moves right — the 'wrong' way to (−20, −120).] Oh grumble.
>
> Bob: Hmmmm.
>
> Miriam: Then I'll do plus 40 —
>
> Bob: [Interrupting] Hold on.
>
> Miriam: On my next X.
>
> Bob: What you have to understand, Miriam, when you say plus or minus, it doesn't tell you how much to move the gun, but it tells you the name of the place where it's going to go.

Miriam: Where?

Bob: What you have to figure out is what's the name of that place, where the carrier is. It's kind of like using MAKEDOTS.... [Points to the carrier] Right now, we're waiting to put in minus a hundred twenty for Y.

Miriam: Yeah.

Bob: O.K. [Keys it in; the gunsight doesn't move.] So let's AIM again, and we know minus one hundred was pretty close [pointing to the marks on the coordinate scale] and this way [left] gets bigger minus.

Miriam: [Puts hands on the X axis to count the division] Minus a hundred twenty [as she drops the line down from the X axis].

Bob: Give it a try.

(1) Miriam: [Keys] Minus 1, 2, 0 [Keys enter; the gunsight moves over the carrier].

Bob: Right on. If you can keep Y in the same place ...

Miriam: A hundred twenty!

Bob: Plus or minus?

Miriam: Minus [Keys

Miriam: Minus [keys −120 and enter].

Miriam's first suggestion to keep the gunsight fixed was 'Y zero'. At that time, she still thought of the Y coordinate as a state-changing quantity. But when that option was blocked, she accepted the previous value of Y [−120] as an alternative. In this second instance, when the X coordinate was so specified as to bring the gunsight over the target, she *volunteered* the correct value for keeping the Y coordinate fixed. Here is the essential contrast in the simplest case: do you maintain a thing by doing nothing (Y = 0, the coordinate seen as a change operand) or by doing what you did before (Y = −120, the coordinate seen as relative to the extrinsic reference point [0, 0]). When Miriam tried to modify the X coordinate from −100 to −120, she 'naturally' thought of −20 as the appropriate change specification. Her correction, when −20 was proven faulty, was +40, that is, the 'compensation' for the error plus what 'must' be required to achieve the original objective. Once more the coordinates were seen as change operands. After I told her that 'it's kind of like using MAKEDOTS' and 'We know minus 100 was mightly close and this way [left] gets bigger minus', Miriam for the first time *without prompting or correction* got her own solution to a problem in terms of X and Y coordinate values (at (1) above), first locating the gun on the target with X = −120, then keeping it there with Y = −120. I hold that this change of behavior signals an insight, an intellectual breakthrough.

Miriam showed at this point two competing interpretations for XY coordinates. The dominant one explained a coordinate value as an operand for change. There were many cases where Miriam's good success at a target followed my correction of her first candidate, as in the citation above. Did she ever go so far herself as to reject her 'natural', state change interpretation of what coordinates might mean? She did. This excerpt (from Logo Session 65, age 6;5;6) begins with the gunsight at [15, 50] and the carrier at [100, 100]:

Miriam: Over forty, plus forty.

Bob: Is that the name of the place?

Miriam: [Looking puzzled.]

Bob: It's not how much you're going to move it.

Miriam: [Looks at the terminal, slapping her forehead] No! [Putting her hand on the large marker of the X axis] It's exactly one hundred. So we just say 100.

Bob: You think that's right?

Miriam: Yeah. [Keys 100; the gunsight lines up.]

Bob: Beautiful.

(2) Miriam: Ahhh.... Up. Up 50, but ... I [moves her finger from the gunsight to the Y axis, then up to the target height; then moving her hand from the target back to the Y axis, holding up her forefinger] One hundred! [Keys 100; the gunsight moves into the center of the target] Yeah!!

Bob: Oh, I hope you're gonna get it here. You think so?

Miriam: [Keys] FIRE.

Bob: [Reading from the display] 'Congratulations Ace'. Good for you.

At (2) above, Miriam spontaneously corrected her first state-change proposal herself, without my intervening.

Discussion

In her introduction to coordinate geometry, three confusions dominated Miriam's thought. First, she did not consistently identify the X and Y coordinates with their respective axes. This was a superficial confusion. But the second and third are essential confusions in the sense that they derive from and express Miriam's ability to imagine what the coordinate values might mean. The second confusion related to interpretation of plus and minus signs as signifying operations which had import for changing the location of the gunsight. When her candidate values did not have expected consequences, Miriam chose to fault the action-sign correspondences she had chosen (these correspondences were clearly, then, an empirical element superadded to a perspective, a 'way of looking at things' and deciding 'what's what', which came from somewhere else). For example, when she keyed -11 for a Y value and the gunsight rose from $Y = -60$, Miriam concluded 'minus goes up'. The third confusion was identification of the coordinate quantity as a value by which a state variable would be changed. Miriam analyzed a form such a $+35$ or -60 into two constituents, an operation signifier and operand signifier (with sign omitted, the quantity was interpreted as having an implicit or default operation specified). She interpreted the quantities as having a structure they do not have. Why? There are several reasons. A first one would be called a lexical convention. Plus means 'add'; minus means 'take away'. Both are operations whose operands change the value of the terms to which they apply. A second reason is the task itself. One object, the gunsight, is to be moved over another, airplane or carrier. The salient difference is that they are apart. Action is the way to reduce such a difference, i.e. move the gunsight from here to there.

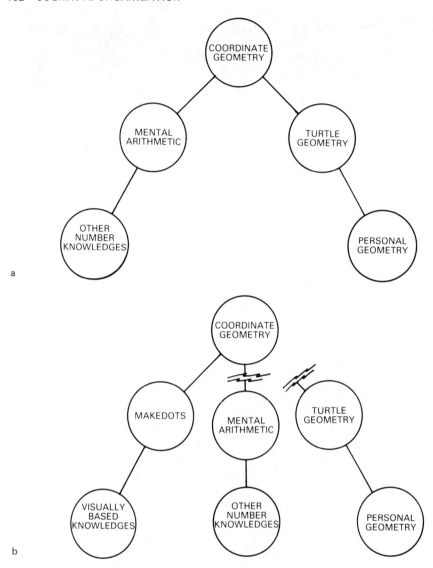

Fig. 5.3 — Two microview filiations. (a) The coordinate view as descended from turtle geometry.[6] (b) The coordinate view as descended from MAKEDOTS.

The microviews of experience which Miriam called on to do turtle geometry and coordinate geometry are sketched in Fig. 5.3(a) (the coordinate view as descended from turtle geometry). At any locus in such a genetic cluster of microviews, the temporally earlier microviews can be called the *ancestors* of those developed later. Thus the view of personal geometry is ancestral to turtle geometry. That personal geometry microview, developing from a coordination

6 The 'Mental Arithmetic' microview of this diagram is described more precisely by the structures and their organization as analyzed in Chapter 2.

of the somatic and locomotive sensorimotor subsystems, has those subsystems as its ancestors. To the extent that number knowledge gave form to Miriam's (erroneous) conceptions in the Coordinate Geometry microview, that arithmetic knowledge ('+' and '−' themselves as signifiers of state change) indicates non-geometric ancestors. If the Turtle Geometry microview and Arithmetic microviews are considered as separate, one might call them *cognate* microviews.

Miriam's basic confusion was to conceive of coordinate geometry as essentially like turtle geometry and arithmetic and that from them she could infer what were the significant operations and the character of elements in that coordinate geometry domain. Miriam assumed such a relation obtained when in fact it did not. That is, her ancestral microviews of arithmetic and turtle geometry were providing, through analogy, strong hypotheses for 'what was what' in this new domain. Is it possible she could have thought of the coordinates of READY, AIM, FIRE as something other than she did? If coordinate geometry is unnatural as turtle geometry is natural, maybe she had, in effect, no choice. How can I make a statement seem sensible?

Let me put you in Miriam's position. Suppose you confront a problem beyond your experience. That system of perspectives (the parsing into part and whole relations) and procedures you need even to comprehend the problem is inchoate. You can only begin to make sense of a more-than-trivial problem if you can see it through the perspective of an ancestral microview, which provides a preliminary parsing of the relevant forms into parts and wholes with which you can attempt to reason. Such ancestral views will also communicate strong hypotheses about what functional procedures might be appropriate for experimental testing. If you lack, in fact, exprience which might have provided you with relevant ancestral microviews, what will happen? Will you not attach your new problem-context-specific microview to an inappropriate cluster of ancestral microviews? Having made such a commitment, Miriam was not able to take advice wherein the forms (+ 55 or −60) were not analyzable into the constituents as she saw them, i.e. operation code and operand. She abandoned RAF early in the project.

My intention in introducing MAKEDOTS was to provide, although temporally after the fact, an experience that could lead to development of a logically ancestral microview for the Coordinate view. Miriam could not interpret the X and Y coordinates as names when it was possible to interpret them as actions. MAKEDOTS was designed to appear action-free. The only events were the appearing of dots upon their being named. When playing with RAF in Logo session 54 Miriam's insight followed hard upon my advice that 'It's kind of like MAKEDOTS'. If we merely note that 'analogy' was a significant factor in her insight, we miss the central point. This particular advice was not about some transient similarity; it was advice about how Miriam should organize her mind. It directed her to relate coordinate geometry to an experience which assigned meaning to elements by parsing the forms encountered in a way different from that of turtle geometry and arithmetic. And she was able to take that advice − because she now owned a microview wherein her perspective, in fact, fitted the requirements for RAF. That is, MAKEDOTS could serve as ancestral to the Coordinate view though it was temporally a later creation. I name such a microview a *post-cedent ancestor.* This contrasts with the *genetic ancestor* (in this case the microviews of turtle geometry) to which the new structure originally related (in this case, the coordinate geometry view).

Miriam had trouble in Logo Sessions 54 and 55. She still saw X and Y as having an operation—operand structure, but there was a significant advance. When I intervened to inhibit that view of coordinates, she could now interpret their signification through her perspective on coordinates in MAKEDOTS, i.e. she owned a competing, albeit secondary ancestor to her coordinate geometry view. Miriam's achieved self-directed inhibition of the coordinate geometry connection to the personal geometry cluster only at the very end of The Intimate Study core period (in Logo Session 65); this is important precisely because it shows how gradually she broke the dominance of the connection between a coordinate geometry microview and the personal geometry cluster. The MAKEDOTS experience permitted changing the way Miriam saw one small corner of the world. Given the assumption that a change in functions derives from a change in cognitive structures or their organization, this implies that the MAKEDOTS experience created some structure which functioned as a powerful idea for Miriam in the developmental sense. (That is, it played a significant role in respect of organizing her mind, although superficially trivial in itself.)

I want to emphasize the importance of the idea of a *post-cedent ancestor.* The vision of learning implicit in Sussman's work (1975), I paraphrase as 'when you encounter something really new, you *cannot, no never*, get it right the first time'. The corollary is the observation that the coherence of mind depends entirely on the connection of new experience to old either by the immediate, analogous connection to ancestral structures *or* through the intervention of a *post-cedent* ancestor. The next important question then is *how* the wrong connections to preceding experience are supplanted by the better comprehension possible through a later, more logically appropriate microview. One alternative is that suppression takes place, the post-cedent ancestor literally inhibits the interaction of the new microview with its genetic ancestors. A second alternative is that the post-cedent ancestor supplants the genetic ancestor through efficient competition with it. This alternative could explain why the dominance occurs gradually. Such could be one situation in cognitive development where the crisp formulation of an idea or the quintessential suitability of a representation exerts a major functional effect on the control structure and consequently the functioning of the mind. My ultimate proposal here is that post-cedent ancestors are the structures through which the reorganization of mind actually takes place.

Reflections: movement and the eye

If the fundamental law of cognitive development is that nothing comes from nothing (to use a very old formulation), one should ask what are the antecedents of the cognitive structures based on the MAKEDOTS experience. Approaching this question indirectly, I note that it is more or less easy to imagine that turtle geometry experience connects profoundly to body geometry. If we pursue the distributed sensorimotor model of the mind base (the body-parts mind proposal)

MAKEDOTS should obviously connect to the visual component. What that could mean, in detail, depends on how one is able to think of the operation of that subsystem.

The eye is popularly considered primarily a sense organ, but its motor activity is equally important in seeing. It is possible to track eye movements and their relation to the scene within the visual field. Noton and Stark (1971a, 1971b) describe such experiments and propose a representation for the movements of the eye. They noted the targets of looking and described the path of eye movement as a series of saccades.[7] At the vertices of the path, Noton and Stark assume 'features' are detected. Their experimental result is that the path closes and is repeated again and again. This loop of movement and feature detection they name a 'feature ring'. They account for much of their experimental eye movement data as the repeated traversing of the ring. They propose that the currently executing feature ring is in part driven by the information contour of the visual field. Further, they argue that the process of image recognition occurs by matching the currently executing feature ring to a similar feature ring, stored in the past. Consequently, the MAKEDOTS microview — even if it is 'obviously' connected to the visual subsystem — may nonetheless be understood as an outgrowth of the sensorimotor system in a serial, motor and feature detection model (in contrast to an image based model). Although I will not attempt to write any programs to describe what Miriam saw in her play with SHOOT, RAF, and MAKEDOTS, it must be understood that it should be possible, in principle if not in fact, to do so. Further, let me propose that the state variables and commands of turtle geometry could be a simple specification language for such programs.[8] This proposal permits a simple observation which goes to the heart of the commonalities and the differences between the locomotive and visual subsystems. Even if the *movements* of the eye may be described and represented in terms similar to those which apply to that of the body moving through space, the elements of visually recognizable experience exist as entities at a higher level of aggregation than do the movements of locomotion. That is, feature rings are like possibly complex procedures and they cannot be expected to be directly comparable to primitive commands. This simple point suggests that consequently linking together microviews descended from visually-based and locomotive-based sensorimotor components may not be a trivial task. This issue becomes a focal concern of the next section, as we explore Miriam's experiences in creating computer-generated designs.

COMPUTER-GENERATED DESIGNS

The basic pattern of the following story is similar to 'Two geometries': a late-occurring experience created a cognitive structure which helped make sense of

---

7 Saccades are quick movements of the eye by which the gaze is moved from one point to another.

8 A similar suggestion has recently been called to my attention in an unpublished article by Czerny and von Glaserfeld, 'A dynamic approach to the recognition of triangularity'.

earlier experiences. In contrast, however, the experiences reported in this section were more various and developed in a fragmentary, overlapping, and much entangled order. The variety of the material and Miriam's reception of it was considerable. Engagement was balanced otherwheres by rejection, even rebellion. The concreteness of her understanding was in evidence everywhere. Furthermore, many essential elements of these experiences were of a highly particular nature and involved detail no reader could endure. Consequently, for clarity this material will be presented in an order more logical than chronological and descriptions of the experiences themselves will be more summary than thorough.[9]

A central difference between this section and 'Two geometries' is in the use of the diverging aspect of knowledge growing out from the body-parts mind: in 'Two geometries', the analysis used the case material to exemplify the separation of microviews decended from different subsystems; here, the interpretations strive to account for the interconnection of late-developed structures. The evidence for such interconnection is rare; the character of its manifestation is idiosyncratic and more spontaneous than controllable. Further, even noticing the occurrence of events causing such linkages appears to require both enlisting the subject as a co-observer and considerable good fortune. Difficult to observe because rare and beyond experimental control, like stellar novae, such events are nonetheless suitable topics for scientific consideration, not least because their understanding may be required to appreciate how rare and difficult is the achievement of coherence in the mind.

The connection mature minds appreciate between the navigation commands of turtle geometry and computer-generated designs based on them is through some understanding of iteration — by which I mean here some programmed process for repeatedly executing a sequence of commands with controlled variation. What preceding knowledge, what 'ur-concepts' of iteration, did Miriam own? At least five: incrementing a counting variable; decrementing a counting variable; repetition until stopped by an external constraint; repeating until necessary elements are used up; repeating until a set of objects completed.[10] These categories and examples indicate how varied and pervasive are ideas of iteration which a child typically might bring to an encounter with computer procedures. What we find as this story unfolds is that *none* of these available models of iteration intervened powerfully. Instead, Miriam engaged in activities — both provided by me and spontaneously invented by her — which specifically linked together the microviews derived from her particular experiences.

9 Further details can be found in Lawler, 1979.
10 Recall first Miriam's initial interpretation of 'RIGHT 90' by counting the turns she made. Second, note that Miriam's favorite song, 'Little Rabbit Foofoo', involves decrement-controlled repetition: the fairy godmother warns the misbehaving rabbit that he has three more chances, then two, then one, then she 'bops him on the head'. Next, repeating an action till stopped is pervasive, as in the 'spinning dizzy' game children enjoy, where they stand with outstretched arms and spin on and on until they can do it no more, then stagger about giggling and disoriented. Repetition to exhaustion must be very basic. One eats candy until she has no more, then stops. Completing a set of objects is represented in Miriam's composing the 'backwards' alphabet (Logo Session 13, 6;1;16).

MPOLY

Miriam's appreciation of angles, as turning in turtle geometry navigation, has been discussed in 'Two geometries'. Here I focus on a second and very different use of the word 'angle' — as the name for a number input a Logo design procedure — which engaged Miriam early in The Intimate Study. When her closest kindergarten friends joined her individually for an afternoon at the Children's Learning Lab, they most enjoyed using the computer for making pretty designs.

> Earlier in the year, Miriam had made paper copies of the image made by a flower procedure and took one for each member of her kindergarten class; the children colored the designs and took them home. While we waited for her flower picture to come out of the printer, Lizzie saw a six-fold, near-triangular multi-polyspiral (see Fig. 5.4) which Robby had printed from a different terminal. 'Wow! I want one of those. Show me how to do it.' After I started the MPOLY procedure, Miriam and Lizzie worked together for over two hours creating designs for later coloring. Both girls made some very pretty, novel designs.
>
> age 6;6;7

MPOLY is a procedure that makes designs of which the four in Fig. 5.4 are typical. Operating under a set of controlling variables (including 'angle') incremented or decremented from the keyboard, with each keyed change MPOLY procedures a design and prints on the computer log a number, the polyspiral angle. The children took this angle value as a name by which they identified the individual designs they created in their play with the program. This is an application of 'angle' which is only distantly connectible to the use of the term 'angle' as a number that tells how far to turn. Although a mature person's understanding unifies the term used in the both navigation and design applications of turtle geometry, 'angle' *must* be a word of multiple meanings to the child or beginner.

Let Miriam's own words from Logo Session 23 (age 6;2;2) describe her appreciation of polyspiral designs. On one with an angle of 116, 'That's a beauty one'. When asked why she was incrementing by one the angle value input to a polyspiral procedure, 'I'm trying to find the ones I love', she answered. As the angle value passed through the region of 144 degrees, creating various stella-form designs, Miriam declared, 'They're all my favorites!' The preceding citations do not merely testify that Miriam enjoyed 'playing with computers'. They mark part of the quality of her relation to a specific body of knowledge, the MPOLY microview. This view contains knowledge permitting the creation of artifacts both pretty and useful — printed patterns may be colored and given as gifts which, in fact, truly astounded the adults to whom Miriam and Lizzie gave them. Although her comprehension did not penetrate the internal workings of the procedures she manipulated, whatever learning these expriences brought was personally appropriated and not dissociated, in Papert's sense (1980).

Among the many occasions in which Miriam played with MPOLY, Session 27 (age 6;2;15) is one both playful and fecund, as shown by the following

POLYSPI 120   MPOLYSPI 120 9

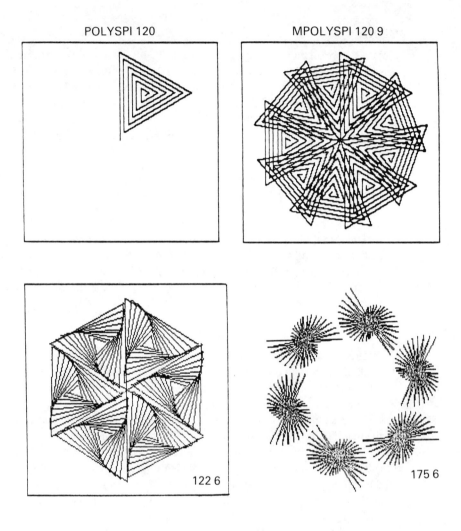

Fig. 5.4 — Four multiple-polyspirals.

highlights. After taking my direction a short while, Miriam went her own way. When I suggested she try an angle of 90 degrees, she keyed instead 60. She was delighted to discover the regular hexagonal maze. Miriam then began a somewhat systematic exploration, trying in sequence the angular inputs 70, 80, 90, 100. Next she began varying the angle by one degree — first trying 101, then 59 and 58. After a break in the session, I tried to focus Miriam's attention on the cyclic symmetry, e.g. the identity of designs made with angles of 30, 390, and 750 degrees, instead of following her lead. Miriam backed away from exploration then but not before she described the design variations near 'her' angle of 60 degrees:

Bob: [After Miriam had keyed 58] Why don't you go up by 1? Try 59?
Miriam: I already did it.
Bob: You did 59 and 60?
Miriam: Yeah, 50 and 60.
Bob: Do you remember what 60 looks like?
Miriam: [A positive head shake.]
Bob: What? Can you tell me? Can you describe it?
Miriam: It's sort of like this [she gestures to the polyspi 58], but bigger, and its got a maze, like in it, but it doesn't have the curly things [emergent spiral arms].

Miriam's MPÔLY view at this point was one of fascinating phenomena. The central variable was 'angle', but this angle could not have connected for her in any directly meaningful way with the angle operand of a right turn. Further, the particularity she assigned to angles is staggering to anyone with a more general perspective. How could one imagine 'owning' an angle? I infer her MPOLY view saw the micro-domain of computer designs as one of disorderly but engaging objects. Miriam explored this range of phenomena in a regular way. But incrementing by tens did not suggest some sensible way of separating designs, by the numbers, into her later developed taxonomy of mazes, messes, pretty stars, and 'ones with the curly things'. We can not consider Miriam's use of input variables with MPOLY as any different from her use of operands with the primitive operations of turtle geometry. That is, these input variables were no more than numbers given to an uncomprehended (and very powerful) primitive to make it work its attractive but incomprehensible function. The clearest conclusion from these data is that the phenomena of this microworld can be loved and felt as personally owned, even if not at all comprehended in any well-articulated, analytic sense.

Empirical and analogical problem solving

Miriam's play with MPOLY exemplifies a kind of empirical learning about a small corner of the world. A striking aspect of the knowledge derived from empirical learning is its particularity. In the view of computer designs, Miriam felt she had discovered the angle 60; that the objects it made were hers. Different but similarly particular examples can be found in her views of arithmetic knowledge. She knew the sum '15 cents plus 15 cents equals 30 cents' because the latter was her allowance at six and that for it she could buy two packs of her favorite gum at 15 cents each. Likewise, she claimed to know how to divide, because she knew the specific result that '8 divided by 8 equals 1'.

A second striking aspect of empirical learning is the regular exploration of the space. Thus, in exporing MPOLY Miram tried in sequence decade-multiples for angle values. Similarly, in an early attempt at multiplication (6;11;13) she tried to determine the product of five and seven by keying in the sequence of commands '5 * 7 = 1', '5 * 7 = 2'. etc. expecting the LOGO error message would change from 'you haven't told me what to do with "false"' 'to 'you haven't told me what to do with 'true', thus signaling the correct result when she stumbled across it. This sort of behavior seems like the operation of simple search in a problem space as described by Newell and Simon (1972).

Simple search is not enough to characterize the creativity and complexity of human problem solving. The regular search of empirical exploration should be contrasted with the analogical character of problem deformation, seen in this later attempt to address a multiplication problem (7;7;8):

> Miriam was angry with me — and she wrote therefore a five-column problem on my chalkboard (1916 and 9232). In a mocking tone, I told her how easy it would be for me to solve. She had her revenge: It's not adding — it's *times!*' Agreeing that such a problem was difficult, I refused to do it, and she stomped away, leaving the problem undone.
>
> A day or so later, Miriam set out to show me that she could solve that difficult multiplication problem and completed it as below:

$$
\begin{array}{cccc}
1 & & 1 & \\
1 & 9 & 1 & 6 \\
\times \quad 9 & 2 & 3 & 2 \\
\hline
10 & 8 & 4 & 2 \\
\end{array}
$$

What could be clearer than her method in solving this problem? She substituted multiplication of digits within columns for addition and carried as in addition. In other words, she deformed the uncomprehended problem to fit her existing knowledge, accounting for the problem difference by substituting a new subprocedure within the controlling framework of addition.

Simple search can characterize problem solving in task domains which are remote from a person's past experience. Such domains can be attractive and engaging, as Logo's turtle designs geometry were for Miriam, but exploration within them tends to be domain-dominated and of an empirical character. In contrast, where interactions and ascriptions of meanings are involved, a complex, pre-existing knowledge structure, a cluster of microviews, is involved. In such cases, problems are assimilated to and deformed by that cluster of microviews. To the extent that intelligence involves integrating the knowledge of a multitude of disparate microviews based on domain-dominated experiences, the most interesting problems and explanations of learning must be based on analyses of experiences which reveal the filiations of structures.

Iteration: a lack of comprehension

Miriam was introduced to iteration as a theme of instruction through the use of a procedure generator. TIMES permitted her to repeat any string of turtle geometry commands as the kernel of an iterative procedure.[11] She found it easy to use and wanted to make figures that would 'grow' as did those she made

---

11 TIMES was involved in Miriam's writing her first procedure, as described in Chapter 3.

with MPOLY. We came to distinguish two different types of growing figures. In the first growth pattern, imperfectly closed figures appeared to precess around their centers, and they grew by turning.[12] The second type of growth came through increasing the distance moved forward by the turtle on each forward movement. Miriam wanted to make designs which grew bigger this way, and therefore she needed to know how to use variables.

Three primary means of encoding iterative procedures are step-duplication, looping, and recursive invocation. TIMES produced different forms of procedures depending on the reponse to its question, 'Stop on count or data condition?' The STAR procedure below, one of unbounded tail recursion, was generated by Miriam's ignoring the request for specification of a stop rule.

```
TO STAR
1 FORWARD 100 RIGHT 144
2 STAR
end

TO TRIANGLE
1 IF EQUAL 0 :COUNT STOP
2 MAKE "COUNT (:COUNT – 1)
3 FORWARD 100 RIGHT 120
4 GO 1
end
```

Miriam's failing to discriminate between an iteration controlling variable and one applied as a movement operand value (the distance of a forward command) turned our focus to that task in later sessions.

The over-theme of Miriam's computer experience was that if you want to change or understand a procedure, you must look inside to see how it works, either by execution or analysis. We undertook analyzing procedures in Logo Session 28 (age 6;2;26) to deepen her understanding of variables. I directed Miriam to create a POLY procedure using the fixed count, i.e. step-duplication, option of TIMES with a kernel [FORWARD 200 RIGHT 90 WAIT 30] and a count of 24. TIMES generated a procedure of 24 steps, each of which was [FORWARD 200 RIGHT 90 WAIT 30]. This meant the 'kernel' would be repeated 24 times whenever the procedure was executed. Initially, no variables at all were used by the procedure. Miriam read the lines of the procedure, one by one. I stopped her:

> Bob: What you're saying is that every time the turtle does something [executes a step] it goes FORWARD 200, RIGHT 90, and waits a little.... How many times does it do that?
> Miriam: 24. [Pointing at the last step] I just looked at that.

After seeing the execution of POLY and how many times the kernel was duplicated, Miriam still did not know whether POLY required an input variable to

---

12 This occurred through the non-overlapping of the turtle's path when a partial sum of terms was close to but did not equal 360 degrees.

control its execution. She tried POLY with no number following and witnessed it working. When she described the object created as 'a square' and the activity as 'going around', I proposed we count the iterations to see if the turtle did it twenty-four times. I identified the unit of the turtle's action as the procedure step, but Miriam identified the unit as the making of a square. When we counted its actions, I counted out loud to '6' — that is, one and a half squares. Miriam continued counting under her breath and concluded with '10'. Her count was right in its way: I had counted 6 for six sides; she counted '4' for the remaining eighteen by counting '6' again at eight, '7' at twelve, '8' at sixteen, '9' at twenty, and '10' at twenty-four. When I challenged her because I was confused, Miriam made a joke of her response. I conclude here first that Miriam's idea of iteration was connected to that of an input value and second that the units Miriam deemed significant were shape-defining more than action-specifying. They applied in terms of repeating visually recognized figures, not of navigating with primitive actions.

Can one ask for clearer evidence from behavior that Miriam had not connected comprehensibly the views of movement (personal geometry and navigation) with design? At first I suggested how easy it would be for Miriam (or some other child her age) to understand iteration. Now we have instead an example of how difficult it is to relate a design made from a repeated action to the occurrences of that action. In 'Two geometries', Miriam could not initially make sense of coordinate geometry because she analyzed that world in terms which were in fact inappropriate. In this case, Miriam saw the thing made primarily as a 'square' and not as a shape emerging from the repetition of more primitive actions. She focussed on the emergent form, not on the creative actions of the process. We are left with the question of whether her failure to comprehend was an accident of inadequate instruction or a reflection of some deeper disparateness in the mind. (These options are not mutually exclusive.) We will return to this issue and resolve it as best we may after the following survey of Miriam's later experiences with computer-generated designs during The Intimate Study.

The particularity of local knowledge

Miriam failed to understand how the space descriptions of navigation microviews (and in particular the primitives of turtle geometry) related to the figures created by the TIMES-generated procedures. That her knowledge relating to various Design view procedures did not connect with navigation microviews meant that the knowledge they embodied retained a 'local' flavor. The outstanding characteristic of the local knowledge of isolated microviews is its particularity. What is known is highly circumstantial. This particularity of local knowledge does not imply that the knowledge is insignificant. Conversely, when circumstances indicate extensive particularity in knowledge we are entitled to infer that the microview itself is created primarily through empirical learning and does not inherit its most important knowledge through descent from an ancestor. The particularity of the TIMES microview is most clearly witnessed in Miriam's limited grasp of the idea of variables, a central issue followed closely in our work.

Experiences with variables

Variables are important because of their function, because they permit the use of powerful iterative techniques; understanding iteration presupposes some understanding of variables. When numbers are used, they are used in specific applications. There are five distinct applications of numbers in the Logo language at the introductory level to turtle geometry (procedure line numbers, angles, distances, looping counts, and increments to other values).[13] All but the first of these five uses may appear as variable numbers.

Summary

Miriam encountered these uses of numbers and their uses as variables in the following Logo subsystems. TIMES (described previously) generated various forms of iterative procedures from a kernel of turtle-actions supplied by Miriam. The SLOT system was based on a device — an input terminal which would accept pre-coded cards as commands — designed to render explicit and tangible the sequence of control flow. With that SLOT system, I introduced Miriam to the coding of polyspirals (as in the first design of Fig. 5.4). The SHAPES (polyspiral) programs were a procedural expression of the activities we had pursued with the SLOT system; the procedures applied the value of a quantity *delta* to DISTANCE (the operand of a forward command). In the sessions focussed on *families* of polyspiral designs, I tried to bring to salience for Miriam the issue of the separation and stepping of variables as a powerful idea. Finally, in her experiences with INSPI, she saw the results of applying *delta* to an ANGLE variable. The particularity of local knowledge is most clearly witnessed by examining the detail in specific learning incidents, such as Miriam's effective introduction to variables through use of the SLOT system.

SLOT

In an unhappy didactic discussion, I tried to introduce variables generally though liking them to little boxes (representing specific variables with matchboxes) about whose contents one might inquire. For a variety of reasons, Miriam rebelled against this instruction. Her useful introduction to variables was with the SLOT machine in Logo session 30 (age 6;2;30). She made some interesting POLY class designs with iterative procedures and fixed quantity instructions, then abandoned the session when I mentioned the word 'variables'. Robby in his turn made several POLY designs using both ANGLE and DISTANCE variables. When he finished, Miriam located her 'good number' card and decided:

> Miriam: I want 1, 0, 5.
> Bob: Go ahead.
> Miriam: How do you do it, the number?
> Bob: First we have to type at the keyboard.
> Miriam: [Presses the button of the row containing the keyword card.]

---

13 This statement is true for the Logo implementation used with this study. In more recent versions of Logo, line numbers are rarely used.

Bob: Do you know how to make an angle? ... See, these words DISTANCE and ANGLE, are like boxes, and we're going to put a number in the slot ... Make, space, quotes —

Miriam: [Interrupting impatiently] I know!

Bob: You know how to spell 'angle'? It's here if you don't.

Miriam: [As she keys] Space ... 1, 0, 5 ... new line?

Bob: Now the distance Robby used last was 100. If that's a good one we don't have to change it.

Miriam: Let's keep 100.

After this first success with a SLOT machine POLY procedure, Miriam varied the contents of the variable ANGLE several times.

Two variables at one time

Miriam had not herself assigned a value to the variable DISTANCE in Logo session 30. As the next Logo session began, both ANGLE and DISTANCE were initialized to default values of zero. After arranging a FORWARD and RIGHT loop on the SLOT machine and directing control at the keyboard, Miriam assigned 150 as the value of ANGLE. The turtle circled in place when she initiated the POLY procedure. Miriam interrupted the loop with a clearscreen and keyboard invocation:

Bob: ... Control is now at the keyboard.

Miriam: M, A ... Why didn't the hundred and fifty work?

Bob: What was it was a hundred and fifty? ... The ANGLE box has a hundred fifty in it. Remember, there's a DISTANCE also.

Miriam: [Frustrated noises.]

Bob: You have to tell the turtle how far to go forward.... Do you know how to spell DISTANCE?

Miriam: No.

Bob: Here, I will show you.... Just key MAKE QUOTES DISTANCE some good number.

Miriam: [As she keys] MAKE QUOTES ...

Bob: [As she keys] DISTANCE, yes.

Miriam: Now what?

Bob: What are you going to put in the slot?

Miriam: What slot?

Bob: The slot that's associated with the name DISTANCE.

Miriam: I don't know how to do it.

Bob: Sure you do. You did it yesterday.

Miriam: No. I did MAKE ANGLE.

Bob: Well, now do MAKE DISTANCE. It works the same way. The turtle turns. He goes right and turns a number that's in the slot of ANGLE. When he goes forward, he goes a distance that's in the slot of DISTANCE.

Miriam's first two variable POLY was ANGLE 80, DISTANCE 190. She was delighted with that result and her next trial as well, with ANGLE 150. It is clear that at first she did not know how to MAKE "DISTANCE and did not recognize that it was the 'same' as MAKE "ANGLE which she had done the day before. However, with explanation and some direction, she did find accessible the practice of assigning variable values.

During use of the SLOT system, the angle 60 degrees was frequently prominent. After the introduction of a CHANGER operation card (which incremented the variable operand of a forward operation), we made a set of nested hexagons and a hexagonal maze. Her sense of proprietary interest shows its beginning in this dialogue (Logo Session 36, age 6;2;30):

> Miriam: There ... MAKE ... [Keys MAKE "ANGLE]
> Bob: Do you know any good maze numbers?
> Miriam: I think I'll try 60. [She keys 60.]
> Bob: So you made ANGLE 60. What are you going to make DISTANCE?
> Miriam: [As she keys] ... 1, 0.
> Bob: 10. O.K. What anout *delta*? *Delta*'s 4 now.
> Miriam: How about 4?
> Bob: O.K. Let's leave it alone.
> Miriam: New Line. [A POLYSPI 10-60-4 appears.]
> Robby: Oh wow!
> Bob: That's a beautiful maze.
> Robby: Can we get two prints of it?
> Miriam: Mine. [She keys PRS; this is a PRINT SCREEN command.]
> Robby: Daddy, when it's done, can we get another print of it?
> Miriam: No. . . . Didn't I do a nice thing?
> Bob: That's a beautiful maze, Miriam. What angle was that?
> Miriam: 60.
> Robby: It's really a hexagon.
> Miriam: Isn't that a beautiful maze?
> Robby: Why couldn't we get two pictures of it?
> Miriam: It was my idea.

Later, in Logo session 43, Robby in his turn generated a 'family of mazes', regular polygonal spirals with angles of 120, 90, 72, 60, 45, and 30 degrees. At the end of that session, Miriam entered my office and seeing his pictures displayed on the wall, objected vigorously that he had used 'her' angle of 60 degrees. This complaint could be dismissed as an expression of jealousy at Robby's achievement and my recognition of it except that it was repeated frequently over following weeks. My conclusion is that Miriam looked at ANGLE less as a variable capable of assuming a range of values and more as a class name for a collection of objects. If there is no functional difference in such a distinction, there is a difference in salience: seen as a variable, the function is more forward; seen as a collection of quantities, the particular value is dominant. With the former view, relations of variables to objects would focus on transformations of values to artifacts; with the latter, the mere associations of quantities with artifacts is a quasi-nominal rather than transformational relation.

In Miriam's other experiences with polyspiral designs or polyspiral families, there is no indication that she understood what she was doing in any profound way. In contrast with Robby's work, which showed that he grasped the idea of isolating one variable from a set and exploring the generation of possible designs by stepping (varying incrementally) the value of that variable while holding others constant,[14] Miriam's greatest achievement in this direction was imitating a display of his designs, taping them on the wall 'in alphabet order, by the numbers' as she puts it. Her exploration of possible INSPI designs was interesting to her and engaging but surely empirical in character and in no way integrated with her other turtle geometry experiences. The conclusion at the end of the core period of The Intimate Study was that she had learned many things but had not learned anything about geometry which could effect her mind of thought in a way beyond what is common in everyday experience.[15]

Evidence of later connection

During the core of The Intimate Study, Miriam did not give evidence of understanding how microviews of the Design cluster related to those of navigation. She could use iteration but there was no evidence she understood it as she so obviously did in this later incident (6;11;15):

> As I sat at work in the reading alcove, Miriam came to join me. She offered to sit in my lap, but I protested to being busy and turned her down. Miriam moped a little, then crawled onto my bed and into the center. She began to move and spin in a most puzzling and distracting fashion. 'What are you doing? You're driving me batty!' I complained. My gripe inspired Miriam to explain. Requesting a pen and a 3×5 card, she draw on it a right rectangular polygonal spiral to show what she was doing in her 'crawling on the bed game'. Her verbal explanation was that she was 'making one of those maze things'.

Whence came this connectedness in her knowledge of physical action to pattern? My best answer to that question is as follows.

Because I lived with Miriam, it had been an ever-present temptation to follow her continuing development. Thus, when one day the children pestered me to play with some Cuisenaire rods I had brought home from the Logo Lab, I agreed on condition that we begin with a project of my choosing. My proposal was this: after they sorted the rods by color (and thus by length as well), I would begin to make something; their problem was to describe what I was making and what my procedure was. I began to contruct the object whose development is shown in Fig. 5.5.

---

14 Robby's behavior is reported in 'Extending a powerful idea', (Lawler, 1982).
15 I emphasize that this conclusion applies only to her exposure to turtle geometry. How exposure to programming affected her thinking is analyzed in Chapter 3, 'The equilibration of cognitive structures'.

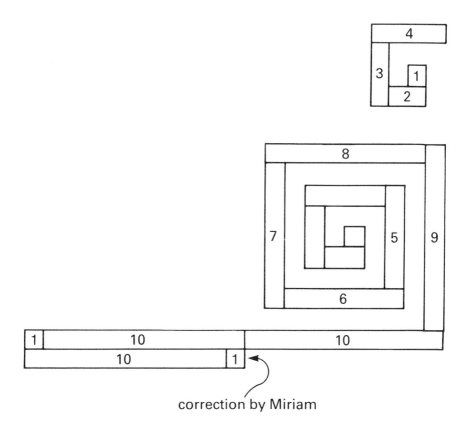

correction by Miriam

Fig. 5.5 – Rod mazes.

After I placed four rods, I asked the children what I was making. Robby answered immediately, 'A swirl, a maze'. Miriam chimed in with his answer. Subsequently, I asked Robby to hold off on his answers until I discussed my questions thoroughly with Miriam. When I had placed eight rods, I asked the children if they could describe my procedure. Miriam could not, at first, but when I focussed her attention on the length of each piece, she remarked: 'You're growing it bigger and bigger'. Upon questioning, she noted the increment was 'one'. After Robby added rods of length nine and ten, Miriam justified his action by arguing, 'It goes in order... littlest to biggest', and finally described my rod selection rule as 'every time you put a rod in, it should be one bigger than the last one'. With the mentioned minimal prompting, Miriam understood well the incrementing of length. In striking contrast, she showed considerable difficulty with the role of turning in the construct.

When I set down the eleven-length (the orange and white pair of rods), I did not orient it perpendicularly to the previous length. Miriam declared the arrangement incorrect but had trouble specifying precisely what was wrong. When she rearranged the rods to place them correctly, she simply interchanged the location of the orange and white rods. From this section, I infer Miriam considered the placement incorrect because two rods of the same color were adjacent to each other — but not because the one rod was colinear with the preceding one. Here I asked Robby to explain what I should have done:

> Robby: You should go a right 90. It could be orange, right 90, white orange.
> Bob: And what should I do after the next orange?
> Robby: You probably could do an orange and red.
> Bob: [Placing the new rods colinear with those preceding.]
> Robby: Hold it! You should do a right again.
> Bob: Oh. Miriam, What should I do next?
> Miriam: A right 90, green and orange.
> Bob: Next?
> Miriam: A right 90, purple and orange.

This is the point at which Miriam brought together in a comprehensive relation the steps and result of a maze-generating procedure.

If we review this rods-maze experience, several aspects stand out. One is the extensive guidance Miriam received from the microculture. The task she confronted focussed on the articulate description of procedures. When she could not begin, I directed her attention: 'Look at the length of each piece'. When she got sidetracked, concerned with color alternation instead of turning, Robby's description of my error definitely redirected her thought. One can say of Miriam's knowledge implicated in the task that she worked with a familiar objective (creating a maze), worked with familiar objects (Cuisenaire rods), and applied familiar operations (adding one to a number, turning right 90, repeating a procedure). I consider these experiences of the rods-maze and turtle on the bed to have integrated and thus culminated in the development of Miriam's knowledge about iteration. The experience was clearly important for Miriam: in later years, whenever offered Cuisenaire rods to play with, constructing a polyspiral maze surfaced regularly as her objective of choice.

I believe this experience with rods helped Miriam better understand her prior computer experiences, but there is no direct evidence to support such a claim. Consequently, the upcoming discussion is admittedly speculative. Nonetheless, I judge it worthwhile because the concrete detail of these experiences permit discussion of issues about the organization of the mind which are much more specific and down to earth than is usually the case.

CONVERGING INTERPRETATIONS

The central issue of human cognitive organization is how long-developing structures become linked in communication to form a coherent mind — at least, an information structure sufficiently unified to exhibit the kinds of mental behavior which we experience personally and witness in others. The studies of preceding chapters focussed on microviews which had much in common. The foregoing incident, 'Evidence of later connection', presents a concrete linking experience as a possible basis for interconnection between essentially remote clusters of microviews.[16] Such a linkage is at least well-exemplified — if not well-established — in this case. I now take the example as empirical guidance for thinking about how this concrete linking can take place between essentially remote bodies of knowledge.

In the preceding studies, I isolated incidents which plausibly could be argued to have been the context of moments of insight where previously disparate microviews were brought into communication. We lack such a certain incident in which this linkage occurred for these turtle geometry microviews. [17] The simplest way of describing the linkage is through seeing that the *Rods-maze* microview plays a mediating role. The *local* character of Miriam's learning in the *rods-maze* incident implies that it was not developed analogically but *de novo* from more primitive components of the sensorimotor system. My proposal for how we should think of that is shown in Fig. 5.6.

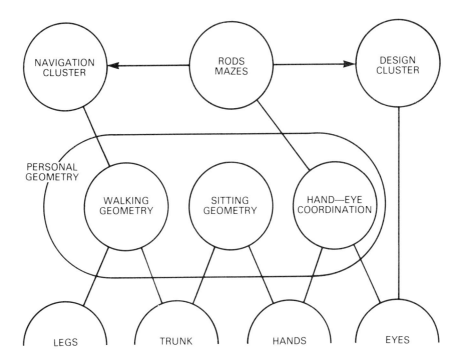

Fig. 5.6 — A mediating microview.

16 Essentially remote refers here to Turtle Navigation's being related primarily to walking and Computer Generated Design's being related primarily to seeing, thus being descended from different sensorimotor subsystems: locomotive and visual, respectively.
17 I could believe that the 'turtle on the bed' incident was itself the context of insight, or at least replicated the original incident in which the connection was made; I have no evidence to support this belief in a substantial way.

What is it about the character of the Rods-maze view that permitted it to function effectively in closing the formerly unbridgeable gap between the cluster of turtle geometry Navigation microviews and the Design cluster? Descended directly from the coordinating scheme which results in hand-eye coordination, the Rods-maze view was effective as mediator for two reasons, which can be brought forward in this simple comparison expressing the activity of the primary agents in these microviews:

Locomotive	*Mediating*	*Visual*
I move from here to there	You (hand) move from here to there	That (thing) goes from here to there
Central agency	Hand as remote agent	Eye as active agent
Difference:	Agent	Agent

As noted at the end of 'Two geometries', the primary difference between the active programs of the locomotive and visual subsystems is the level of aggregation which is significant for their functioning. The body lurches forward, step by step. The eye recognizes an image as an entity by circulating repeatedly in the pattern of a closed loop, a 'feature ring', which defines that object in memory. The feature ring program is a complex recognition procedure, whose primitive elements are like the movements of the locomotive system, going forward and turning right. Because of years of developed hand- eye coordination, the eye can recognize the pattern that emerges from what the hand does whereas it cannot recognize so simply (if at all) the pattern that emerges from the path of body movement. The rods-maze experience was able to function mediatively between descendents of the locomotive and visual subsystems because the hand, as the familiar agent for manipulating remote objects (say little toy dolls some of whom may be thought of as self or other), can make the bridge between an action of movement which a body can make and one which can be coordinated with visual results.

This is not the only possible interpretation. Earlier (Lawler, 1979) I offered another interpretation which I review here because of the more general light it casts on the organization of mind. The alternative interpretation, which I named *the nucleation of* microview, Clusters, is a generalization of the idea of a Post-cedent Ancestor. Consider all Miriam's computer-generated design experiences as a cluster of related but uncomprehended microviews. I suggested the special effect of the rods-maze experience could be explained if it was able to function as a 'post-cedent' ancestor for all those views. The inference was drawn that over time those empirical microviews would be reconstructed as 'logical descendents' of rods-maze. The explanation offered for why this particular experience acted with such force was that it represented in concrete form 'powerful idea'. Since it would be capable of acting as a post-cedent ancestor for all the members of a cluster of formerly related but unlinked microviews, it would be the nucleus of a microview cluster. Here the idea of cluster nucleation was able to link up with another image of cognitive organization from Minsky's 'Frames' paper (Minsky, 1975). The mind can be seen as an information network wherein the nuclei of microview clusters play the role of geographic capitals in the great world.

In a city, any person should be able to visit any other, but we do not build a special road between each pair of houses; we place a group of houses on a 'block'. We do not connect roads between each pair of blocks, but have them share streets. We do not connect each town to every other; but construct main routes, connecting the centers of larger groups. Within such an organization, each member has direct links to some individuals, mainly at his own 'level', mainly to nearby, highly similar ones; but each individual has also at least a few links to 'distinguished' members of higher level groups....

...

As our memory networks grow, ... our decisions about what we consider primary or 'trunk' difference features and which are considered subsidiary will have large effects on our abilities. Such decisions eventually accumulate to become epistomological commitments about the 'conceptual' cities of our mental universe.... The selection of capitals corresponds to selecting stereotypes or typical elements whose default assignments are unusually useful.... We need not invoke any mysterious additional mechanism for creating the clustering structure. Developmentally, one would assume, the earliest frames would tend to become the capitals of their frames would tend to become the capitals of their later relatives, unless this is firmly prevented by experience.... Acquisition of new centers is in large measure forced upon us from the outside: by the words available in one's language; by the behavior of objects in one's environment; by what one is told by one's teachers, family, and general culture.... (Minsky, 1975)

The identification of these capitals not as prototypes but as post-cedent ancestors of microview clusters is a unification of the structural metaphor of Minsky with Papert's theme of powerful ideas — a unification based on my empirical observations about the interacting roles of construction and reconstruction in the everyday processes of natural learning. At this point, even as I abandon the specific interpretation as applicable to this particular case, I maintain the coherence and importance of this idea as a component of a computational vision of cognitive organization.

Why is it necessary to supplant the former interpretation of the rods-maze experience with a new one, the channelled description conjecture? There are two reasons, first, the nucleation of microview clusters did *not* explain why this experience was more powerful than some other might have been in effecting the cognitive reorganization I impute to it, second, it did not address a major gap in the description of powerful ideas, a gap which I became convinced was was essential to close. Specifically, following Papert, I described the Rods-maze microview as a concrete model of a powerful idea by attributing to it the characteristics of simplicity, generality, and utility. That is, the objects of the experience (Cuisenaire rods and the square maze) were easily recognizable and distinct entities; the generality of the discovery made through the experience — that through a series of comprehended steps one could create an unexpected but easily recognizable result ... the idea of emergent form[18] — and its specific utility to Miriam in rendering comprehensible the relation of turtle navigation to computer-generated designs, all qualify the experience as the concrete embodiment of a powerful idea. But there is another dimension to ideas to which I had long been sensitive (from the poetry of G.M. Hopkins and Stephen Crane) that the ownership of ideas is a critical element in their power for the individual. When completing the thesis 'One child's learning', I was not able to create a theory which would embrace this observation but still I marked it as an essential element of a theory of mind.

> The leitmotif of ownership [of ideas] running through this disquisition has not emerged clearly as a theoretical theme, but it is irrepressible as an issue because, when the mind is seen as an autochthonous construction of the person, ideas-to-be-incorporated will be intimately owned as few other things in life are.... (Lawler, 1979, p. 720)

In *Mindstorms*, Papert labelled this dimension of ideas 'syntonicity' and emphasized the importance of ideas being personal, but advanced no explanation for why this sometimes occurred and other times did not, and no proposal for how such a thing might work within a computational vision of mind. The channelled description conjecture does offer such a proposal: concrete embodiments of ideas are personally owned because they are not remote form the shaping structures of the soma itself. Experiences such as those of rods-maze are powerful precisely because they provide the links between late-developed structures and the coordinating schemata (the primary integrations of the sensorimotor subsystems achieved during the sensorimotor period). They are important because they link the concrete structures of body knowledge to the more abstract descriptions of external things that blossom as the cognitive network of the mind.

The question of what constrains the possibility of some ideas being powerful and others not so is the crux of the channelled description conjecture. In strong form, it proposes that only those concrete embodiments of ideas which link together descendents of disparate sensorimotor subsystems can be powerful; it claims that such models are the correlate in concrete thought of the correspondence schemata of the sensorimotor period and that on them depends the developing coherence of the individual's cognitive structure. Further, such microviews provide the bases of construction of the more extended cognitive nets of developed minds, functioning as the ancient cities, the geographic capitals of personal importance. In contrast with a goal-oriented attempt to link feelings and thoughts — say upon a basis of disparate need systems as seen in ethology — and with a Freudian focus on the conflict between competing, even conflicting homunculi in the mind, the channelled description conjecture proposes a third model of basically disparate structure, but one better characterized by a pun of Wallace Stevens, 'my anima likes its animal', than by either the needs or coflicts of the other mentioned alternatives.

18 As another example of the importance of this idea to Miriam at this same period, see the discussion 'Precursors of debugging: pretty flower' in Chapter 3.

A final link between two converging visions of mind is the idea of learning through debugging. Sussman (1975) developed a computer-based model of learning which grows out of a simple but profound observation. In my para-phrase, the idea is: 'if you don't understand something, you can't tell that it's different from what you do understand'. The main consequence of this obser-vation is the following general vision of the process of problem solving: not recognizing that a new problem is different from others met before, one first tries old solutions; when these old solutions fail on the new problem, the specific details of the failure provide guidance for the construction of a variation of the old solution which will solve the new problem. The vision of problem solving as learning through debugging faulty procedures shows directly and lucidly how to think of the incremental refinement of local knowledge. The nucleation of microview clusters attempts to perform the same function on the level of cogni-tive organization. Consequently, this idea is a further unification of ideas on learning long developing in the MIT Artificial Intelligence community. Their convergence with the results and interpretations of my empirical psychological research coalesce into a vision of the structure of mind that goes beyond a single modality of mind.

SUMMARY AND NEW DIRECTIONS

In my attempt to address the question of how knowledge is organized in the mind — from a perspective where the constraints of learning are judged most important, I have raised for consideration the body-parts mind, an organization of cognitive structures with these main features:

- the structure of the mind and its development are reciprocally generative, in Piaget's pretty paradox: *pas de structures sans genèse; pas de genèse sans structures.*
- the dominant aggregations of knowledge are a specific type of schemata, one which I have called 'microviews' (competing, pattern-activated procedures); such structures are internalized 'descriptions' of the situ-ations and activities of encountered reality.
- interpreting confusion between two different descriptions of space has led to an uncommon emphasis on the role of cognitive reconstruction in the construction of mind (the importance of cognitive reconstruction should not, however, surprise anyone who takes seriously the memory studies of Bartlett (1932)).
- the novelty of this work is the proposal to take seriously the fact that the body is made of parts and reflect this fact in a vision of body-derived cognitive structures; a key observation has been the reasonably precise sense in which body motion and vision are different and interrelated: visual scan paths (the patterns of eye movement involved in figure recognition) can be thought of as procedures of greater or less complexity formed from movement primitives for the foveal target of the eye similar to those of turtle geometry that can describe the movement of the body in space; where Freudian or Loenzian models of mind focus on

functional structure, I have advanced a vision with a somatic foundation to explain functional differences and relations.

— the primary affective dimension of cognition is the congeniality of structures among themselves; that is, new knowledge may be taken up and effectively applied if and only if it is connectible to what is already recognized as part of the self; the appeal of abstract ideas has a distinct but related basis: the structures of which such ideas are expressions are less intimately owned than concrete microviews but can be more thrilling when their power is realized and can be accepted as most intimate, in fact, when one experiences powerful ideas as the root of personal coherence.

— finally, in our attempt to answer the question of why particular experiences proved effective in learning and others did not, we have formulated the 'channelled description conjecture' which in its strongest form states: the connections between late-development cognitive structures can *only* occur through the mediation of cognitive descendents of the coordinating schemata of the sensorimotor period.

Modalities of mind

What are they, these modalities of mind? Galton's famous survey of his colleagues uncovered the phenomenon named after him, that people can generally describe a dominant mode of the most productive of their thought processes. Einstein thought with images. Piaget held internal dialogues. The three dominant modes are the visual (thinking with images), auditory (thinking with words), and motile (thinking in which the sense of body movement and tension plays a significant role). These introspectively witnessed modes of thought map directly onto the major sub-systems of the body-parts mind. The linguistic and visual systems are the most discriminated, and thinking in their modes is clearly reported by the subjects of Galton and those of others who have found his phenomenon robust. Those whose bias is motile have not discriminated so finely between the various kinesthetic subsystems. Only extremely handicapped people might be expected to exhibit thought uniformly dominated by a single mode. Whole people, through the varieties of their experiences, can be imagined to develop quite various minds, each with its own particular balance of thought modalities. With such a point of view one may go beyond thinking about mind as a uniform thing — without making the overly simple direct association of modes of thought with 'halves' of the brain. One may accept the evidence of dispersion of representations and procedures within the brain by adopting a richer framework of developmental possibilities, one which saves the fundamental insight of Piaget, that through the activity of the individual the mind constructs itself.

What are the appropriate research questions to ask if one takes seriously the body-parts mind?

— Is it possible to represent the mind, in the large, in a coherent way with such assumptions? Can one assemble an empirical base for cognitive mapping on a large scale within the individual? For a specific application of the channelled description conjecture, a reasonably complete cognitive history of an individual would be required, a very different record to create. If such a direct test is infeasible now, the body-parts mind organization nonetheless presents a new description of mind onto which behavior can be mapped to address questions now most difficult even to raise.

— what are the modes of an individual mind and why? How do specific life experiences create the Galton phenomenon? Is the body-parts mind useful in explaining why and how people are different from one another?

— Is it possible to develop structured information-processing models of mind? (Such would not be constrained to the single mode models of past decades and would be less amorphous than unstructured cognitive networks.) How would one detail the relations of one subsystem to another and what, precisely, would coordinating schemata have to be like? (The specific interest in coordinating schemata derives from the central role assigned them by the channelled description conjecture.)

Farther from the paradigmatic research of contemporary psychology are endeavors that might be considered cognitive history and anthropology, asking and trying to answer questions such as how the life experiences of different cultures affect the organization of minds possible within them and to what extent technological change and social intervention may foster homogenization or more extensive differentiation between individual people and different peoples of the world.

6

Summary

The unifying theme of this entire work has been the search for a deeper theory of structural emergence. I have judged this task essentially to involve specifying how local changes lead to globally significant results and how local changes within the individual's mind relate to his social context and to the organization of the individual's mind on the large scale. My focus on interactionist, empirically based structural models of natural learning has led me to put different tasks, methods, and ideas in the foreground than are common in most of the contemporary cognitive sciences.[1] The accompanying Table 6.1 summarizes the primary conclusions from this work under headings appropriate to the analyses where they are developed.

---

1 My approach is one of many rational ways of studying the human mind. It contrasts with Fodor's program to establish the psychological reality of the transformational grammar (begun with a worked out theory of syntax for which no psychological claims were originally made), with the Newell–Simon strategy of starting with conclusions selected from a state-of-the-art survey of traditional, American academic psychology, with the cross-sectional/state-descriptive approach of Piaget's later years, with the task and setting dominated approach of ecological psychology, and with the a-structural but learning-focussed behaviorist psychology. It also contrasts with the AI work which addresses central problems of mind but denies any claims of applicability to humans (the early work of Sussman is an example).

Table 6.1 — Theme-based summary table.

Chapter 1: The development of objectives

Assumptions:
- a more 'human' rather than 'goal-driven' model of behavior guidance is needed

Questions:
- where do objectives come from?

Assertions:
- objectives come from elaboration of recent achievements (one's own or other's)
- objectives come from demonization of failed elaborations
- abstracted failures become demons capable of symbolic realization; abstracted successes become generalized tools

Chapter 2: The progressive construction of mind

Assumptions:
- task domain derived structures develop from interactions between what is already in the mind and the particular details of experience
- these structures compete among themselves to interpret subsequent problems by deforming them to fit what they can recognize as objects to which they apply

Questions:
- how do complex mental skills develop?
- can we disentangle the relations between prior knowledge and the circumstances of the experience in the formation of new knowledge?
- if diversity comes from the world, whence comes coherence?

Assertions:
- complex skills develop from the integration of task-specific knowledge and its application through problem deformation
- control element insertion can 'explain' developing coherence
- case study can be fruitfully applied to a new level of cognitive analysis through tracing the learning of the particular individual

Chapter 3: The equilibration of cognitive structures

Assumptions:
- major 'stylistic' differences in thought exist, e.g. concrete versus formal.

Questions:
- how does 'formal' thought relate to 'concrete' thought?
- what is it like to learn something really new?
- how does new knowledge effectively replace competing old knowledge?

Assertions:
- Piagetian stages do not develop from completion of predecessors: formal

Table 6.1 – *continued.*

thought is an epistemologically separate system of knowledges which achieves late dominance over the concrete system by chance in some cultures
— task-specific knowledge has an association-like character but is different from stimulus—response couples in this major sense: behaviorists' associations are solutions responding to problem- specific cues; on balance, active knowledge is more like solutions looking for problems to solve
— inhibition of obsolete knowledge (local reorganization via affect): new knowledge ultimately suppresses old knowledge through various techniques of 'distancing' obsolete knowledge from one's self-image.

Chapter 4: The articulation of complementary roles

Assumptions:
— two-person games are a more complex problem environment than spontaneous learning about addition or taking instruction, worth investigating and able to be investigated

Questions:
— how does knowledge of interactive problem situations get built up?
— how does knowledge about people and things interact?
— how does pattern-oriented, associational/classificatory thinking turn into serial deductive thinking; how do these relate to more systematic thought and to penetrating understanding of a problem domain?
— how does one get a major new idea?

Assertions:
— the desire for social interaction is the motive for multi-role mental play which in its turn is cognitively productive; one's model of the other derives from the obsolete self
— serial deduction is the new application of adequate old knowledge to new problems; the only other alternatives are instruction and the top-down creation of a structure which could *ab initio* be able to 'see' a new problem as different from others already encountered
— major new ideas, like minor ones, are accidents prepared for by the establishment of individually adaptive precursors

Chapter 5: Cognitive organization

Assumptions:
— there is no necessity for assuming that the uniformitarian hypothesis of mind holds; but non-uniformities can be based on other models of division than on simple 'hardware' division (right versus left brain halves); the functional division of mind in service of the body parts is more significant than physical lateralization of hemispheres.

Table 6.1 – *continued.*

Questions:

- why do some experiences act with force in enhancing the coherence of mind and not others?

Assertions:

- concrete structures are close to the body-specific ancestry and are quite disparate; more abstract structures are less ancestry-constrained than the early predecessors and can emerge as elements of a general semantic network; thus the mediating structures of coordinating schemata give way to the nuclei of microview clusters in more abstract cognitive networks.

In summary, the principles applied and the conclusions drawn from these analyses can be categorized under the two general headings of structure and process.

STRUCTURE: PRINCIPLES AND CONCLUSIONS

I began with the primacy of self-construction through individual activity in a resistant environment, not the shaping of a resistant albeit marginally plastic creature by an active environment. This primary activity is the ground of elaboration through which new goals are generated and knowledge becomes more broadly and precisely applicable. Behavior and the 'self' are emergents of self-activating cognitive processes; cognitive styles are surface emergents of interactions of large-scale clusters of such cognitive structures. Denying the existence of central, universally capabilities (such as Sussman's 'hacker') committed us to seek local, stepwise changes in cognitive structures even though some steps may be below the threshold of manifest behavior. The development of mature skills through interactions of imperfect but adaptively effective predecessors requires that those intermediate cognitive structures be at least metastable. The distinctness of computational primitives of the diverse components of mind and their possibilities of relation through a kinesthetic foundation of some of the major subsystems imply that multi-modal descriptions of mind should be initially preferred unless they can be demonstrated to be inadequate. The uniformitarian description of mind should be that which requires support by argument. Within an assumed competitive structure of mind, the emergence of hierarchy is what must be explained. Within an assumed disparate structure of mind, the emergence of any coherence is what must be explained.

For describing both states of knowledge and transformations between them, I have found it useful and compatible with data of The Intimate Study to assume of cognitive structures that:

- they originate through particular experiences and have a derived, highly specific character;

- they may be sub-dominant; this means they may exist and function but only become manifest in behavior under very special circumstances, such as experimental interventions;
- they are disparate; that is, structures developed from experiences in different task domains do not communicate among themselves except as a consequence of separately formed linkage through organizational development;
- they are competitive complexes of:
  - specific memories derived from particular experiences;
  - specific procedures derived from imitation (of uncertain use in most cases until the scope of constraints on their application is worked out): the Perspective of a cognitive structure is the collection of pattern matching, value-specifying demon procedures which judge its fitness for a problem; the Functions of a cognitive structure is the network of transformations of slot values activated by the filling of the structure's slots;
  - demonic objectives derive from failed elaborations of successful procedures; the collection of such objectives is the structure's Agenda;
- the class of situations upon which a structure can function is progressively uncovered and the definition of the structure is refined incrementally though the many interactions of the structure with situations to which it variously applies.

Organization

Assuming that organization is fundamentally competitive means disparate structures compete among themselves to solve problems as each can. Further, this permits reorganization to be seen as taking place through the more effective competition of later-developed cognitive structures which can and do thus function as logical ancestors to temporally preceding structures. Further, if the primitives of structures derive from movement primitives of fundamentally different body-parts, this implies:

- structures descending with compatible primitives comprise a cognitive mode; such structures may be interrelated more easily than those of different modal systems;
- direct descendents of coordinating schemata are central in advancing coherence of the mind.

Interactions with others

Society presents individuals with frameworks for interpreting situations and scripts for activities which include categorizations (descriptions of what's what) and with central issues resolved on conventional or negotiated bases. In process terms, these issues provide nodes of decision at which the individual can later assert different (often more flexible) decisions; this is a functional insertion of a control element in a network. Simulation of another person becomes possible only with the structures of the self. This implies that dialog-like activities which take place within one mind involve developing control over subsystems originally used differently.

PROCESS: PRINCIPLES AND CONCLUSIONS

I assumed initially that problem solving began as a race among structures competing to solve presented problems through the use of well-known results and familiar procedures. The first Piagetian aspect of processing was represented through the possibility of invocation of ancestral knowledge at need. Equally important was the notion — equivalent to the idea that experience is interpreted through imperfect structures — that on encounting a novel situation, structures deform problem to models derived from past experience and, when all past models fail, the mind goes into constructive mode, piecing together a new solution from fragments of earlier models and specific failure-provided guidance.

The mind generates new problems for itself. This is a central aspect of mind which permits its progressive development. New problems are proposed first through elaboration of problems currently solvable successfully, next through activation of demonic objectives created from earlier failed elaborations. I have named this proposition 'The Unified Generalization Proposal': when elaboration leads to the successful application of a working procedure to a new problem, this implies the effective generalization of the procedure; when the failure of a procedure on a problem leads to its suspension and later reactivation with possible symbolic realization, the broader class of objectives which the procedure may serve constitutes a goal-related analog of procedure generalization.

Learning

Beyond the fundamental association of one thing with another, learning is dominated by the cleavages of cognitive structures. Insulation is the cutting apart of structures; amalgamation is their joining together into new organizations. There are at least four amalgamation processes: the elevation of control, the correlation of perspectives, cross-modal coordination, and cluster nucleation. The coherence of related domains of knowledge is achieved either through linkage of formerly disparate structures or through the reorganization of prior experience via the development of temporally later, but logically antecedent structures when they are competitively more effective. Two insulation processes (there may be others) are progressive discrimination and the repression of obsolete perspectives. Learning by example, by instruction and by discovery are typically of the progressive discrimination sort because the hypotheses about what are the relevant kinds of things to attend to are given, either by programming, as in Winston's work, by society through instruction, or by ancestral experiences in human learning through discovery. Humor takes part in the repression of obsolete perspectives, as does assignment of a less-preferred role to another, for both serve to separate the image of the self as an agent from the use of specific structures derived from one's authentic experience.

Interactions with others

People learn by taking instruction from other people in their environment because they enjoy being engaged with them. Such information of simple associations is homely binding. But society is intrusive as well as engaging. By forcing new questions on structures developed for other purposes, other people engender changes of behavior which may be so remarkably different in effect as to manifest 'changes of stage'. When deprived of social engagement, the individual, to redress that loss, recreates the interaction by simulating his former colleagues; this in turn leads to elevation of control and the increased lability of procedures (generalization).

CONCLUDING COMMENTS

The mind has a structure such as I describe *because* the interaction of multiple ancestral structures, channelled by action and consequences within the task domain, provides the creativity for cognitive adaptation. The adaptivity of cognition is what unites the development of mind with the evolution of all things, for the mind evolves through the interaction of the individual's emerging objectives and opportunities. Those emergent opportunities are constrained by reality. More importantly, some interactions are so powerful that creatures who seize the opportunities they present completely dominate all competition (language and social organization is one such interaction). In this sense, some interactions create a new dimension of being — as flight literally brought a new dimension of life to our planet.

Under such a view, doing psychology is more like a combination of epistemological analysis and history than physics. This argues such psychology should not be expected to be a science in the narrowest sense of that term — however much we might hope to describe, even model, the processes of change of specific configurations of ideas.

In the study of human learning, as in evolution and cultural development, we should address the kind of specific questions Kurt Lewin proposed fifty years ago: 'what are the interactions of individual tendencies and environmental opportunities, and what are powerful synergies among environmental laws which permit such opportunities to exist'. It is possible to answer such questions. Even though the concreteness of experiences undergoing the skillful and deceptively abstract processes of mature thought are hidden by the processes of amalgamation, they may still be traced through the details of thought, for the particularity of knowledge gives away the path of its genesis and thus reveals the processes of learning. A more detailed appreciation of human learning will contribute to our understanding in general how is it possible for an idea to become embodied in a thing.

7

The genesis of microviews

A COMPACT SKETCH OF MICROVIEWS

The aim of this research has been to apply ideas from structuralist descriptions of knowledge to the interpretation of learning-related behavior observations. The objective is theory development. I make no claim to propound a complete theory of mind. I struggle to describe coherently some of the processes that may obtain in the development of mind. In its weakest description, this 'theory' is a cluster of ideas, richly exemplified, exhibiting what it might mean if one saw mind as a system of disparate, active structures. I call such structures microviews. The important idea encoded in the term 'micro' is the centrality of fragmentation in the process of knowing: the external world can only be experienced as a collection of disparate microworlds; the challenge of learning has as an essential ingredient coming to understand the unities behind what we experience in so fragmentary a fashion. Microviews are internal, cognitive structures built through interacting with such microworlds and reflecting that fragmentary process of knowing.[1] Three outcomes summarize how the microviews formulation proves valuable. The first is that certain kinds of insight can be understood as the experienced correlate of modifications of the organization of microviews. A second is the description of some forms of guidance available to microviews from which effective procedures

1 The term 'microview' is a change of nomenclature for me. The term 'microworlds' was used equivocally to refer both to the external world and internal structures by Minsky and Papert in the '72 progress report', an error in which I myself continued in later work (Lawler 1979, 1981, 1982). This change has been made necessary by Papert's popularization of the word with a specific and limited sense defined in *Mindstorms*. It should be clear that the intellectual position implied in the use of the terms 'microworld' and 'microview' has nothing to do, logically, with the existence of microcomputers.

may develop and be fixed as well-known results or procedures. A third outcome is some examples of how particular experiences interact with specific cognitive structures at the moment of insight. In these examples, the insights which occur are seen to derive from a specific configuration of the problem encountered and the control structure of the mind.

There are four primary characteristics of microviews. They are disparate, in the sense of being essentially different, one from another. Microviews are active cognitive structures. They have a genetic history. Finally, they have an internal structure evolved from this history of their genesis.

Internal structure

The internal structure may be divided first into a perspective and functions. I use the term perspective in a secondary sense of the term, that is, as the aspect of an object of thought from a particular standpoint, as in 'a historical perspective'. A *perspective* is the recognition mechanism by which a microview analyzes a problem into elements its functions can cope with. It determines the aspect of a problem from the standpoint of a particular microview. As the historical perspective is owned by the historian, so the microview's perspective is of the microview. A perspective is composed of *slots*, which may be thought of as variable names to which are assigned values from the problem context by procedures associated with each slot. Microviews differ from each other because their perspectives are comprised of different slots bearing different functional relations to one another. The *functions* of a microview relate slots to one another. They may be either well-known results, procedures, or primitives. Well-known results are things remembered. Procedures relate slots of the perspective to one another through simple transformations.

Primitives are the operations from which procedures develop. *Anchoring with variation* is an example of a primitive – but one that in turn needs explaining. Anchoring with variation is a basis for progressive achievement of a result.[2] In counting a pile of coins, when the value of a second coin is added to some first, the calculation is anchored at the intermediate result and varied by the value of the next coin to be added. The history of prior, intermediate steps is irrelevant and is obliterated in anchoring. The variations possible from an anchor are a direct consequence of the quiddity, the essential character, of the values apposite for specific perspective slots. That is, one can add number or coin values, but one can not rotate them as one can with shapes drawn on a computer graphics display. There are at least three forms of this primitive operation, each form reflecting a specification of the dominant source of guidance in the variation: difference reduction, bricolage, and detour.[3]

2 See the extended citation 'Tversky and Kahnemann: One Anchoring with Variation' (p. 253).

3 *Difference reduction* is a form of anchoring with variation: in a context of explicit commitment to a specific goal, that variation is selected which most reduces the discrepancy between the anchor state and the goal state. The more common situation in human experience is one where both objectives and means are negotiable. This is the variation aspect of *bricolage*. In the third form, the *detour,* an indirect path from the anchor to the goal state takes its form from circumventing an insurmountable obstacle.
Trying to prove a theorem, mathematicians oft-times work backward from the result to

The filiation of microviews

Some knowledge is a prerequisite of other knowledge. This empirical observation, which is obvious in simple cases, is also true in more complex ways in more complex situations.[4] I will treat the observation as a theoretical assumption and relate it to the internal structure of microviews. An *ancestral* microview (or *ancestor*) is one whose perspective functions as a template for the perspective of another, which is defined by this relation as the *descendent* of the former. This filiation of microviews creates the control structure of the mind through specific learning processes. Notice that this filiation is epistemic and not temporal. That is, the local ancestor in a more mature mind may be different in fact from that first genetic ancestor of the original microview.[5] It is clearly possible for a microview's perspective to be inadequate for the problems it confronts and to be later modified so as to create better registration between the cognitive structures and the problem situations of which it attempts to make sense.

More ideas on internal structure

In response to questions at a lecture advocating his production system as a representation of mind (MIT, 1978), Alan Newell noted there was no such thing as a satisfactory learning theory, that every one he had examined contained a 'big switch' which, when thrown, caused learning to happen. My focus on how interaction between internal structure and external circumstances can be seen as an attempt to move the 'big switch' out of the mind as a closed system and into the arena of interaction between a system and an external context. The word 'microviews' names structures for which this empirical study has indicated a need. It would be possible to create production systems which would function as the microviews I have described. But such models would be inadequate because the structures would exist only as emergent phenomena of interacting rules.

All workers in the field hope for the simplest adequate representation scheme, but I require one that is designed to permit the straightforward and explicit representation of learning. Because the genetic filiation of cognitive structures is an important idea for understanding learning, a system of microviews should be able work by 'analogy' both in deforming problems (assimilating them to internal structures) and in constructing new component microviews. Similarly, they must be locally complete and self-contained because the disparateness of structures representing fragmentary knowledge is an important idea. Further, the analyses of Chapters 2 and 4 have shown how valuable can be the notion that self-constructing systems should complete an output-proposing cycle

the assumptions they need in order to prove the theorem. This 'backward chaining' still exhibits anchoring with variation. A common, powerful technique for solving complex problems doubles up forward and backward chaining of anchors and variations, then uses difference reduction in searching for bridges between nearest anchors. This is problem solving by *negotiation* among all constraints that actually apply in a given context. These complications are introduced here only to indicate how the elaboration of this procedure germ, anchoring with variation, can lead first to procedures and upon reflection, to methods of solving problems.

4 A detailed analysis of such a situation appears in the section 'Two geometries' of Chapter 5.
5 Issues about this distinction are exemplified and addressed in Chapter 5, 'Cognitive organization'.

in parallel even when behavior is serialized (as in moving in a single game cell in tic-tac-toe or speaking a single answer to an addition question); unusual output conditions are the primary cue that a problem-solving situation is novel in an interesting way. Furthermore, microviews must be such as can permit the growth of organization because dealing with the issue of emerging coherence is central to understanding mind. Finally, one needs a kind of structure that can begin simply enough to represent Miriam's first use of the tic-tac-toe 'three corners' strategy (initially no more than an imitation of an action coupled with a conviction that the action would lead to a specific result). But microviews must also have the potential to develop continually over a long time into something as complex as frame systems.

Elements for a system
The logical structure embodied in the most common kinds of rules used in cognitive modelling are condition action rules, of which the productions of Alan Newell may be taken as the most widely used type. A formulaic expression of such a rule might be: IF condition-x then DO action-y. Demon procedures mentioned through the text as the essential components of microviews can be contrasted with such IF—(then) DO rules in a comparable formula: WHENEVER condition-x DO action-y. Cognitive models using demon procedures depend upon the simultaneous condition-testing of many such demons for their effects. Parallelism of demons is the most salient aspect of such systems. A final contrast may be made with an element which one might call the *action-plan,* represented by the formula: FOR purpose-x DO action-y. Here is a simple summary table to highlight what is most salient about each of these entities:

Element	*Formula*	*Foremost aspect*
production	IF x DO y	conditionality
demon	WHENEVER x DO y	parallelism
action-plan	FOR x DO y	active purpose

The aspects of purpose, conditionality, and action execution sequence are engaged by systems of each of these kinds of elements. Purpose is usually implicit in rule-based models. Conditionality needs to be handled by any system of action-plans that can be resource limited. The fact that each of these elements is a two-part structure does not mean that system elements must continue to be so limited. Indeed, one should expect that a system constructed out of slightly more complex elements could have significantly more developmental potential. I propose one consider constructing learning-oriented systems based on a three-part element, which I call the GAC (an acronym for Goal Action-plan Constraint). The GAC can be contrasted simply with these other structures by summarizing which aspects are explicit in the element or implicit in the architecture of a system made up of the elements:

Element	Purpose	Conditionality	Parallelism
production	implicit	explicit	only at activation
plan	explicit	implicit	non-committal
demon	implicit	explicit	essential
GAC	explicit	explicit	through output[6]

GAC's can be described most simply as demons with explicit purposes.

For an aspect of a structure to be changeable, either it must be explicitly represented or else there must exist processes within the organization of the system for the modification of that organization itself. I believe developing models built around elements such as GACs will permit a significant advance in cognitive simulation through separating out components of what must be learned for effective action. More specifically, one can recognize a new goal without knowing how to achieve it through a specific plan. Similarly, one may learn a procedure by some form of imitation before developing a well-articulated understanding of the goals it will achieve. Finally, constraints upon the achievement of goals with given procedures can be a later acquisition; in Chapter 4, Miriam learned how to achieve a three-corner fork and only later came to appreciate her plan's vulnerability to counter move.[7] Learning separately goals, action-plans, and constraints should prove to be a much more tractable challenge for computer modelling than learning such relatively complex things as if–then rules.

Such a simple structure as the GAC can by itself be the beginning of a microview. For example, one could represent Miriam's initial strategy for achieving a fork in tic-tac-toe by these three elements: a set of three cells numbers which comprise her markers in the fork; a list of three cell numbers which comprise her plan for achieving the form; an empty list of constraints. As it becomes more complex through variabilities introduced by self-generated elaborations or by interactions with the environment, two of a GACs separate parts come to function as the perspective of the microview: the goal becomes a demon procedure looking to satisfy its conditions for activating the plan; constraints become demon procedures looking to inhibit goal demons. Since the functioning of a microview is an activation cascade, what originally was a purpose-driven GAC may cross over in situations of under-constrained activity to function as a

6 The condition–action rule is comfortable to the essential novelty of the serial programmable computer, the ability to branch in instruction sequences. Their extensive use has been supported by the influence of the LISP dichotomies as well. Such structures map all too easily into stimulus–response kinds of behavior descriptions. The deep resonance between the computer architectures of today and the psychological theories of yesterday has permitted inadequate theories to go farther and to appear more powerful than they should. Programming structures with multi-part elements have been advocated and developed before. I trace this idea back to conversations with Minsky and Papert in the mid-seventies. An early computer implementation was Ira Goldstein's extension of simple if–then rules with a 'caveat'; he argued rules should have the form 'IF x, DO y, UNLESS z' to limit applications under known exceptional conditions. At a more fundamental level, the programming environment developed by Wertz (1982) involves a LISP variant where the language operates on triples instead of the standard two-component element.

7 I am now applying these ideas in computer-based simulation studies and more general explorations based upon the observations of this book.

stimulus responding structure: this is how *bricolage* emerges as a consequence of the internals of a purpose-driven structure. With a multitude of such GACs competing, purposes would be quickly selected by and appear to be driven by conditions and possible actions. Response to a stimulus can thus be seen to be a highly developed reaction by a complex structure — not the primitive thing itself from which structures have to be built up.

When necessary for an action to be modified because it doesn't work a primitive form of learning through debugging can occur. A local constraint can be thought of blocking one path of the net. Others become possible to try; they are tried because they are still driven by an integral purpose. Under such conditions, the inversion of order of subgoals becomes conceivable without remote, complex, and reflexive interventions.[8]

If we discuss the activity of microviews in terms of the question 'What sort of computer is the mind?' we conclude that the mind is not 'a computer', but a network of microviews. The activity of microviews implies that they are networks, each node of which is an independent, purposeful demon, always ready to perform its function whenever it can. If we think of these nodes as little men, we can imagine microviews as little societies of some sort, with the diversity of objectives and negotiations such as the name implies. It is here that we make contact with the idea of problem solving in the greater world as a negotiation between goals and givens through permissible functions; in such a circumstance, actions, conditions, and purposes are all modifiable through local interactions.

More complex structures

There appear to be two paths to greater complexity, different in principle. Complexity can develop through elaboration of structures based on those sorts of experiences which permit the more refined specification of what circumstances facilitate the activation and completion of information processing functions in the mind. The second path to greater complexity of structures is the one this study has pursued, exploring how learning can be seen as the discovery of coherence through achieving more effective organization of prior structures. The following discussion is a scaffolding for thinking about such issues.

CONTROL STRUCTURE

The main tactic of my research has been to correlate particular experiences with changes in how disparate microviews relate to each other while problems are being solved. The issue of control structure is central: some basic learning processes derive directly from the control structure of the mind.[9] The common, usually implicit assumption is that the problem-solving mind has an executive control structure. There is some decision-making process (call it 'I') that selects one method or another for trial application to a problem at hand. Such an assumption fits well with the surface coherence and permanence of the individual.

---

8 Such as would be required in a learning system with Sussman's hacker structure.
9 To call this assumption or strategy a discovery, or even a conclusion, would be to beg the question.

One quintessential novelty in the Freudian theory of mind was the vision of an apparently coherent personality emerging out of the contention of three psychic entities: Ego, Id, and Superego. With structures of such a type, the central issue is how control emerges from the interaction of parts.

What sorts of things need we assume to make a computational explanation go? We begin with demonic activity and genetic filiation of microviews. How might these microviews interact to solve a problem? The assumption of demonic activity leads us to assume a fundamentally competitive interaction obtains between microviews. Such a system is described as having a *heterarchical* control structure. When confronted with a problem, the entire mind may be alerted, but I don't insist on that. A *cluster* of microviews is the set whose disparate knowledges might apply to the problem.

Here is a sketch of how a three-microview cluster might respond to an addition problem with *simple contention.* Let us propose the problem 'How much is 75 plus 26?'[10] One way of answering the question is with counting operations, e.g. representing the quantities by hashmarks and reciting the number names. These sorts of mental operations are characteristic of the counting microview discussed in Chapter 2. A second answer might come from applying the standard algorithm of vertical-form addition: that is, '5 and 6 are 11. Put down the 1 and carry. 7 and 2 are 9 and the carry make 10. The answer is 101'. A third answer might come from money-based calculations: 'Four quarters make a dollar, and a penny's 101'. If the control structure were simple contention, the 'fastest' microview would produce the answer. Which microview wins the race depends on the problem. For 75 plus 26, a *money* world wins in my mind, but for 36 plus 59 other worlds of mental computation come to the fore. The state of knowledge in the microview obviously determines the outcome; for example, you can not use the standard algorithm if you do not know it. How such disparate, competing microviews can be integrated to form a coherent understanding of number is addressed in Chapter 2 and described in terms of the general processes set out in the following.

LEARNING PROCESSES

Here is a general scheme for describing the splitting apart and joining together of microviews. Call such processes *cleavage* processes.[11] The two sub-classes of cleavage processes are insulation and amalgamation. The latter implies a mixing together of elements which maintain their identity. Insulation implies the separation of things which should still be thought of as joined at a level below the surface. (A peninsula becomes an island through insulation). Cleavage processes generate new microviews.

---

10 This example is drawn from the study of Chapter 2.

11 This is a serious pun, calling upon both senses of the auto-antonym 'cleave', which means in one sense a cutting apart and in another sense an intimate joining together. Thus in my use cleavage means both separation and conjunction.

Insulation

Insulation is the creation of a new microview through a splitting off of a new perspective through penetration of a prior perspective by a distinction. The ancestral perspective is *syngnostic* with respect to the descendent, i.e. it views as wholes entities which are analyzed into parts in the descendent perspective.[12] The new knowledge that this additional perspective indicates does not render the ancestral and prior knowledge obsolete. Because there are indications that microviews become distinct, we *choose* to view this process of distinction as the genesis of new structure rather than as the complication of a prior structure.[13] How does a descendent structure relate to its ancestor? *The Genetic link becomes the path of analogy.* Let me be more precise.

A descendent microview may directly invoke the knowledge of an ancestor, and this is an essential, supportive role. Confronted by a query 'How much is 27 plus 46?', a counting microview would not respond quickly. A newly developed microview, in which decade numbers (30, 70 etc.) were the salient objects, would not contain as a well-known result '20 plus 40 equals 60'. But if its perspective breaks down the original problem to a subordinate one, 'How much is 2 plus 4?' (which this new microview likewise would not know), that subordinate query could readily be answered by its ancestor, the counting microview.[14] *Supportive analogy* names the case where the perspective analysis of one microview reduces a query into components which may be resolved by the response of an ancestral microview. *Constructive analogy* names the case where supportive analogy creates results which have such salience for the applications of the new microview that they become well-known results of that world.

The general problem addressed by constructive analogy is the question 'Where does guidance come from in hypothesis formation?' Genetic filiation is the primary answer I propose. Supportive analogy provides a weakly held, speculative method of solution which is then subject to confirmation or refutation by trial. An example of procedural analogy may help here.[15] A year or more after the end of The Intimate Study, Miriam, angry with me for some reason, challenged me with a difficult calculation problem, writing 1916 and 9232 on my chalk board. When I scoffed that the sum was easy, she had her revenge: 'It's not plus', she said bitingly, 'it's *times*'. I refused to do the problem. The next day Miriam returned, entirely without the intervention of anyone else, and worked the problem thus:

---

12 The word /sin/os/tik/ is a neologistic back-formation; the idea is that one knows as alike things which are epistemologically distinct; a suggestive and analogous English word is synaesthesia. The formation of the *decadal* microview (detailed in Chapter 2) exemplifies the process. Let this summary suffice here. One may know that 50 plus 50 is 100 and that 3 plus 3 is 6, yet be confounded by the problem of 53 plus 53. To appreciate that one may catenate the two results of 100 and 6 requires a perspective which divides 53 into decadal and units parts and which implies a specification for the re-integration of the part-sums into the compound entity 106.

13 For a succinct discussion of why one would want to make such a choice, see the extended citation 'Papert: On the Elevation of Control' (p. 247).

14 Miriam's use of finger counting to solve such decadal problems in turtle geometry exemplifies the reality of such a linkage.

15 The following example is discussed further in Chapter 5.

$$
\begin{array}{c|c|c|c|c}
 & \overset{\prime}{1} & 9 & \overset{\prime}{1} & 6 \\
\times & 9 & 2 & 3 & 2 \\
\hline
1 & 0 & 8 & 4 & 2
\end{array}
$$

That is, she mutliplied within columns and accounted for columnar interaction by 'carrying' as in addition. This invention is illuminating because it is so wrong. The perspective of this multiplication microview witnesses its descent from addition knowledge. The interaction procedure, carrying, derives from the ancestral procedure knowledge of addition microviews. When supportive analogy creates a procedure (correct or not) which dominates microview functions, it is constructive analogy.

With the examples of insulation and constructive analogy behind us, we can now discriminate *two different kinds of learning:* processes of insight and processes of construction. The former generate new microview perspectives; the latter fill out the functional capabilities of microviews. Let me describe groping, another function-filling process, before returning to the processes of insight. *Groping* is a more general term for learning by trial-and-error, more general in that it covers trial-and-success. Given the preceding description of anchoring with variation, groping can be described as the kind of behavior that results from the absence of a procedure effective to achieve an objective. If there is strong goal commitment, difference reduction guides the path of problem solution (or failure). If the objective is unspecific, bricolage will lead to its negotiated adjustment of means and ends. If there is strong goal commitment, and the process meets an insurmountable obstacle, the detour will take guidance from the obstacle which blocks direct achievement of the goal. Since the variation required by any specific problem depends upon the quiddity or 'what-ness' of the objects of thought, the groping process is responsive to genetic filiation through the descent of the perspective. With that qualification, groping can be seen as an intra-world process for problem solution and for the establishment of microview-specific procedures with whatever mnemonic reinforcement repetition provides.

Amalgamation

Amalgamation processes, the second category of insight processes, bring formerly unrelated microviews into relation with one another. The two to be discussed, the elevation of control and the correlation of perspectives, both indicate a knowledge of other microviews, but of different kinds. The *elevation of control* names a process where the creation of a new microview perspective subordinates other microviews (for some range of problems) through supportive analogy. This subordination is functionally equivalent to direct invocation of those microviews. This process has been exemplified in detail in case studies of Chapters 2–5. What is most striking in the elevation of control is that a significant increase in power (in terms of calculation range and completeness of coverage, for example) results without an increase in the abstractness of the description involved. The 'knowledge about knowledge' implicated in the elevation of control is purely functional in character. Contrast this aspect with the more declarative character of the knowledge implicated in the following.

The *correlation of perspectives* names a process which provides guidance for the refinement of the perspective of an imperfectly functioning microview from slot correspondences between it and a second microview perspective. That is, there exists no supportive analogy in the sense of an invocable function, but there exists an analogy of signification, a semantic analogy specifying relations between parts and the wholes of the two perspectives.[16] The knowledge of the guiding world is reflected into the second for refining its perspective. 'Reflection' is meant to suggest (though the suggestion be equivocal) that such correspondence knowledge without direct function is a rudimentary form of structures which eventually permit the reflexivity of mind.

It is tempting to squeeze these processes into a uniform and balanced framework for their better comprehension. (Should there be two forms of insulation, for example, to balance the two forms of amalgamation?) To do so would be unwise at this point, for several reasons. There is no reason to believe the processes are uniform or balanced. Insulation involves two microviews, and amalgamation, three. The processes go on simultaneously, and both insulation and amalgamation may be implicated in an insight. Finally, this sketch is intended as scaffolding for analysis and interpretation, not as a cage.

Re-learning: cognitive reconstruction

After cleavages of microviews, groping and supportive analogy result in the construction of new procedures. But *re*-construction also occurs in this circumstance. For example, before she understood place value, Miriam invented an idiosyncratic carrying procedure, one giving incorrect results, which was subsequently displaced by a standard procedure.[17] Of more concern here is the reconstruction of mind in the specific sense of changes in the organization of microviews. The descriptions of the cleavage processes all concerned knowledge that reflected what it was about, accurately albeit imperfectly. In such a case the organization of microviews is basically progressive even if within a microview erroneous procedures develop from a syngnostic perspective. It is a different question to ask, 'How does the structure of mind get corrected after it has gone wrong?'

It is very difficult, if not impossible, to understand a problem which is unlike anything you have ever encountered. If it is a law of mind that there can be no genesis of new knowledge without attachment to prior cognitive structures, that attachment may frequently be made in error. It is essential, then, to address those misapprehensions deriving from the inappropriate attachment of one microview to another. The clearest example appears in Miriam's computer-focussed experiences and is analyzed in detail in the 'Two geometries' section of

16 When this semantic analogy concludes in the refinement of one perspective by another, it is a second type of constructive analogy. The outstanding example of this process, detailed in Chapter 2, is witnessed in Miriam's sudden comprehension of vertical-form addition through her quite different knowledge of mental calculation. Only after appreciating the specific correspondence between the 'places' of vertical-form addition and the processes of her mental calculation could Miriam construct a correct notion of carrying that made sense to her.

17 Notice that my use of 'reconstruction' is more like that of Bartlett's *Remembering* than that of Piaget.

Chapter 5. There I argued that she made specific mis-interpretations through seeing the problems as like those she encountered in turtle geometry *because* she had no ancestral microview built on experiences with the appropriate epistemo- logical character. Only after I later provided a specific such experience was Miriam able to cope with this class of problems; further, my instruction in this case was most effective precisely when I called her attention to the similarity of the problem domain to that prior experience. The process of reorganization, involving a later group of experiences and an insight of the relevance to a long-standing misapprehension, I name *the closure of a genetic gap*. In biological filiations, ancestors are temporally antecedent to descendants. In cognitive organizations, the genetic filiation is epistemologically and fundamentally atemporal. The closure of a genetic gap is achieved by the retro-active insertion of a *post-cedent* ancestor in the filiation between the microview of the originally misapprehended problems and the prior structures to which it becomes connected.

There is a more general form of closure of a genetic gap. Imagine there is a microview of primary importance to its descendants, as is the Count microview of Chapter 2. Count and the set of its descendants comprise a Cluster of micro- views. Now imagine further such a cluster without the Count world in it. One can think of Miriam's computer-based experiences during The Intimate Study as having generated such a chaotic cluster of microviews without a coherent core. If there were a specific experience she had which in turn created a microview which could serve as a post-cedent ancestor to those microviews, such would be an example of what I speculate is a major process of learning, which I named the nucleation of microview clusters in 'Converging interpretations' of Chapter 5.

If one asks 'What makes it possible for one microview and not another to serve as the nucleus of a cluster?,' an answer of a general sort must depend more on the character of the domain than upon that of the person (as was the case with the mediating microviews discussed in Chapter 5). In 'One child's learning' (Lawler, 1979), I argued that Miriam's learning about the relation of computer designs to her microviews of navigation exemplified nucleation process. Recall that at the end of The Intimate Study Miriam, her brother, and I assembled a square spiral design, familiar from her computer experience, but made in that case with cuisenaire rods. Let's assume that through this activity she was able to appreciate how the repetition of the basic operations produced the result because of the special character of the domain;[18] the microview embodying knowledge of such a domain I call an *archetype*. What makes an archetype special is the degree of transparency relating the objects which can serve as slots' potential values, the operations performable on them, and the results of those operations. The results can be appreciated as the necessary outcome of performing those operations on such objects. For example, if one arranges increasing lengths of cuisenaire rods at right angles, it is obvious when a 'square maze' appears where it came from. This sense of accessible necessity is the hall- mark of the archetype. In other microviews, conclusions are hard won by chains of inference. In the archetype, the conclusions possible (which may be few)

18 This assumption is at odds with the interpretation of Chapter 5 which I now prefer; my intention here is merely to use the detail of this incident to illuminate the ideas by example.

are 'intuitively obvious'. A second characteristic of archetypes is that relations in them are capable of ramification. That is, whatever is obvious in that particular microview instantiates an epistemologically more general idea whose exemplary archetype is, in fact, capable of illuminating problems proper to other microviews in the cluster. This is the sense in which an archetypical microview embodies a powerful idea. The *nucleation of microview clusters* names the retro-active insertion of an archetype in a cluster of microviews. When such an event occurs, the re-constructions of individual microviews within the cluster need not be immediate following the reorganisation. If that reconstruction occurs, i.e. if the problems involved are encountered again (either in the world or in thought) and re-solved, the effect of nucleation is profound, for the post-cedent archetype becomes the common ancestor of a cluster of microviews and thus renders them all coherent and comprehensible. The conclusion to which I drive is that the nucleation of microview clusters describes the process through which order emerges from the variously aggregated experiences of life. This is the process through which specific microviews come to serve as the 'geographic capitals' in Minsky's metaphor for the structure of mind. The idiosyncratic system of archetypes develops, atemporally, as the skeleton of the mind. Coherence of mind is an achieved articulation of archetypical microviews. What permits communication, uniting the experience of one individual with another, is the epistemological generality of the ideas instantiated in the various archetypes of diverse minds.

Control structure: a more elaborate view
The quintessential commitment of the cleavage theory is characterizing the mind as fundamentally active. This previously proposed formulation (I will refer to it as the *query* formulation) suffers two apparent flaws. In the first place, it portrays the mind as re-active, not active; that is, the mind merely responds actively to queries put upon it without generating queries itself. Secondly, the activity is located in the slots of microview perspectives, but the competition is portrayed as between microviews; this description either is vague or contains an implicit assumption about how active slots interact, about how their activity is integrated proximately. In neither case can the issue of integrating demon activity be ignored. We will turn first to how questions might arise within the mind.

What follows is unusual and may even strike some readers as bizarre. Therefore I want to be especially clear about what the aim is and why the attempt is necessary. I must now confront the issue of motivation in problem solving. Without resolving this issue, I cannot hope to achieve a general theory of the active mind. My uneasiness at this obligatory task may inspire in me some caution and in you, I hope, some extra willingness to suspend your disbelief while the analysis and explication proceed.

Grand theories of motivation reduce man's needs to essentials (think of the famour four F's: feeding, fighting, fleeing, f. . .) and derive behavior by long chains of inference from them. Justification is by appeal to man's continuity with other orders of life. In depending on what is common to man and animals, we risk attending too little to what is distinctive in the human mind. My approach is more differential than axiomatic. I do not ask 'What comes first?' but rather 'What comes next, and how does that relate to what just went before?' For the assumption of fundamental activity, and for the sake of coherence, I strive for explanations in terms of demons and anchoring with variation. In these terms we will try to explain the *development of objectives*. The basic idea is this: when a problem fails to be solved that 'should' have been solvable (most likely created by elaboration as described in Chapter 1), a demon is created; call it a *puzzled* demon. This demon proposes objectives for mental activity at later times. Because the perspective under which the solution fails is syngnostic relative to what is required for the problem's solution (and possibly because the specificity of the original problem is incompletely preserved), the slot values necessary at a later time for the problem to proceed further are underdetermined. This underdeterminacy of slot value assignments permits the appearance of symbolic realization of an objective with respect to the original problem inspiring it. The collection of puzzled demons within a microview is the *agenda* of that microview; the agenda is not a list but a pandemonium of things-to-be-done. Agenda is a term at the same level of generality as perspective and functions; thus it names a third major microview component. *The flowing interests and curiosity of a mind are the observable counterpart of interacting agendas of puzzled demons.*

One cannot escape the problem of drives and the mind's being driven, but it is very much an open question of how important, quantitatively, drives are. One is not always hungry, frightened, angry, or lustful. How important are drives? A simple mechanical model helps there: think of a freewheeling transmission between the other systems of a person and the mind. When the going is tough, the motor controls the machine's progress, but when the going is easy, the motion goes on regardless of what the motor is doing. However much life is unpleasant and filled with nasty surprises for a man, there is little reason to believe that life is hard — in the sense of so subjugating body and mind that man is a driven creature. This stance argues that the human mind is fundamentally freewheeling.[19] Man's behavior may be seen as entirely determined (if one is so inclined) but *not* by drives, rather so through the incremental elaboration of his past successes or through plunging into symbolic encounters with his past failures under the guidance of his present ignorance. The agendas of microviews are primary determinants of behavior.

But how, precisely, do these agendas act, and interact among themselves and between themselves and perspectives? If the agendas of microviews propose queries to which the affiliated perspective of each world responds, is it not circular in extreme to claim that their organization is well described as involving the competition among microviews? Further, there is a basic sense in which commitment is a precursor of problem solving at the detail level we shall consider. For example, this succession of narrowing questions represents the decision steps and commitments through which Miriam came to confront problem solving on a typical day of The Intimate Study:

---

19 A formula for this position might be that man is continually but not continuously driven.

(1) Do you want to go to Logo today? Or stay home? Or go elsewhere?
(2) [At Logo] What do you want to do? (The basic and obvious choices were from these possibilities: use the computer, do puzzles, socialize, get snacks, run around.)
(3) [When using the computer] What sort of activity interests you today? Would you like to use a game, e.g. Shoot, or an interface, e.g. Draw+? Would you like to use the Logo interpreter directly?

If one is interested in a particular kind of problem, is not the competition of microviews a distraction, and even more, a primary source of confusion? Here we seem to have an essential paradox. That very competition of active knowledge which can illuminate learning is simultaneously a source of pervasive confusion. In a profound sense, then, this theory of learning must be coextensive with a theory of confusion. I grapple with that general problem through exemplifying two specific kinds of confusion, genetic and nominal.

Genetic confusion is possible when one microview derives from multiple ancestors. Each ancestor could provide guidance, and how could a microview decide beforehand which to prefer? The descent of the DRAW+ (see Chapter 1) program from SHOOT (see Chapter 2) and EEL exemplifies this condition. EEL is a shape manipulation Logo interface, with which Miriam was fimiliar. A child moves a shape by keying direction characters (U for up, D for down, etc.). Shape size is altered by keying B for bigger and S for smaller. Miriam was familiar with EEL. These command characters were incompatible with Logo language. In DRAW+, a new and Logo-compatible interface with the same system appearance, shapes were located by presetting the turtle's location before invoking the shape-drawing procedure by name. Miriam understood my explanation of this difference, but even after assigning input values to specify the shape's size, she asked, 'How do I make it bigger? B?' How does such incorrect advice get suppressed? Just raising that question focusses attention on the assumed impermeability of microveiw boundaries, even with respect to ancestors. We will return to this question after discussing a second kind of confusion.

This second major confusion, less essential perhaps in respect of structural genesis but nonetheless more pervasive, might be described as linguistic, but I choose not so to describe it. I will call it *nominal* (by which I mean name-based) confusion. There are many more things in the the world and relations among things than there are words. The mind experiences more things more differently than it can remember words of the common tongue. Because they must represent more than a single meaning, words cannot be unique labels for slots in perspectives. This situation is the source of nominal confusion, but it is more, much more. Let me return to a specific example before we plunge on to the theme of nominal confusion and its relation to concept formation.

Both the knowledges constructed from Miriam's use of SHOOT (a game) and MPOLY (a design program) were among the earliest of The Intimate Study. Each was a world disparate from the other. In both, *angle* was the dominant focus of attention. The turtle was aligned with the target by turning through an *angle* as a precondition to using the SHOOT procedure. For every use of SHOOT, several turns through angles were common. In the SHOOT world, turning RIGHT 90 meant turning to the right a little bit, 90 times. The question to resolve was one of scale, how much was 'a little bit'. In the designs of the MPOLY programs, there was a whole lot of turning going on, but it is beyond imagining that Miriam connected her own RIGHT 90, when we played at SHOOT, with the quickly generated, massively complex, and incomprehensible designs of MPOLY. She sought to establish correspondences between input angle values and specific designs judged attractive. We call both these things 'angle', but Miriam could not possibly have seen them as 'angle' with a common meaning. We ask, 'Was Miriam confused by this usage?' 'A ridiculous question!' any critic might reply. 'Every child solves this puzzle of multiple meanings at an early age and wends his tortuous way through the accidents of language history to the concepts important in his world'. Precisely so — but — each new occurrence of a meaning is another confusion to be puzzled out. We may own a concept of *angle* which permits us to unify these two diverse experiences of turning into a single abstract description, but a person who owns no such concept can not be other than puzzled by the particular problem. The point is this: before it exists, there can be no influence from an abstract description, even to the essential minimum guidance of proposing what sorts of features of a situation ought to be explored to solve a particular problem or to make sense of experience. I propose, however, that the genetic path of experience and the confusion of multiple meanings of words are fecund and complementary influences through which the language-capable mind raises itself to the plateau of abstract meanings where the language of its culture has committed the vocabulary.

Let me turn a trifle analytic. The nomenclature of the language is not perverse. Usually, if two things you fail to see as related are similarly named, the naming indicates that your perspective relating to both name applications is not so developed as the cultural standard. Of course, occassionally the commonality is an accident. In this latter case, when confusion arises implicating a word of multiple meanings, the accident (that culturally embedded nominal confusion) provides the mental contexts which permit disambiguation. Consider this simple joke, the first pun Miriam claims to have invented.[20]

> Miriam: What should you do if your toe falls off?
> Victim: I don't know.
> Miriam: Call a tow-truck.

Here the disambiguation of meanings in her mind is highlighted by a joke as two uses of /to/ which must not be permitted to interact (except in this new mode of relation, punning). The interaction prohibition of multiple word meanings is an argument why the separation of microviews is necessary. It is also the most pervasive and natural example of a situation calling for that hypothetical process in concept formation advanced by Winston (1975), the substitution of emphatic forms for particular descriptions. The initial description is one of an

---

20 'Learning and making jokes', R. Lawler, 1978 (unpublished). The point of the example does not depend upon her claim being true, in its strongest sense.

object; the last is one of a concept. The change from one to the other is defined as substituting a proscription or prescription for a description. In Winston's words:

> I want to make clear a distinction between a description of a particular scene and a model of a concept. A model is like an ordinary description in that it carries information about the various parts of a configuration, but a model is more in that it exhibits and indicates those relations and properties that must and must not be in evidence in any example of the concept involved. (Winston, 1975, p. 185.)

The language-capable mind receives significant culturally given guidance through the necessity of applying abstract names to varieties of entities in particular experiences. The nominal confusions derived from abstract nomenclature provide exactly the kind of focus needed for learning concepts based on the modification of descriptions. Further, the embedding of labelled slots in descriptions constructed through specific experience of the application of the label in varied contexts constrains to a manageable number the possible hypotheses of a generalized concept through the requirement that those hypotheses be coherent with the existing microview perspectives.

In contrast with Winston's focus on learning through a prototype and a series of acceptable variants and 'near-misses', the description of knowledge as disparate microviews of thought focusses on 'far-misses'; for example, on *angle* encountered in SHOOT and *angle* encountered in MPOLY. Good numbers for one world are rarely good for the other. In effect, the different worlds where the same name would be culturally assigned as a slot label must not relate lest confusion result. But paradoxically, the commitment of the language to a common label argues that there exists some perspective within which the lable used in these disparate worlds constructed from experience can be seen as *the* name for a generalized and unified concept.

The importance of not relating is profound. Winston, focussing on a crisp formulation of learning through near-misses, did not mark the asymmetry of the emphatic and negative emphatic forms. In particular, a *must-not-confound* link between two descriptions distinguishes two entities from each other without the necessity of specifying a relation-based on some common abstracted character. This is important in avoiding logical complications. But more important is the illumination the negative emphatic form brings to the question of microview boundaries. It is sufficient for the separation of microviews that all slots which are potentially confusable be blocked by *must-not-confound* links. Such refinement is surely a powerful tool for controlling confusion in exquisitely articulated microviews of knowledge. With less developed microviews, as in the mind of a child or of an adult beyond his familiar experiences, other means of confusion control must be employed. The most common of these is reasoning through actions performed on specific objects. Undeveloped microviews, without a concrete system accessible for anchoring thought to, will suffer frequent confusion through inappropriate demon interruption. If a microview's boundary system of *must-not-confound* links is imperfect or not rigid, analogical reasoning will be pervasive. If the boundary system is strong and the microview well articulated, analogical reasoning will be constrained, but it will also be controlled in a second sense; it will appear in the guise of reasoned problem deformation guided by the relaxation of *must-not-confound* links. A third character of the *must-not-confound* link between confusable entities is that its very existence is a goad, perhaps even a puzzled demon. The fact that one observes an empirical suppression of confusion is an implicit criticism of his mind. Microview boundaries purchase coherence by admitting ignorance, one's incompetence of mind. Thus learning, as it unifies disparate knowledges, is not merely an increase in power; it is a personal victory.

Relating this subject to other studies

The general purpose of this appendix is to broaden the characterization of Miriam's intellectual performances in such a way as will permit comparison and contrast with others. Many of us have observed young children learning to read and to write. For that reason I include material on these themes here, although it is not integrated with other studies of this book. The cognitive profile which follows the language-oriented studies will help to place Miriam with respect to a series of well-known experiments from the Piagetian repertoire. The appendix closes with a detailed analysis of Miriam's performance on an IQ test. The value of this material is less to place Miriam on a linear scale with other children (though it does do so) than it is to relate her performance on that test to the particulars of her experience.

READING SKILLS

Her learning to read was something, as I recall it, pretty much of Miriam's own doing. Of course, she was read to and we played word games at our supper table, but Miriam early showed an interest in reading as her brother was first learning to do so at school. While he played with sets of 3 × 5 cards of words with common terminal digraphs (e.g. *gun, sun, fun*), Miriam also learned her letters and some of the sounds the consonants make. Miriam's view of her learning to read is this:

> Miriam: I learned how to read from *Hop on Pop*.
> Bob: You did? How did that teach you to read? I don't understand.
> Miriam: I started with the easy books and went to the harder ones.

My recollection is a little different, that she learned to read by sight a large number of words (about 100) from a set of cards I made containing all the words of *Put me in the zoo*. I recall a period of two weeks or so in which Miriam gradually mastered those words, after which she was vastly surprised to find herself capable of reading her brother's first reading book. Upon completing that book, in the fall of 1976 (age 5; 6), Miriam declared herself a reader.

About the same time, Robby's interest in the Second World War impelled him into a range of material Miriam could not approach. So the reading to them of common bedtime stories ceased and each began to pursue his interests. Miriam typically brought home from the library books by Sid Hoff (*Thunderhoof, Who will be my friends?*), and read them to herself or anyone who would listen. Instead of sleeping when she first went to bed, Miriam carried with her a stack of *Peanuts* cartoon books and read them till she fell asleep.

Summary: reading level at 6;0;18

The second grade series of Dick and Jane books seemed appropriate for assessing Miriam's reading ability and proved so.[1] In this examination, Miriam read fluently and with good comprehension stories from each of the three sections of the book. Her execution of exercises from the companion *Think and do* book showed her awareness of how context selects between potentially ambiguous meanings of words and how idiomatic meanings of phrases dominate those of words.

Miriam's typical word-level error was substitution of a context-compatible word with similar initial and terminal characters for words she could not read. At the sentence and paragraph level, her lack of knowledge of punctuation's function led her into inappropriate divisions of running text. Such limitations, till overcome, would prevent her from reading more difficult material.

The material and the level of challenge engaged Miriam's interest. The same evening at home she did exercises from the workbook and informed me afterwards. Over the next several days, Miriam read us parents bedtime stories from the book and took it to school for reading to her friends in kindergarten.

Even though I do not attempt any significant integration of this material with the four primary analyses of this book, I conclude this summary with a sketch of her performance at six and a half years.

Summary: reading level at 6;5;16

During the six months of The Intimate Study, Miriam's reading was dominated, at her own choice, by *Pogo* and *Peanuts* books (her mother owns an extensive collection of both). I could not, on the basis of her casual reading, judge what would best test Miriam's capability at 6;6. When we discussed the problem, Miriam characterized *Friends old and new* as 'easy-bezy.' 'Was it so back in April?' I inquired. Miriam answered that the book had been pretty hard for her to read earlier. We agreed that the solution to my problem was for her to select

1 *Friends old and new* (Book 2, Part 1 of the New Basic Reading Program, published by Scott, Foresman and Company) contains simple stories; the companion *Think and do* book provides exercises in areas such as inference and context.

the book for her final reading evaluation. At an educational materials supply store, Miriam checked out the sixth and fifth grade readers, declared them too hard. Examining the fourth and third grade readers, she selected *More road to follow*[2] (a book for the second half of third grade) as having a level of difficulty comparable to the book she used six months previously. Her judgment was verified subsequently; she proved able to read the book but showed some difficulty. The outstanding problems were with syllabification and phonetic pronunciation of unfamilar words. I conclude that Miriam's skill level had advanced by three half-grades during the six months of our research. This is a significant advance about which I intend to make *no* strong claims. Although it is reasonable to say that 'computer reading' shared centre stage with *Pogo* and *Charlie Brown* during the period of development, it would be rash to claim any special impact on her reading skill, as the following incident suggests. While I was passing through a room where she was watching TV, I was stopped by Miriam's question 'Daddy, what does choreography mean?' Miriam had been reading movie credits. This extreme of lexical exploration argues that she was reading all the time.

INTRODUCING WRITING WITH A COMPUTER[3]

Writing before The Intimate Study

Miriam didn't write much before she was six, in any standard sense of composition. There were, however, two kinds of activities in which she engaged that can be seen as the precursors of the stories and letters she wrote later. One was a kindergarten activity where the teacher or one of her helpers asked a child to tell the story of a picture the child had drawn. She then wrote the story on a piece of paper and attached it to the picture. My favorite of the genre:

> It's a sunny day in my picture.
> People are sailing on the river.
> A boy and a girl are happy together.

In the year preceding The Intimate Study, a large portion of Miriam's drawings took the form of 'presents' she made for others. A typical example of this second precursor is this: after drawing a picture of 'football Fred' from Ed Emberley's *Drawing book of faces,* Miriam prepared it as a gift for her playmate Brian. Miriam wrote at the side 'football Fred' and at the top 'To Brian/Love/Miriam'. (The '/' indicates a new line.) Miriam spoke of such drawings as presents many times. One formal element of those notes reflects that character. Each typically bore a 'tag' with conjoined salutation and closing.

Writing stories

The central idea of the writing experiences in The Intimate Study was to segregate the content and structure of writing by use of a computer language interface.

---

2 Book 3, Part 2 of The New Basic Reading Program published by Scott, Foresman and Company.

3 A longer version of this analysis appeared as an article in *SIGCUE*, July, 1980.

The strategy embodied in the idea of a computer language interface is to pre-establish the structure of a piece of text and to form the content of the text from the writer's direct expression; the final end, to be hoped for if not achieved, is that the writer in reading and re-reading her own composition will first perceive the structure vaguely as an envelope surrounding her content and later as a specific form into which she can cast her content for its effective communication.

Effective natural learning requires that material to be learned relate simply to the learner's past, personal experiences. I was fortunate in being able to present Miriam, as a generalized story structure, a specific joke-script by which she had recently victimized me:

Miriam: Would you like to hear a short story?
Bob: Sure.
Miriam: Once upon a time, the end. That's a *short* story.

Through the WRITER interface, Miriam encountered a story template whose first line was 'Once upon a time', and whose last was 'The end'. In between these two lines, Miriam was able to interpolate any story lines she might wish. The WRITER interface generated a procedure whose execution would display on the video terminal the text of the story (after which it could be simply copied to a printer). When I introduced the WRITER interface, Miriam objected of the template story 'That's not any nice story!' Agreeing with her, I was able to argue that we had a beginning and an end, all we had to do was write the middle part.

Miriam confronted two major difficulties: choosing what to write, and ignorance of spelling. The content of Miriam's early stories is idiosyncratic:[4]

        P STORY
ONCE UPON A TIME
P WAS TIRED OF FOLLOWING Q.
HE STARTED AT THE BEGINNING OF THE ALPHABET.
PABCDEFGHIJKLMNOQRSTUVWXYZ.
THE END.

My prejudices would have judged this P STORY as uninteresting to a child. But it did engage Miriam, as is witnessed by her later claim of authorship when she showed the text to Robby and he said it was nice. In the first month of our study, she made several minor variants of this story.

I found Miriam's elaborations of 'P STORY' sterile and boring and intervened in major ways to alter her writing. First I removed the spelling burden by taking on the role of amanuensis and put the composition task in an oral context by introducing a variation of WRITER as a special tool for writing out the text of songs. While Miriam recited her favorite kindergarten song ('Little Rabbit Foofoo/Hopping through the forest/Scooping up the field mice/And bopping

---

4 This is not to say it is unrelated to common activities among bright, adventuresome children. At the age of 4;3, having mastered typing the alphabet, Miriam undertook the elaborate variation of typing it backward. Such an activity is not at all uncommon. See Simon and Simon (1973).

them on the head,/. . .'), I keyed the text and produced printed output which Miriam copied and shared with her kindergarten classmates the following day. In the next writing session, I followed Miriam's lead. She composed orally — and I keyed at her dictation — a version of the Goldilocks story as a play-script for her kindergarten classmates.[5]

The most fully developed story

These two interventions liberated Miriam's conception of what it was possible for a computer-written story to be like. The next week she asked to write another story. This story, SCURRY, was her most developed story made during The Intimate Study.

> SCURRY
> ONCE UPON A TIME,
> WE GOT A DOG NEAR VALENTINE'S DAY.
> AND WE DID NOT KNOW WHAT TO CALL IT
> AFTER A WEEK WE DECIDED TO CALL IT SCURRY.
> AND WE FIGHTED OVER IT.
> THE END.

The protocol of her composing SCURRY shows Miriam with a much more liberal conception of what a story may be but with her production of text still much encumbered by the need for extensive spelling advice.[6]

Effects beyond the computer laboratory

How much of this script became Miriam's property, in the specific sense that she used it spontaneously? Two incidents of succeeding days showed the **WRITER** template used outside the laboratory:

> Robby called me from Miriam's bedroom: 'Dad, come see the puppet show'. They have played with, even made, hand puppets for a while and enjoy giving shows — whose typical script has been 'Hello. My name is Owl. Goodbye'.
>
> Walking through the door unsuspecting, I found the children were playing 'Ambush' — both were lying under covers on the top bunk. They cried *'Bam! Bam!'* as I walked through the door. Riotous laughter.
>
> Suffering only flesh wounds, I managed to return their fire, then said I thought it a dirty trick for them to call me to see a puppet show and shoot me. Miriam responded, 'This was our puppet show:
>
> > Once upon a time,
> > There were two guns.
> > Bang. Bang.
> > The end'.

5 Miriam's script proved of limited use (the other actresses couldn't read), but the next day in kindergarten and subsequently when a friend came to play at Logo, the children dutifully carried their copies about as they were 'supposed to'.

6 She asked the spelling of these words: got, near, valentine's, know, what, call, after, week, decided, Scurry, fighted.

Her joke was a spontaneous expression of the **WRITER** program's story format. Her use of it in this explanatory way shows her recognition that it was a shared model of story structure. That same evening, Miriam, who had recently been making 'late mother's day presents', brought me an 'early father's day present'. The present was a drawing of one of her typical flowers with this story:

> Once upon a time,
> A flower was stitting on a hill.
> And someone came and pick it.
> The end.

Miriam could not spell the words, I was told, and had dictated the story to her brother after drawing the picture.

Long-term effects

Miriam recalls writing no stories at all during her two years of public school after The Intimate Study. Before entering third grade in a different program, she took an entrance examination which required her to write a composition. She selected the theme *My Dog* from a list of ten very general suggestions. Not only the theme, but her initial text as well shows the influence of the earlier composition. Her episodic continuation beyond the earlier Scurry material derived directly from the requirement that the composition be one hundred words long. Other compositions as well show the residual influence of the earlier story script. More importantly, that experience provided a shared, albeit simple, idea of story structure which permitted her understanding my structural criticism of stories she wrote.

My conclusion is that Miriam's early experience with the **WRITER** interface at Logo left her with a stereotypical form for short story and even default thematic elements (which were easily overridden if occasion required it). Further, I speculate that the early presentation of a form with a beginning, middle, and end permitted Miriam's comprehension of my criticism of the form of one story, as shown by the presence of a summarizing conclusion in her next composition.

Computer use and the simple procedures I wrote for her were tools for introducing Miriam to writing. Critics might argue that such an approach as I used is entirely cosmetic, disguising the child's real ignorance with a covering of some other person's knowledge, mechanically reproduced. However reasonable such criticism, its focus is more on the finished product than on the genetic intent of the tool. A programmed machine permits presenting the structure of written material as conventional scripts into which a child can insert personalized content. The intention is to engage the child in the creation of nearly conventional artifacts through which activity she might come to perceive what the organization is, typically, and what the significance of the elements is. These observations and others on her letter writing witness Miriam's ability to learn in such an environment.

A COGNITIVE PROFILE AT 6;0

The Intimate Study began with a series of quasi-standard experiments. These had two general purposes: first, to provide means for 'calibrating' information about Miriam's knowledge and learning with more general studies in the literature; second, a subset of these experiments were intended to provide a baseline against which I could explore the extent to which her computer experience might alter Miriam's inclination to think in a more formal fashion.[7]

One to one correspondence (Age: 6;0;10)

Once the subject makes a judgment that two sets have the same number of beads, the experimenter determines whether or not the subject changes that judgment when the beads in one set are moved closer together or further apart.[8]

Miriam did not change her judgement as the configuration was changed. She exhibited operational correpondence with lasting equivalence despite rearrangement of members of the sets. In addition to justification through the standard argument 'you didn't take anything away', she invoked the equivalence of the residuums of the two sets as supporting evidence.

Conservation of continuous quantity (Age: 6;0;10)

The experimenter gets the child to concur that two quantities of liquid are the same. Pouring those same volumes of liquid into containers of different shape and into multiple containers, he explores whether or not the child knows that the quantity of substance remains unchanged.[9]

Miriam's judgments show her a conserver of continuous quantity. The justifications she offers exhibit arguments of compensation, history, and reversibility.

Conservation of substance: Clay (Age: 6;0: 12)

After gaining the subject's concurrence that two balls of clay weigh the same (using a balance), the experimenter changes their shape and inquires whether or not they still weigh the same after the deformations.[10]

Miriam expects weight to be conserved despite transformations of a material's shape and its division into pieces. Her conviction that weight will be conserved is not firm (she does not 'know' that it will be conserved but will so venture a 'guess').

---

7 These experiments were audiotaped and videotaped. The protocols have been analyzed in detail, but only summary descriptions are presented here. The standard experiments are presented first, followed by those focussed on formal thought, and lastly by others of a more idiographic character.

8 References: Jean Piaget, *The Child's Concept of Number*, Chapter 3; J. Flavell, *The Developmental Psychology of Jean Piaget*, p. 313.

9 References: Jean Piaget, *The Child's Concept of Number*, Chapter 1; J. Flavell, *The Developmental Psychology of Jean Piaget*.

10 Reference: J. Flavell, *The Developmental Psychology of Jean Piaget*, p. 299.

Conservation of displacement volume (Age: 6;0;19)

The experiment tests whether or not the child knows that the volume of a liquid displaced by a solid does not vary when the shape of the same solid is changed. This conservation is typically a late achievement of the concrete period.[11]

Miriam did not expect the displacement volume of an object to be conserved when its shape was changed by deformation or breaking into fragments. She did expect immersion of an object in water to raise the water level in the container, qualitatively at least, in proportion to its size.

Notions of movement and velocity (Age: 6;0;12)

By asking the subject to judge a race between two small dolls, the experimenter determines the extent to which the child distinguishes between velocity and the length of paths covered in equal times.[12]

At six, Miriam conceives of movement at different velocities in a framework of homogeneous time. She distinguishes between duration and extension in space. It is probable that this distinction recently became operational for her; it is possible the insight occurred during the experiment itself.

Combinations of bead families (Age: 6;0;14)

The experimenter probes the subject's spontaneous use of systematic procedures in constructing the combinations of small numbers of objects taken two and three at a time. Systematicity is characteristic of children at the threshold of formal operational thought (eleven or twelve years).[13]

Miriam's combinatorial skill, as seen in this experiment, was clearly pre-operational. She discovered neither all the two-bead nor all the three-bead combinations. Whatever small amount of systematicity may be inferred from the sequence of bead family formation may equally plausibly be explained as an artifact of very simple, local transformations. A close analysis of the protocol detail permits the argument that she failed to distinguish between black and dark brown beads. For this reason, the conclusions of the experiment on combinations of shape families is more dependable.

Combinations of shape families (Age: 6;0;18)

The experimenter probes the subject's spontaneous use of systematic procedures in constructing the combinations of small numbers of objects taken two and three at a time. Systematicity is characteristic of children at the threshold of formal operational thought (eleven or twelve years).[14]

11 Reference: J. Flavell, *The Developmental Psychology of Jean Piaget*, p. 299.
12 Reference: J. Flavell, *The Developmental Psychology of Jean Piaget*, p. 320.
13 Reference: Piaget and Inhelder, *The Origin of the Idea of Chance in Children*, Chapter 7.
14 Reference: Piaget and Inhelder, *The Origin of the Idea of Chance in Children*, Chapter 7. The experiment conducted was a superficial modification of Piaget's task, with a variety of shapes substituted for colored beads.

Miriam's assembly of shape combinations shows characteristics of systematicity expected in the Piaget–Inhelder stage II. Restriction of this systematicity to the generation of families and the failure to apply it to the exclusion of duplicate family combinations argue that Miriam's apparent systematicity may be an artifact of a simple pair generation procedure unrelated to any global understanding of the task.[15]

Multiple seriation (Age: 6;0;21)

The experimenter explores first whether or not a child uses seriation in more than a single dimension to organize collections of objects and second, whether or not the child can use an array structure to locate a specific object defined by two characteristics.[16]

Miriam did not spontaneously seriate a collection of 32 leaves by both size and color. When asked to put her initial four color-based collections of leaves in better order, she ranged the leaves from small to large within each collection. She was able to make use of the doubly ordered array to locate specifically described leaves directly.

Implicit multiplication with the balance (Age: 6;0;18)

The experimenter probes the subject's problem solving with a balance to determine the extent to which the child appreciates the implicit multiplication of length times weight along the balance arms.[17]

Miriam's comprehesion of relation between weight and distance, interpretable as a set of simple procedures, was rudimentary. On this task, her performance is characteristic of substate IIA (concrete operations on weight and distance with intuitive regulations) as described by Inhelder and Piaget.

Abstractness of the object concept (Age: 6;1;10)

The experimenter determines the abstractness of the child's object concept. The subject uses weights to cause bending of metal rods clamped in a stable apparatus. There are four dimensions of variation in the flexibility of the metal rods used in this experiment (material, length, thickness, and cross-sectional shape).[18] The experiment attempts to discover whether the subject analyzes the behavior of individual rods in terms of these four dimensions of variation or not. Only with such a feature analysis can one develop the systematic procedures in this domain characteristic of formal thinking.[19]

---

15 More detail on her performance can be found Chapter 3, 'The equilibraton of cognitive structures'.
16 Reference: Piaget and Inhelder, *The Early Growth of Logic in The Child*, Chapter 12.
17 Reference: Inhelder and Piaget, *The Growth of Logical Thinking from Childhood to Adolescence*, Chapter 11.
18 Reference: Inhelder and Piaget, *The Growth of Logical Thinking from Childhood to Adolescence*, Chapter 3.
19 For an example of how computer experience might affect such mental abilities, see the article 'Extending a Powerful Idea' (Lawler, 1982).

Miriam's performance on this task placed her at the concrete operation level (substage IIA) as described by Inhelder and Piaget. Her understanding that added weights must be the same when comparing two rods and her predictions based on 'skinniness' put her clearly in substage IIA. She showed none of the factor multiplication characteristic of substage IIB.

The most striking characteristic of her predictions was her willingness to subject them entirely to empirical test. For example, though she believed that skinnier rods bent more, she was willing to consider it possible that a fatter rod might bend more than a skinnier one. Her conviction of the dependability of her judgments was weak, with one idiosyncratic exception: she was convinced that color was not implicated in flexibility. If her primary conception of color was as a superficial property, not an intrinsic one of some substance, her adamant refusal to assign it an effective role would be comprehensible. Miriam did not have an abstract object concept. Commitment to an abstract object concept requires a conviction that characteristic features of objects interact in a lawful way. With such a view, existing objects are instances of possibilities resulting from the specification of their interacting features. For Miriam, those bending rods were each unique objects which exhibited certain properties able to provide guidance for hypotheses about their behavior. But guidance is not the law-like regularity which the abstract object concept leads one to expect.

Nonstandard interpretations
Class inclusion relations (Age 6;0;11)
The experimenter explores how the subject deals with problems of class inclusion.[20] Younger children may judge, for example, that a collection of five horses and three cows contains more horses than animals. More mature children will not make this non-standard judgment.

Miriam was capable of handling the class inclusion relation. When the general term referring to the including class was modified by a universal quantifier (for example, 'all together'), Miriam concluded the intent of the question relates to inclusion. Otherwise, she apparently assumed the intended use of the general term was for disjunctive reference to a secondary class too variegated for specification.

The phenomenon Genevan psychologists uncovered with this experiment is robust, but precisely what its significance may be is not clear.[21] The experiment was designed to probe a subject's comprehension of class inclusion relations. But the material of Miriam's particular experiment may be more richly viewed in terms of another issue, how a child uses specific and generic labels.

Miriam's ability to grasp inclusion relations does not imply that all her applications of general terms, or even her preferred applications, are for specifying inclusion relations. For example, she showed in this experiment an unexpected and intense disinclination to use a generic name when she knew a specific name

20 References: Piaget and Inhelder, *The Early Growth of Logic in the Child*, pp. 100–110; J. Flavell, *The Developmental Psychology of Jean Piaget*, pp. 303–309.
21 More recently, this task has been dropped from the repertoire of Genevan experiments and other tasks substituted for it. See *Learning and the Development of Cognition* Inhelder, Sinclair, and Bovet (1974).

which could be applied. Her specificity bias was so extreme that Miriam considered it a mistake to use a term such as flower when one knows that a thing is 'really' a tulip. Although admitting that tulips should be included if one planted a flower garden, she denied that tulips are flowers. Although adults may use general terms primarily for specifying hierarchical inclusions, this does not imply that such is their primary use by children. A more important use of general terms, for children, may be as default labels for classes of objects when the specific name is unknown.

The volume of solid objects (Age: 6;0;12)

The experimenter probes the subject's ability in logical multiplication by asking the child to construct a building of volume equal to an exemplar but on a different base; thus, height must compensate for differences between the product of the two other dimensions.[22]

Miriam's performance on this experiment was atypical. She was instructed not to count the component blocks of which larger shapes were made, but did so anyway. Her heavy dependence on counting and its adequate use prevented engaging the issue of the logical multiplication of spatial dimensions.[23]

Separating translation and rotation in backspinning a ball (Age: 6;0;18)

The experimenter explores the subject's ability to separate conceptually two contrary motions. A backspinning ping-pong ball on a smooth table skids forward until the spin countervails and the ball returns to the person who propelled it.[24]

Although the phenomenon was completely new to her, Miriam easily succeeded in backspinning a ping-pong ball. She found the phenomenon very engaging and showed and described it to other children in the laboratory. Her explanations of the phenomenon are those Piaget classifies as stage IB. Although she described the motions of the ball in detail, Miriam was not able to provide an explanation of why the ball first went away and later returned.

When challenged with a proffered 'magical' explanation, Miriam rejected it, then proposed that there was something inside which got 'wound up'. She then explained further; this interpretation came from observing an elastic-driven airplane belonging to her brother which would fly in one direction and occasionally circle back.

Miriam was clearly far from conceiving of the phenomenon as an adult would. She distinguished between the ball's rotational and translational motions and remarked early that the ball skipped on the outbound path and rolled on returning. Convinced that the ball's action derived from what one did to it, and having observed these specific critical features, how could she possibly fail to understand backspinning? Miriam did not attempt to explain backspinning by analyzing the action's features of which she was aware. Instead, she explained the phenomenon through analogy to another situation with which she was

22 Reference: J. Flavell, *The Developmental Psychology of Jean Piaget*, pp. 341–342.
23 See question 2 of the set for age 10 years in the Binet test. Miriam's performance on this Piagetian task sheds light on her unusual performance for the Binet test item.
24 Reference: Piaget, *The Grasp of Consciousness*, Chapter 3.

familiar. She even speculated that an unseen mechanism, analogous to the elastic band in the airplane, caused a comparable result in this case. Her theory was pre-analytical, in character more like Peirce's abduction than any combination of inductive and deductive processes. *If Miriam was a little scientist investigating the interesting phenomena of her world, she was less like Galied – or Aristotle – than like Empedocles, who explained the world as compounded out of diverse, familiar elements.*

BINET TEST at 6;1;17

Miriam had known for over a week that our next trip into Boston would be for taking a test. I had introduced her to the idea with the explanation that nearly everyone takes such a test some time and that she was simply taking this test earlier than most other children. So, after kindergarten and a rousing two hours with her play group, Miriam put on a dress and we took the Green Line into the centre of Boston.

Miriam had earlier expressed concern that she didn't know how to get ready for this test. (The only other test formally so defined to her was having her ears checked. She apparently does not think of our experiments at Logo as being tests.) This concern surfaced again as we waited for the trolley car. 'Daddy, what kind of questions did they ask you?' I could recall only one question from an early intelligence test (25 years before). 'They asked me who was the president before Franklin Roosevelt'. 'Who was it?' Thinking she now had the inside track, Miriam asked who was the president before Carter, and before him, and before that one. We stopped at Eisenhower when the trolley came.

It was a beautiful day as we strolled through the Common, stopped at an ice-cream store, and continued to the testing centre. Miriam was clearly content and relaxed when she went with the tester. She was also relaxed and pleased with herself when she had finished.

Although we needed wait another week or two for a formal evaluation, the tester offered these general comments: since Miriam had just turned six, she began with the age six series; Miriam had to be confronted with questions from the eleven-year-old series before she failed to get at least some of them correct; they had never had to go through so many series with such a young child in their laboratory.[25]

In the evening before going to bed, I asked Miriam if the questions were difficult or easy and if she tried hard to answer them. She responded that she tried as hard as she could, but that some of the questions were just too difficult for her to answer. She was pleased with her performance – having overheard the comment about never having to go through so many tests with a child her age; she was proud that she 'did better than anybody else'. Her only gripe was that they didn't ask her a single question about the presidents.

25 The comments need to be put in this perspective: the laboratory (Tufts–New England Medical Centre Neuropsychology Section) typically is called upon to diagnose problems. Thus, they do not see as a matter of course so young a child as Miriam who has no immediately caused requirement for such a test.

ANALYSIS OF DETAIL DATA

Herein is presented the detailed material on the Binet test taken by Miriam at 6;1;17. I have collated a description of the questions Miriam confronted[26] with her responses and their scoring. The detail data are followed by the summary evaluation of the test administrators and by my observations thereon.

Miriam took the examination under ideal conditions and by her own later report tried hard to do her best. The test had been scheduled four days earlier but had been rescheduled at the request of the administrators. This had the effect of changing Miriam's chronological age from 6;1 to 6;2. The test series began at age six because that was Miriam's chronological age and there were no problems suggesting an earlier test age would be more appropriate.

Age 6 test

Question 1: This question is a vocabularly test whose result is reflected in the year scores for ages 6, 8, and 10 although given once. The standard question format is this: 'I want to find out how many words you know. Listen, and when I say a word, you tell me what it means. What is an orange?' The question format is varied over a small repertoire: 'What does . . . mean? Tell me what a . . . is'. If the child's response is unclear, a simple request for further information is made. The test appears to have been discontinued after four sequential responses of 'I don't know'.

Test word	Score	Response
orange	+	a kind of fruit
envelope	+	something you mail things with
straw	+	something you drink with
puddle	+	you splash around in it
tap	−	I don't know
gown	−	I don't know
roar	+	a lion roars
eyelash	+	[Miriam points to hers]
Mars	−	I don't know
juggler	+	someone who juggles balls
scorch	−	I don't know
lecture	+	something where people talk
skill	+	got a way to do something that is hard to do
brunette	−	I don't know
muzzle	−	I don't know
haste	−	I don't know
peculiarity	−	I don't know

Total 9+

---

26 From Stanford–Binet Intelligence Scale, Manual for the Third Revision, Terman and Merrill, 1960. The test was administered by a psychologist at the Tufts–New England Medical Center Neuropsychology Unit; the generosity of the Director of that unit, Homer Reed, made it possible for Miriam to take the test. The raw examination data were recorded in a Record Booklet, Form L-M, published by Houghton Mifflin Company.

Commentary

Several specific points are worthy of note. Miriam makes a consistent distinction between what she knows and what she is willing to speculate about. In the experiments performed at Project Logo, where her first response was 'I don't know', a request that she guess frequently brought forth speculations as often correct as not. The pursuit of such responses lies, of course, outside the standardized procedure which the designers of the Stanford–Binet test believe is essential to its validity (cf. Terman and Merrill, 1960, p. 47).

Driving home from Logo yesterday, Miriam, in the back seat of the car, was making up a story. It was about a family who lived under a glass dome and always had to have oxygen tanks strapped on their backs whenever they went outside... because they lived on Mars. Further information: Miriam enjoys using my slide projector. She primarily shows for herself pictures of her and her brother when they were babies. I have an extensive collection of slides showing views of the Earth, the Moon, and Mars made during space flights. Miriam has seen them all several times. How could Miriam not recognize 'Mars'? My dialect is Philadelphian, purified by a longstanding habit of precise enunciation. My wife hails from northern New Jersey. Escaping the influence of the New York accents, her speech is similar to mine. I find difficulty in comprehending those who talk of buying their groceries in the /Stah Mahket/ and get there by /cah/. Miriam might well not recognize Mars after its vowel has lost the 'r' coloration.

Miriam's special involvement in Logo at MIT has made the words 'juggler,' 'lecture', and 'skill' salient for her. She has attended a number of Seymour Papert's lectures. I, and several friends, know how to juggle. One friend, Howard Austin, had completed a doctoral thesis on physical skills, of which his prototype was juggling.

The comments do not, of course, argue that Miriam would not have learned such words otherwheres, but they do exhibit one way in which her engagement in the Logo subculture at MIT might have biased, entirely accidentally, her performance on this task. In other circumstances one might speculate her performance range could have been from a low of 6 to a high of 10. The former would reduce calculated mental age by two months; the latter could leave it unchanged.

Question 2: The standard form of the question is 'What is the difference between . . .'

Comparands	Score	Response
bird and dog	+	bird flies but a dog runs
slipper and boot	+	slipper is something you wear inside and a boot you wear outside
wood and glass	+	glass you can see through but wood you can't

Question 3: The experimenter shows Miriam cards with mutilated pictures and asks: 'What is gone in this picture? or 'What part is gone?' Miriam observed 5 of 5 missing parts.

Question 4: The experimenter places a pile of blocks before Miriam and asks her to place a specific number on a piece of paper: 'Give me . . . blocks. Put them here'. Miriam gave the correct numbers on request 4 of 4 times.

Question 5: Miriam was asked to complete this set of analogical statements:

Statement	*Completion*
A table is made of wood; a window of . . .	glass
A bird flies; a fish . . .	swims
The point of a cane is blunt;	
the point of a knife is . . .	sharp
An inch is short; a mile is . . .	long

Question 6: The experimenter shows the child the maze and says: 'This little boy lives here, and here [pointing] is the schoolhouse. The little boy wants to go to school the shortest way without getting off the sidewalk. Here is the sidewalk [pointing]. Show me the shortest way. Mark it with your pencil, but don't go off the sidewalk. Start here and take the little boy to school the shortest way'. The second and third maze problems are introduced similarly but in a shorter form of reference.

Conclusion

Miriam was judged to have completed all the tests at the age six level satisfactorily. The standard procedure continues in an attempt to establish three conclusions: first, the highest age question series the child completes — this is the basal age; second, the age at which the child fails to complete any questions — this is the ceiling age; third, that scattering of questions which the child answers satisfactorily despite having failed to answer questions at that age grade.

Age 7 test

Question 1: The experimenter confronts the child with a series of pictures which contain absurdities and asks: 'What is funny (or foolish) about that picture?'

Picture	*Score*	*Response*
man with umbrella	+	the man is getting wet, isn't holding the umbrella over him
man with saw	+	he's sawing upside-down
dog and rabbit	+	dog is trying to catch the rabbit but he's going the wrong way
man and woman sitting in rain	+	they're sitting outside in rain, but they should go inside
cat and mice	+	mice drinking out of cat's dish

Question 2: The experimenter asks: 'In what way are . . . and . . . alike?'

Comparands	Score	Response
wood and coal	—	can't see through 'em; they're hard
apple and peach	+	round
ship and automobile	+	both move; big and heavy
iron and silver	—	I don't know

Commentary

The response on 'wood and coal' was scored negatively because the similarities apply too generally.[27]

Question 3: The experimenter points to a diamond shape and asks Miriam to 'make one just like this' in the booklet.

Question 4: The score of this question series is also used as a Question 5 at age level eight. The experimenter asks a series of questions and asks Miriam how she would respond to the situation.

Score	Question	Response
+	What should you do if you found on the streets of a city a three-year-old baby that was lost from its parents?	Look for its parents
+	What's the thing for you to do when you have broken something that belongs to someone else?	Buy them a new one
+	What's the thing for you to do when you are on your way to school and see that you are in danger of being late?	Run
+	What makes a sailboat move?	Wind
+	What's the thing to do if another girl hits you without meaning to do it?	Tell her that she should say she's sorry
—	What should you say when you are in a strange city and someone asks you how to find a certain address?	Read all the addresses in the telephone book

Question 5: The experimenter requests a series of opposite analogies by asking:

Question	Score	Response
The rabbit's ears are long; the rat's ears are . . .	+	short
Snow is white; coal is . . .	+	black
The dog has hair; the bird has . . .	—	wings
Wolves are wild; dogs are . . .	?	not

27 The response on 'iron and silver' is coherent with Miriam's lack of discrimination about metals as also witnessed in the 'Bending Rods' experiment. See 'Abstractness of the object concept' in Cognitive Profile at 6;0.

Commentary

Miriam's performance here was judged as meeting the seven year standard (2+). Scoring the fourth question is difficult. The directions of the scoring standard seem to focus strongly on the verbal antonym 'tame'. Miriam clearly recognized the logical opposition but did not produce the verbal form.

Question 6: The experimenter asks Miriam to repeat a string of five digits. She succeeds at the first attempt: 3 1 8 5 9.

Conclusion

Miriam was judged by the test administrators to have answered adequately all six questions at this age level.

Age 8 test

Question 1: Miriam's performance on the vocabulary test at age level six was adequate for her passing the eight year criterion.

Question 2: The experimenter reads Miriam a story and assesses her memory of it. She introduces the story thus: 'Here is a story about "The Wet Fall". Listen carefully while I read it because I shall ask you questions about it'. The experimenter reads:

The Wet Fall

   Once there was a little girl named Betty. She lived on a farm with her brother Dick. One day their father gave them a Shetland pony. They had lots of fun with it. One day when Dick was riding on it, the pony became frightened and ran away. Poor Dick fell into a ditch. How Betty laughed when she saw him. He was covered with mud from head to foot.

The experimenter asks these questions:

Score	Question	Response
+	What is the name of the story?	The Wet Fall
+	What was Betty's brother's name?	Dick
+	Where did they live?	On a farm
+	Who gave the pony to them?	Father
+	What did the pony do?	Got frightened
+	What happened?	Dick fell off of it

Question 3: The experimenter reads to Miriam a series of statements, then asks: 'What is foolish about that?'

Score	Statement	Response
+	A man had the flu twice. The first time it killed him but the second time he got well quickly.	'Cause he'd be dead from the first time!
+	Walter now has to write with his left hand because two years ago he lost both arms in an accident.	'Cause he doesn't have any arms

+	A man said, "I know a road from my house to the city which is downhill all the way to city and downhill all the way back home."	'Cause you can't go downhill both times. You have to go down once then back up.

Question 4: The experimenter asks: 'I'm going to name two things and I want you to tell me how they are alike and how they are different. In what way are . . . and . . . alike, and how are they different?'

Comparands	Score	Response
baseball and orange	+	Both are round. You can eat an orange but not a baseball.
airplane and kite	+	Both fly. Kites don't carry people; airplanes do.
ocean and river	−	Both blue and have water. You can't go on an ocean in a sailboat 'cause if you tip over something will eat you.
penny and quarter	−	Both round and money, but one's gold and one's brown.

Commentary

The test administrators scored Miriam's performance on this test as below criterion (3+) for age level eight. Not meeting this age level criterion implies the basal mental age for Miriam is seven. This interpretation is contestable, and in the light of the general interpretation I will offer subsequently, is worth contesting.

Consider first Miriam's response to the question comparing a penny and a quarter. What are the acceptable similarities and differences? What 'should' she have said? The following examples comes from Terman and Merrill, 1960, p. 166:

(1) They are money, and one is silver looking and the other looks like brass.
(2) Both round. A quarter is silver.
(3) Penny is red and quarter is gold − a quarter is silver and they're both round.

These show either being money or being round is acceptable as similarity. Miriam cited both. The judgment thus must hinge on differences. Miriam's specification does not say whether the penny is brown and the quarter gold or vice versa. Neither does example 1. But a quarter is not gold. Example (3) shows an initial description of a quarter as gold, subsequently corrected to 'silver'. No specific, non-silver description of a quarter is cited as acceptable . . . but could that be the only acceptable description? Ask yourself if a penny is red. We speak of copper loosely as a red metal. Is the difference between silver and gold greater than that between red and brown? I would incline to mark this response as adequate.

Miriam cites as similarities between river and ocean that both are blue and have water. This is an adequate specification for most of the examples cited in

Terman and Merrill (1960, pp. 165—166). The difference must, then, be what makes the difference. Every day we ride to MIT across the Charles, more often than not seeing sailboats and sculls as we proceed down Memorial Drive. I make jokes about this or that novice who's about to tip over. Miriam has asked me whether anything in the Charles will eat such an unfortunate. The children have both seen the sharks at the Mystic and New England Aquariums. They know that the Sound is home to sand sharks. I am sure Miriam has seen advertisements for 'Jaws'. Her response indicates a significant difference between river and ocean, albeit one not so forward in the general consciousness of the fifties (when these tests were described) as the shark-infested fears of today.

Question 5: When exposed to this task at age level six, Miriam performed well enough to meet the eight-year-old criterion.

Question 6: The experimenter asks Miriam: 'Name the days of the week for me'. Following her response, Miriam met two of three checks made in this form: 'What day comes before . . .?'

Conclusion

The test adminstrators scored Miriam's performance as meeting five of six criteria, therefore establishing seven as a basal age and crediting her with ten months additional as an addendum to the calculation of mental age. I suggest that a basal age of eight would more accurately reflect her performance.

Age 9 test

Question 1: The experimenter folds a piece of paper, makes a cut in it, and requests Miriam to draw a picture of what the piece would look like when flattened; the drawing should show both creases and holes. The test administrator marked Miriam's booklet as indicating she performed well enough to meet the criterion of age level nine for this question.

Question 2: The experimenter reads Miriam a set of verbal absurdities, then asks: 'What is foolish about that?'

Score	Statement	Response
—	Bill Jones' feet are so big he has to pull his trousers on over his head.	Then his feet get wet but his head doesn't
+	A man went one day to the post office and asked if there was a letter waiting for him. 'What is your name?' asked the postmaster. 'Why', said the man, 'you will find my name on the envelope'.	He doesn't know the name so how can he find the envelope
+	The fireman hurried to the burning house, got his hose ready, and after smoking a cigar, put out the fire.	'Cause the fire just got bigger and he was just wasting his time

| + | In an old graveyard in Spain, they have discovered a small skull which they believe to be that of Christopher Columbus when he was about ten years old. | 'Cause he didn't die when he was ten! |
| — | One day we saw several icebergs that had been entirely melted by the warmth of the Gulf Stream | 'Cause it's warm, the water, if it's in the sun |

Question 3: The experimenter shows a card to Miriam and says: 'This card has two drawings on it. I am going to show them to you for 10 seconds, then I will take the card away and let you draw from memory what you have seen. Be sure to look at both drawings carefully'. For each of her drawings, Miriam received half credit.

Question 4: The experimenter assures herself that Miriam knows what rhymes are, then proceeds to ask for rhymes as specified below. Miriam produced four out of four.

Tell me the name of a color that rhymes with lead.
Tell me a number that rhymes with tree.
Tell me the name of an animal that rhymes with fair.
Tell me the name of a flower that rhymes with nose.

Question 5: The experimenter asks: 'If I were to buy four cents' worth of candy and should give the shopkeeper 10 cents, how much would I get back?' The same for twelve and fifteen and four and twenty-five cents. Miriam failed to subtract properly 12 from 15 and 4 from 25. This does not meet the age level nine criterion (2 of 3 correct).

Commentary

Miriam was just beginning to learn about subtraction at the time of the test. Two elements in the presentation format could have impeded her performance. She is more likely to subtract correctly when presented with an abstract problem, e.g. how much is 15 take away 12, than when confronted with a word problem which she must translate into numbers. Secondly, her preferred format has the minuend preceding the subtrahend. Asking for change would have required a change in the ordering of terms which could disturb her still not robust procedures.

Question 6: At the second attempt, Miriam was able to repeat four digits reversed: 8 5 2 6 (fail); 4 9 3 7 (succeed)

Conclusion

The test administrators scored Miriam's performance as not meeting the age level nine criteria. She failed at that age level because of her inability to perform two of the three change-making problems she confronted. She was credited with ten months for incrementing her mental age from the age level nine.

Age 10 test

Question 1: Miriam's vocabulary score of 9 is below criterion for a ten-year-old.

Question 2: The experimenter presents Miriam with a card having pictures of piles of cubes. On the first three piles, Miriam is introduced to the task and specifically instructed to count the hidden blocks. The experimenter then asks: 'Now count them and tell me how many there are in each square, beginning here [at left] and working along each row'. The criterion for a ten-year-old is 8 out of 14. Miriam counted correctly 12 out of 14.[28]

Question 3: The experimenter asks Miriam the meaning of a series of abstract words. She replied 'I don't know' to the question 'What do we mean by . . . ?' for the words 'pity', 'curiosity', and 'grief'. She was not asked the meaning of surprise.

Question 4: The experimenter asks Miriam to provide two reasons for the following statements:

Score	Statement	Reasons
+	Give two reasons why children should not be too noisy in school	1. 'Cause they can't hear each other 2. 'Cause it upsets people when they try to work
?+	Give two reasons why most people would rather have an automobile than a bicycle	1. 'Cause they don't have to pedal 2. 'Cause if you want to go a mile it's too far to pedal

Commentary

Although the test adminstrators credited Miriam with meeting this criterion, they acknowledged that lack of clarity in her response leaves considerable doubt that the second question received two distinct reasons in answer.

Question 5: The experimenter asks to 'see how many words you can name in one minute. Just any words will do, like 'clouds', 'dog', 'chair', 'happy'. When I say 'ready', you begin and say the words as fast as you can and I will count them'. Miriam was able to recite 16 words. 28 words are expected of a ten-year-old.

Question 6: Miriam was able to repeat six digits without error on the first try: 4 7 3 8 5 9.

Conclusion

The test administrators credited Miriam with six months toward mental age from the age level ten, i.e. she met the criterion on three questions. On two of those three, her performace was clearly adequate (if not superior). Question 4 may have been too liberally interpreted.

---

28 The test adminstrator added an editorial exclamation point after the score. Compare this performance with her earlier experiment on the volume of solid objects in 'Cognitive Profile at 6;0'.

Age 11 test

Question 1: This question is the re-application of memory for designs test of age level nine. Miriam's score there was below age level eleven criterion.

Question 2: The experimenter asks Miriam 'Why is that foolish?' after the following statements. To the first Miriam responded, 'I don't know'.

> The judge said to the prisoner, 'You are to be hanged, and I hope it will be a warning to you.'

> 'A well known railroad had its last accident five years ago and since that time it has killed only one person in a collison.'

> Miriam responded, 'There must have been only one person in the train'.

Question 3: Of five abstract words [connection, compare, conquer, obedience, revenge], she knew only that conquer means 'someone takes over something'.

Question 4: The experimenter asks Miriam to repeat the following two sentences verbatim.

> At the summer camp, the children get up early in the morning to go swimming.

> Yesterday we went for a ride in our car along the road that crosses the bridge.

Miriam failed to repeat either sentence exactly (both must be repeated exactly to meet the eleven year criterion). In the first she omitted 'in the morning'. In the second, she substituted 'on' for 'along'. In both cases, the alterations are semantically neutral (at the extreme, one might contrast the test sentence with 'The children get up early in the afternoon to go swimming'; otherwise, the omitted phrase must be admitted to be redundant).

Question 5: The experimenter says: 'Listen and see if you can understand what I read'. Then she proceeds with this story:

> Donald went walking in the woods. He saw a pretty little animal that he tried to take home for a pet. It got away from him, but when he got home, his family immediately burned all his clothes.

The experimenter asks, 'Why?'
Miriam didn't recognize that scenario.

Commentary

In a practical sense, it is a test of experience to know a polecat from a possum. Miriam was raised in the woods and could tell a skunk from a possum. As presented in the standardized Stanford–Binet, however, this is more a test of a child's familiarity with a story convention than with inferential capabilities.

Question 6: The experimenter asks Miriam to specify similarities in sets of three items. Of the five sets, she succeeds at one, noting that the rose, potato, and tree all grow in the ground.

Comparands	*Response*
snake – cow – sparrow	snakes and cows walk on the ground
wool – cotton – leather	feel soft
knife blade – penny – piece of wire	sharp
books – teacher – newspaper	books and newspaper have paper

Commentary

As a child schooled only in nursery school and kindergarten, Miriam had not yet been exposed to the claim that teachers – and even books – are part of a fundamentally didactic system. For Miriam at six, teachers and books were friends. She read the funnies and children's sections of newspapers but not much else. Entertainment was more the salient feature than was the transmission of information.

Conclusion

Since Miriam failed to meet the criterion of any question at this age level, it was taken as the ceiling of her mental capacity at six. Is it clear, entirely, that she failed to meet the criterion for every question? One could argue against the grading of questions 4 and 5, but let's not do so.

Summary of administrator's conclusions

Calendar age at date of test: $6;1;17 = 6-2 = 74$ mos.

mental age	years	months	
basal year	7		
8		10	
9		10	
10		6	
total	7	26	$= 9-2 = 110$ mos.

intelligence quotient $= 145$

Concluding comments

This estimate of Miriam's IQ is just the kind of thing to have in one's records. For those who go by such measures, it should indicate she is bright enough to do whatever she may want to do. It is also low enough that she will be spared the burden of being expected to perform miracles. Viewing Miriam as a subject in the experiments of this project, I find an IQ of 145 quite satisfactory. I can claim my subject is as bright as anyone could wish and is ignorant because of her young age. What could be better characteristics for the subject of an experiment wherein the hope is to trace in fine detail the development of ideas?

The following variations are my attempt to probe the variability of the standard estimate in terms of what exploring the test has led me to learn. I begin by finding that 110 divided by 74 does not yield a ratio of 145, but of 148.5. Consequently, one would expect (if rounding were involved) the reported IQ to be 150. Another possible interpretation of this discrepancy occurred to me: perhaps there was some non-linearity in the tests that required correction by a table of which I was ignorant. This plausible assumption left me happy with the reported score.

When I acquired the Terman–Merrill book, there was such a table. To my dismay, in checking out the discrepancy, I found the correction goes the other way. The Pineau revised IQ tables show for a child of 6–2 with an MA of 9–2 an IQ of 154. (The reported score of 145 may be a simple case of reversed digits.) But aren't there other variables? What of my argument that Miriam should have been scored as passing Question 4 at age level 8 (recall those sharks in the ocean and her description of pennies as brown and quarters as gold). Wouldn't that not only change her basal age to 8 but also set her mental age at 9–4? To make the extreme case – let's pretend she had taken her examination when scheduled, four days earlier (thus having a calendar age of 6–1). The Pineau tables then show an IQ of 159.

Reflect, then: from this accidental change of schedule and a single uncertainty of interpretation, in conjunction with the recommended use of Pineau's tables to calibrate IQs on the basis of a uniform standard deviation, we see a change in the reportable test score of 14 points – nearly a standard deviation itself! I rest content with the estimate of the professionals who administered the test, but I have a much more profound sense than ever before of just how funny are these numbers.

Let's back off a bit from this number manipulation to see what other use can be made of these data in helping to characterize Miriam's cognitive state. There is a document generally available[29] which classifies the questions of the Binet test into these six categories:

General Comprehension
Visual-Motor Ability
Arithmetic Reasoning
Memory and Concentration
Vocabulary and Verbal Fluency
Judgment and Reasoning

Let us adopt my interpretation that Miriam's basal age is 8 and examine where the 'deficiencies' appear as the test progresses from age level to age level. The one question Miriam failed at age level nine was in applying subtraction to a word problem. I interpret this to mean she can function much as a nine-year-old who is accidentally lacking in certain arithmetic knowledge.

Miriam failed three questions at age level ten, questions 1, 3, and 5. All of these Valett characterizes as measures of vocabulary and verbal frequency. You will recall that her block counting was 50 per cent above the ten-year-old criterion (this is visual–motor ability according to Valett); her repetition of six digits succeeding on the first attempt (where three are permitted) testifies to her competence in the category of memory and concentration at the ten year level. Her responses to both Questions 2 and 4 argue her capability in judgment and

29 *A profile for the Stanford–Binet* (L–M),   Robert E. Valett, Consulting Psychologists Press, Palo Alto, Calif.

reasoning. By the ten year level she has shown in tests that her performance is deficient in word processing and arithmetic but is otherwise adequate.

What does one make of such arguments? How seriously can one take them? How seriously should one take them? Miriam at six was a relatively mature child who was lacking in specific knowledges. The characterization of that maturity and ignorance is beyond addressing by the Binet examination. On the other hand, the detail data of this independent examination are quite compatible with the other materials of The Intimate Study.

Extended citations

Extended citation seems to me a more useful appeal to authority and expression of actual intellectual debt than is the piling up of secondary and rarely followed references. I have chosen material for the following citations because the ideas embodied in them are essential to understanding this book. The ideas are better expressed in the original than they could be in any summary of mine; perhaps these samples will lead you to the original.

CITATIONS

Goodman: On Rightness of Rendering
Goodman: On Multiple Worlds

Langer: Against Physicalism
Papert: On Learning in a Machine: Heredity versus Epistemology
Langer: On Objectivity
Lewin: On the Pure Case
Papert: On the Elevation of Control
Papert: On Classifying Theories of Learning

Lévi-Strauss: On Bricolage
Jacob: On Bricolage in Evolution
Tversky and Kahnemann: On Anchoring with Variation

The texture of behavior

GOODMAN: ON RIGHTNESS OF RENDERING

A profound theme in the work of Nelson Goodman is the attempt to go beyond a too-narrow conception of truth to a criterion of rightness of rendering as the standard for our descriptions of an unapproachable reality. Beginning his contrast of truth, validity, and rightness with the well understood case of deductive logic, Goodman notes:[1]

> Among the most explicit and clearcut standards of rightness we have any-where are those for validity of a deductive argument; and validity is of course distinct from truth in that the premisses and conclusions of a valid argument may be false. . . . A deductive argument is right in a fuller sense only if the premisses are true and the inference valid. Thus rightness of deductive argument, while involving validity, is still closely allied with truth.

He then proceeds to the more difficult issue of induction.

On induction

> Now consider inductive validity. Here again, neither truth of premisses nor truth of conclusion is required; and inductive like deductive validity consists of conformity with principles that codify practice. But inductive validity is one step further removed from truth than is deductive validity; for valid inductive inference from true premisses need not yield a true conclusion. On the other hand, while inductive *rightness* like deductive rightness does require truth of the premisses as well as validity, it also requires something more. To begin with, a right inductive argument must be based not only on true premisses but upon all the available genuine evidence. . . . No parallel requirement is imposed upon a deductive argument. . .
>
>   Still, inductive rightness is not fully characterized as inductive validity plus use of all examined instances. . . . Even if all examined emeralds have been grue,[2] still inductive argument to the hypothesis that all emeralds are grue is wrong. Inductive roughness requires evidence statements and the hypothesis to be in terms of 'genuine' or 'natural kinds – in my terminology, to be in terms of projectible predicates like 'green' and 'blue' rather than in terms of non-projective predicates like 'grue' and 'bleen.' Without such a restriction, right inductive arguments could always be found to yield count-less conflicting conclusions. . . .
>
>   In sum, then, inductive rightness requires that the argument proceed from premisses consisting of all such true reports on examined instances as

---

1 In Chapter 7 of *Ways of World Making*.
2 Goodman introduced the term 'grue' and others like it to name examples of non-projectible predicates he invented. For example, 'grue' might mean 'green whenever observed before the year 2000 and blue after that'. 'Bleen' is defined as the converse of grue. For an appreciation of the importance of the projectibility of predicates, see Putnam's intro-duction to the Harvard Press edition of *Fact, Fiction, and Forecast*, by Nelson Goodman. The persistent scholar might enjoy examining Peirce's discussion (in *'How to make our ideas clear'* in Peirce (1956)), of what prevents us from saying that all hard bodies are soft until they are touched. He concludes that it would involve no arrangement of facts different from what it is, merely an arrangement of facts which would be exceedingly maladroit.

are in terms of projectible predicates. Thus inductive rightness, while still demanding truth of predicates, makes severe additional demands. And although we hope by means of inductive argument to arrive at truth, inductive rightness unlike deductive rightness does not guarantee truth. . . . Any feasible justification of induction must consist rather of showing that the rules of inference codify inductive practice – that is, of effecting a mutual adjustment between rules and practice – and of distinguishing projectible predicates or inductively right categories from others.

This brings us, then, to the question, what are inductively right categories, and so to a third kind of rightness in general: rightness of categorization? Such rightness is one step further removed from truth; for while deductive and inductive rightness still have to do with statements, which have a truth value, rightness of categorization attaches to categories or predicates – or systems thereof – which have no truth-value. . . .

In such a context, I am not so much stating a belief or advancing a thesis or a doctrine as proposing a categorization of scheme of organization, calling attention to a way of setting our nets to capture what may be significant likenesses and differences. *Argument for the categorization,* the scheme suggested, *could not be for its truth, since it has no truth-value, but for its efficacy in world making and understanding.* An argument would consist rather of calling attention to important parallels between pictorial representation and verbal denotation, of pointing out obscurities and confusions that are clarified by this association, of showing how this organization works with other aspects of the theory of symbols. *For a categorical system, what needs to be shown is not that it is true but what it can do.* Put crassly, what is called for in such cases is less arguing than selling.

Our descriptions of reality are an imposition *we* make. Our investigations may disturb whatever might have been there otherwise. As evolved creatures, we are limited by the experience of our species to ideas at a range of sensation and conception which is effective but very partial. We can only hope our descriptions go with the grain of an unapproachable reality. I try to offer a fair sample of empirical detail to show how my vision of mind applies to behavior and how it can be applied powerfully to the comprehension of human learning. The question is less whether my description of mind is true or false than whether or not I make it work on important problems.

GOODMAN: ON MULTIPLE WORLDS

The prestige of science is such today that its method is respected as the primary means of settling differences of opinion. C. S. Peirce offers what may be taken as the core description of the nature of scientific truth and reality. Beginning that a man should consider that he wishes his opinions to coincide with the facts of things, he argues that such a result is the prerogative of the method of science:[3]

3 His position is set out in two charming and profound essays, 'The fixation of belief' and 'How to make our ideas clear' (Peirce, 1956).

Different minds may set out with the most antagonistic views, but the progress of investigation carries them by a force outside of themselves to one and the same conclusion. The activity of thought by which we are carried, not where we wish, but to a foreordained goal, is like the operation· of destiny. No modification of the point of view taken, no selection of other facts for study, no natural bent of mind even, can enable a man to escape the predestinate opinion. This great law is embodied in the conception of truth and reality. The opinion which is fated[4] to be ultimately agreed to by all who investigate, is what we mean by the truth, and the object represented in this opinion is the real. That is the way I would explain reality.

However attractive one finds Peirce's vision, is it not clear that profound problems exist? His definition of truth and reality depends upon a convergence over all time and even extra-human intelligences as well.[5] His definition of reality finesses the issue of its characterization. We may *choose* to believe in the eventual convergence of opinion to a possible singular truth if we are able to take the viewpoint of eternity. But our everyday world of science, as Kuhn (1962) describes it,[6] seems more like 'a darkling plain where ignorant armies clash by night'. Too often Peirce's assumed convergence with its implication of progress supports in practice an extreme sort of physicalist reductionism — where works are judged scientific only if they grow directly out of or attach directly to the canonical theories of the hard sciences.[7] After Peirce, other notable philosophers have struggled with the same issue. Among these, the perspicuous and profound effort of Goodman is most congenial to the presuppositions of my work.[8]

Countless worlds made from nothing by the use of symbols — so might a satirist summarize some major themes in the work of Ernst Cassirer. These themes, the multiplicity of words, the speciousness of 'the given', the creative power of the understanding, the variety and formative function of symbols — are also integral to my own thinking. . . . In just what sense are there many worlds? What distinguishes genuine from spurious worlds? What are worlds made of? How are they made? What role do symbols play in the making? And how is world making related to knowing? These questions must be faced even if full and final answers are far off.

The reality of multiple worlds
We are not speaking in terms of multiple possible alternatives to a single actual world but of multiple actual worlds. . . . Consider, to begin with, the

4 Fate means merely that which is sure to come true, and can nohow be avoided. It is a superstition to suppose that a certain sort of events are [sic] ever fated, and it is another to suppose that the word fate can never be freed from superstitious taint. We are all fated to die. (*Note of Peirce.*)
5 See the full text in 'How to make our ideas clear' (Peirce, 1956).
6 See *The Structure of Scientific Revolutions*.
7 See the extended citation Langer: 'Against physicalism' (p. 240).
8 These citations are drawn from *Ways of Worldmaking*.

statements, 'The sun always moves' and 'The sun never moves' which, though equally true, are at odds with each other. . . We are inclined to regard the two strings of words not as complete statements with truth-values of their own but as elliptical for some such statements as 'Under frame of reference A, the sun always moves' and 'Under frame of reference B, the sun never moves' — statements that may both be true of the same world.

Frames of reference, though, seem to belong less to what is described than to the system of description. . . . But if I insist you tell me how it is apart from all frames, what can you say? We are confined to ways of describing whatever is described. Our universe, so to speak, consists of these ways rather than of the world or of worlds.

The alternative descriptions of motion, all of them in much the same terms and routinely transformable into one another, provide only a minor and rather pallid example of diversity in accounts of the world. Much more striking is the vast variety of versions and visions in the several sciences, in the works of different painters and writers, and in our perceptions as informed by these, by circumstances, and by our own insights, interests, and past experiences. Even with all illusory or wrong or dubious versions dropped, the rest exhibit new dimensions of disparity. Here we have no neat set of frames of reference. . . we turn from describing or depicting 'the world' to talking of descriptions and depictions, but now without even the consolation of intertranslatability among or any evident organization of the several systems in question.

While we may speak of determining what versions are right as 'learning about the world', 'the world' supposedly being that which all right versions describe, all we learn about the world is contained in right versions of it; and while the underlying world, bereft of these, need not be denied to those who love it, it is perhaps on the whole a world well lost. . . .

On reduction

Since the fact that there are many different world-versions is hardly debatable, and the question how many if any 'worlds in themselves' there are is virtually empty, in what non-trivial sense are there. . . . many worlds? Just this, I think: that many different world versions are of independent interest and importance, without any requirement or presumption of reducibility to a single base. The pluralist, far from being anti scientific, accepts the sciences at full value. His typical adversary is the monopolistic materialist or physicalist who maintains that one system, physics, is preeminent and all-inclusive, such that every other version must eventually be reduced to it or rejected as false or meaningless. If all right versions could somehow be reduced to one and only one, that one might with some semblance of plausibility[9] be regarded as the only truth about the only world. But the evidence for such reducibility is negligible, and even the claim is nebulous since physics itself is fragmentary and unstable, and the kind and consequence of reduction

---

9 But not much, for no one type of reducibility serves all purposes (N. Goodman).

envisaged are vague. . . . A reduction from one system to another can make a genuine contribution to understanding the interrelationships among world versions; but reduction in any reasonably strict sense is rare, almost always partial, and seldom if ever unique. To demand full and sole reducibility to physics or any other one version is to forego nearly all other versions.

So long as contrasting right versions not all reducible to one are countenanced, unity is to be sought not in an ambivalent or neutral something beneath these versions but in an overall organization embracing them.

So it is also, I believe, the case with mind.[10] Goodman continues that Cassirer sought unity through cross-cultural study; Goodman's own focus is analytic study of the types and functions of symbol systems. My approach is the empirical probing of his opening questions: What are worlds made of? How are they made? And how is worldmaking related to knowing? In this study of the human mind, the conclusion is clear: *The constructability of knowledge depends upon the integrability of the systems of symbols through which we come to choose to represent the disparate experiences of our everyday lives.*

LANGER: AGAINST PHYSICALISM

Kurt Lewin drew profound lessons for the science of mind from contrasting them with the development of physics as a science, [11] but his own theory of a 'dynamic psychology' became vulnerable to severe criticism because it permitted itself to be excessively influenced by inappropriate analogies, as Langer notes in her more general diatribe against physicalism.[12]

The social sciences, originally projected by Auguste Comte in his sanguine vision of a world reformed and rationally guided by science, have finally come into recognized existence in the twentieth century. They have had a different history from the natural sciences which grew up chiefly in the seventeenth and eighteenth centuries under the name 'natural philosophy', and gradually took shape as formal and systematic pursuits. Astronomy, mechanics, optics, electronics, all merging into 'physics', and the strange kettles of fish that became chemistry, had a free and unsupervised beginning; and the most productive thinkers of those maverick days ventured on some wild flights of fancy. Not so the founders of the 'young sciences' today. They cannot indulge in fantastic hypotheses about the aims or the origins of society, the presence of sentience or intellect in anything but the investigator himself, the sources of fantasy, the measures of human or animal mentality. They began their work under the tutelage of physics, and — like

10 To the question of what sort of organization might provide unity in a mind developing from a structured center but confronting experiences of extensive variety, I offer my conjecture in Chapter 5, 'Cognitive organization.'

11 See the extended citation, 'Lewin: One the Pure Case' (p. 245).

12 These excerpts are from Chapter 2 'Idols of the laboratory', in *Mind: An Essay on Human Feeling*, vol. 1 (Langer, 1967).

young ones emulating their elders — they have striven first and hardest for the signs of sophistication; technical language, the laboratory atmosphere, apparatus, graphs, charts and statistical averages.

This ambition has had some unfortunate effects on a discipline for which the procedures of classical physics, for instance, the experimental techniques of Galileo, may not be suitable at all. It has centered attention on the ordering and collating of facts, and drawn it away from their own intriguing character as something distinct from the facts encountered by the physicist, and perhaps differently structured. The main concern of early physicists was understanding puzzling events; each scientific venture grew from a problem, the solution of which threw unexpected light on other problematical phenomena. It was always in such a light that the concepts of physical science were set up. But the chief preoccupation of the social scientists has been with the nature of their undertaking, its place in the edifice of human knowledge, and — by no means last, though seldom candidly admitted — their own status as scientists. For decades, therefore, the literature of those new disciplines, especially of psychology, has dealt with so called 'approaches', not to some baffling and challenging facts, but to all the facts at once, the science itself. . . .

In proportion to the effort spent on all these 'approaches', the harvest of interesting facts and systematic ideas remains meagre (which, of course, is not to say that there are none). By comparison with other biological sciences, both the method and the findings of laboratory psychology look extremely simple. Their essential simplicity is sometimes masked by a technical vocabulary, and even an algorithmic-looking form of statement; but when we come to the interpretation of 'variables', their values prove to be such elements as 'somebody', 'some fact', 'some object', without formal distinction between a person, a fact and an object, which would make it logically not possible to interchange them, as it would have to be to assure the formula any sense. . . .

The cult of borrowed mathematical terms is especially pernicious when it invades serious original thinking, where there are really fundamental psychological concepts in the making, which are obscured and turned from their own implicit development by the unessential though enticing suggestiveness of scientific words. In a sober but trenchant article, I. D. London has shown even so influential and important a venture as Kurt Lewin's 'field theory' to be only verbally modelled on the field theory of relativity physics, since Lewin's key concept, 'force', has no real analogue in real topology, and his psychological 'field' conforms to no known geometry. The result is that Lewin can use none of the powerful principles of substitution that make topology reveal new facts in physical science. . . . The host of theorems that form the actual machinery of topology should have been made to function and so to take over the work of rigorous deduction. Lewin in reality does not utilize one single theorem of topology.

Here, I think, we have the central and fatal failing of all the projected sciences of mind and conduct: the actual machinery that their sponsors and pioneers have rented does not work when their 'conceptualized phenomena' are fed into it. It cannot process the interpretations that are supposed to be legitimate proxies for its abstract elements. . . . The reason for the failure. . . is that abstract concepts borrowed from physics, such as units of matter — even with the adjective 'living' to qualify them — and their motions do not lend themselves readily to the expression of psychologically important problems. . . .

Understanding learning is a psychologically important problem. Reasons to believe that Artificial Intelligence ideas will help with this problem are twofold. The representation of knowledge is a main issue of that discipline itself. Further, and more importantly, if new cognitive structure emerges from the functioning of pre-existing cognitive structures, the building of computational models will provide an experimental ground where new ideas can be simulated with clarity until they are sufficiently well understood that their value in explaining psychological phenomena can be reasonably evaluated. My work strives to provide a plausible ground of samples of learning — a characterization of one significant state in human cognitive development and the processes which early on shape its formation — from which basis one might explore how the more complex processes of adult thought developed in order to address learning, the essential problem of the human cognitive sciences.

PAPERT: ON LEARNING IN A MACHINE: HEREDITY VERSUS EPISTEMOLOGY

Does heredity — with the richness of the genome's structured chemistry — or epistemology — the implicit logic of ideas in concert — offer the more fruitful explanation of what makes learning possible? Usually this problem is too difficult to decide, but Papert offers a single, compelling example which argues that the power of ideas *must not* be ignored in discussing the roots of knowledge and the processes of learning.[13] The central question is what must be considered in inferring that an idea is 'innate' in a thinking thing. Papert describes a machine called a perceptron as follows:

Its structure is quite simple: it has a retina on which pictures can be projected, and the purpose of the machine is to recognize whether or not this image has a certain property called 'the predicate' (for example, 'is a square'). It has a large number of submechanisms, each of which can compute the answer, to be expressed as 'yes' or 'no' to any well-defined question about a tiny region of the retina. Collectively, these submechanisms (called 'the local function') cover the whole retina, but none of them has any global knowledge. In particular, none of them can see the whole figure.

There is also a central organ, which has access to the answers given by the local mechanisms; but this organ is constrained to a particular simple algorithm to generate the global decision (for example, it is a square!) from

13 For the extended argument in the context of which this sketch was presented, see Chapter 3 in *Language and Learning*, edited by Piattelli-Palmarini (1980), the report of a conference where Piaget and Chomsky each advocated his position.

the local functions, namely the 'linear threshold decision function': the binary yes/no outputs of the local functions are represented as 1 and 0, respectively; the machine forms a weighted sum of these numbers using weighting coefficients characteristic of the particular perceptron; it then makes its decision according to whether the sum comes out to be more than or less than a certain quantity called 'the threshold'.

Finally, the perception is equipped with a 'learning mechanism', which works like this: when the machine says 'that's a square', it will be told whether it is right or wrong, and if wrong, will use this feedback to alter its weighting coefficients.

What can a perceptron learn? The answer is not always immediately obvious, either from an examination of its 'innate structure' or from simple experiments. It is easy enough to see that a perceptron could learn to distinguish between dichotomies such as *square* versus *triangular*; in this case, the local functions recognize the presence or absence of at least one angle which is not a right angle, and so the hypothesis *square* can be eliminated on local grounds. But there are cases where it is much harder to see whether the global decision is reducible to such local ones. The classic example is the predicate 'is connected'. The picture is assumed to be a black figure on a white ground, and the question for the perceptron is whether the black figure is made of one or several pieces. Is such a decision reducible to local observations? Intuition still says that a perceptron should not be able to tell whether there is only one blob or several. But a deep mathematical theorem by Euler can be adapted to show that the perceptron can learn any predicate like 'the number of blobs is less than k'.

Let us now imagine an investigator who does not know the Euler theorem and happens to be concerned with whether blob-numerosity (in the sense of the predicate just mentioned) is innate in the perceptron. One can easily imagine such a person being very puzzled when shown the wiring diagram of the perceptron. He would see nothing there which (to his mind) even remotely resembles numerosity. He might conclude that something must be missing from our wiring diagram (so one of the cautioning morals of the story is that one has to be very careful about conclusions like this). But the even more important, if more subtle, conclusion is that even with full knowledge (of the wiring diagram and the mathematics), it is not at all clear whether one ought to say that numerosity is innate. In some senses of 'innate' it is, and in other senses it is not. The conclusion for me is that we need a much more carefully elaborated theoretical framework within which to formulate the real questions that lie behind formulations such as, 'Does the subject X have the notion Y?' or 'Is Y a property of the initial state of this subject?' or 'Is Y innate?'

Papert concludes from his argument by example that the key problem of learning theory should be to reduce the sense of miracle induced by the power of the mind both to think and to grow. Euler's theorem can do this for a student of perceptron-learning. The more precise articulation of the processes Piaget named 'assimilation' and 'accommodation' is the best hope for achieving this end in the case of human learning. By providing crisp examples of how functionally labile cognitive structures can be seen as changing through their local interactions, we move in such a direction.

LANGER: ON OBJECTIVITY

Adopting Bacon's label 'idols' for those major categories of errors of thought which undermine scientific work,[14] Langer attacks the Idols of the Laboratory.[15] In her own words:

> Another source of idolatry is the cultivation of a prescription methodology, which lays down in advance the general lines of procedure — and therewith the lines of thought — to be followed. According to its canons, all laboratory procedures must be isolated, controllable, repeatable, and above all 'objective'. The first three requirements only restrict experimentation to simple responses, more significant in animal psychology than in human contexts; but the fourth is a demon. The Idol of Objectivity requires its servitors to distort the data of human psychology into an animal image in order to handle them by the methods that fit speechless mentality. It requires the omission of all activities of central origin, which are felt as such, and are normally accessible to research in human psychology through the powerful instrument of language. The result is a laboratory exhibit of 'behavior' that is much more artificial than any instrumentally deformed object, because its deformation is not calculated and discounted as an effect of the instrument.
>
> Here indeed is a critical spot where haste to become scientific destroys the most valuable material for investigation. It completely masks the radical phylogenetic change induced by the language function, which makes one animal species so different from others that most — if not all — of its actions are only partially commensurable with those of even the nearest related creatures, the higher primates. For the revelation of subjectively felt activities through speech is not a simple exhibit from which the observer infers the action of external stimuli on the observed organism; in a protocol statement, the dividing line between the observer and his object is displaced, and part of the observation is delegated to the experimental subject. . . .
>
> The relativity of the subject—object division, which lets that division come now at the eye, now at the lens of the microscope, or — in psychological observation — now between the experimentor and the experimental subject, now between the latter's report and its matter of reference, is one of the serious instrumental problems for scientific psychology. But it is more than that; it is one of the most interesting phenomena characterizing human material itself. . . . To exclude such relationships for the sake of sure and safe laboratory methods is to stifle human psychology in embryo.

14 In *Magna Instauratio,* Bacon inveighs against the Idols of the Tribe (failings that fall to our lot because we are human), the Idols of the Cave (personal idiosyncrasies), Idols of the Marketplace (jargon, the trafficking in empty words instead of meanings), and Idols of the Theatre (premature systematization).
15 Chapter 2 in *Mind: An Essay on Human Feeling* (Langer, 1967).

I have tried to follow the path of the problem regardless of how the centre of activity meandered across the boundaries of individual action in the studies of this work. My use of mechanical recording was twofold, as defense against ingrained biases and to permit accounting for my deformations of Miriam's behavior. If my work is not objective, so be it.

LEWIN: ON THE PURE CASE

Arguing from the contrast between Aristotelian and Galilean modes of doing physics, Lewin proposes a program whose primary themes are three: the assumption that psychological phenomena are fully lawful; the advancement of an apt representation; and a commitment to the analysis of the concrete case in full detail.[16] He begins with an appreciation of Galilean physics:

> Galilean physics tried to characterize the individuality of the total situation concerned as concretely and as accurately as possible. This is an exact reversal of Aristotelian principles. The dependence of an event upon the situation in which it occurs means for the Aristotelean mode of thought, which wants to ascertain the general by seeking out the like features of many cases, nothing more than a disturbing force. . . . The step from particular case to law, from 'this' event to 'such' an event, no longer requires the confirmation by historical regularity that is characteristic of the Aristotelian mode of thought. This step to the general is automatically and immediately given by the principle of the exceptionless lawfulness of physical events. What is now important to the investigation of dynamics is not to abstract from the situation, but to hunt out those situations in which the determinative factors of the total dynamic structure are most clearly, distinctly, and purely to be discerned. Instead of reference to the abstract average of as many historically given cases as possible, there is a reference to the full concreteness of particular situations. . . .
>
> The increased emphasis upon the quantitative which seems to lend modern physics a formal and abstract character is not derived from any tendency to logical formality. Rather, the tendency to a full description of the concrete actuality, even to that of the particular case, was influential, a circumstance which should be especially emphasized in conjunction with present-day psychology. . . . It was the increased desire, and also the increased ability to comprehend concrete particular cases, and to comprehend them fully, which, together with the idea of the homogeneity of the physical world and that of the continuity of the properties of its objects, constituted the main impulse to the increasing quantification of physics.

In psychology

The concept formation of psychology is dominated, just as was that of Aristotelian physics, by the question of regularity in the sense of frequency. This is obvious in its immediate attitude towards particular phenomena as

16 In 'The conflict between Galilean and Aristotelian modes of thought in contemporary psychology' (Lewin, 1935).

well as in its attitude towards lawfulness. If, for example, one shows a film of a concrete incident in the behavior of a certain child, the first question asked of the psychologist usually is: 'Do all children do that, or is it at least common?' And if one must answer this question in the negative the behavior loses for that psychologist all or almost all claim to scientific interest. To pay attention to such an 'exceptional case' seems to him a scientifically unimportant bit of folly. . . . The individual event seems to him fortuitous, unimportant, scientifically indifferent. . . . that which does not occur repeatedly lies outside the realm of the comprehensible.

The field which is considered lawful, not in principle but in the actual research of psychology — even of experimental psychology — has only been extended very gradually. If psychology has only very gradually and hesitantly pushed beyond the bounds of sensory psychology into the fields of will and effect, it is certainly due not only to technical difficulties but mainly to the fact that in this field actual repetition, a recurrence of the same event, is not to be expected. And this repetition remains, as it did for Aristotle, to a large extent the basis for the assumption of the lawfulness or intelligibility of an event. . . . It is evidence of the depth and momentum of this connection (between repetition and lawfulness) that it is even used to define experiment, a scientific instrument which, if it is not directly opposed to Aristotelian physics, has at least become significant only in relatively modern times. . . .

The fact that lawfulness and individuality are considered antitheses has two sorts of effect on actual research. It signifies in the first place a limitation of research. It makes it appear hopeless to try to understand the real, unique course of an emotion or the actual structure of a particular individual's personality. It thus reduces one to a treatment of these problems in terms of averages. . . . This conviction that it is impossible to wholly comprehend the individual case as such implies, in addition, a certain laxity of research: it is satisfied with setting forth mere regularities. The demands of psychology upon the stringency of its propositions go no farther than to require a validity 'in general' or 'on the average' or 'as a rule'. The 'complexity' and the 'transitory nature' of life processes make it unreasonable, it is said, to require complete exceptionless, validity. According to the old saw that 'the exception "proves" the rule', *Psychology does not regard exceptions as counter-arguments so long as their frequency is not too great*[17] . . . .

Two points stand out: in the field of theory and law, the high valuation of the historically important and the disdain of the ordinary; in the field of experiment, the choice of processes which will occur frequently (or are common to many events). Both are indicative in like measure of that Aristotelian mixing of historical and systematic questions which carries with it for the systematic the connection with the abstract classes and the neglect of the full reality of the concrete case. . . .

The thesis of exceptionless validity in psychological laws makes available to investigation, especially to experiment, such processes as do not frequently recur in the same form. . . . When lawfulness is no longer limited to cases

17 Italics of K. Lewin.

which occur regularly or frequently but is characteristic of every physical event, the necessity disappears of demonstrating the lawfulness of an event by some special criterion, such as its frequency of occurrence. Even a particular case is then assumed without more ado, to be lawful. Historical rarity is no disproof, historical regularity is no proof of lawfulness. For the concept of lawfulness has been quite detached from that of regularity; the concept of the complete absence of exception to laws is strictly separated from that of historical constancy. . . . Since Law and individual are no longer antitheses, nothing prevents relying for proof upon historically unusual, rare, and transitory events, such as most physical experiments are.

A Galilean view of dynamics. . . derives all its vectors not from single isolated objects, but from the mutual relations of the factors in the concrete whole situation, that is, essentially, from the momentary condition of the individual and the structure of the psychological situation. The dynamics of the process is always to be defined from the relation of the concrete individual to the concrete situation, and so far as internal forces are concerned, from the mutual relations of the various functional systems that make up the individual. . . . The carrying out of this principle requires, to be sure, the completion of a task that at present is only begun: namely, the providing a workable representation of a concrete psychological situation according to its individual characteristics and its associated functional properties, and of the concrete structure of the psychological person and its internal dynamic facts. . . .

The accidents of historical processes are not overcome by excluding the changing situations from systematic consideration, but only by taking fullest account of the individual nature of the concrete case. It depends upon keeping in mind that general validity of the law and concreteness of the individual case are not antitheses, and that reference to the totality of the whole concrete situation must take the place of reference to the largest possible historical collection of frequent repetition. . . . It means for psychology, as it did for physics, a transition from an abstract classificatory procedure to an essentially concrete constructive method.

Lewin's analysis is profound. The specific representations he advanced for the psychological situation have not been accepted,[18] but his specification of the requirements for a scientific psychology with concepts appropriate to the arena of human concerns can now advance using the representational techniques developing in the engineering discipline of Artificial Intelligence.

PAPERT: ON THE ELEVATION OF CONTROL

Papert describes the idea which I call 'the elevation of control', emphasizing two points: first, the local grouping of knowledge structures is critical to understanding; second, learning may be explained by the insertion into a complex network of a simple change whose effect is profound.[19]

18 See the extended citation, 'Langer: Against Physicalism' (p. 240).
19 From *Mindstorms:* Chapter 7: 'LOGO's Roots: Piaget and AI' (Papert, 1980).

Children up until the age of six or seven believe that a quantity of liquid can increase or decrease when it is poured from one container to another. Specifically, when one container is taller and narrower than the first, the children unanimously assert that the quantity of liquid has increased. And then, as if by magic, at about the same age, all children change their mind: They now just as unequivocally insist that the amount of liquid remains the same. . . . Why does height in a liquid seem like more to the child, and how does this change?

Many theories have been advanced for how this could come to pass. One of them, which may sound most familiar because it draws on traditional psychological categories, attributes the pre-conservationist position to the child's being dominated by 'appearances'. The child's 'reason' cannot override how things 'seem to be'. Perception rules.

Let us now turn to another theory, this time one inspired by computational methods. Again we ask the question: Why does height in a narrow vessel seem like more to the child, and how does this change?

Let us posit the existence of three agents in the child's mind, each of which judges quantities in a different, simple minded way. The first, *height,* judges the quantity of liquids and anything else by its vertical extent. Height is a practical agent in the life of the child. It is accustomed to comparing children by standing them back to back and of equalizing the quantities of Coca-Cola and chocolate in children's glasses. We emphasize that Height does not do anything as complicated as 'perceive' the quantity of liquid. Rather, it is fanatically dedicated to an abstract principle: anything that goes higher is more.

There is a second agent, called *width,* that judges by horizontal extent. It is not so practised as Height. It gets its chance to judge that there is a lot of water in the sea, but in the mind of the child this is less influential than Height.

Finally, there is an agent called *history,* that says quantities are the same because once they were the same. History seems to speak like a conservationist child, but this is an illusion. History has no understanding and would say the quantity is the same even if some had indeed been added.

In the experiment with the preconservationist child, each of the three agents makes its own 'decision' and clamors for it to be adopted. As we know, Height's voice speaks the loudest. But this changes as the child moves on to the next stage.

There are three ways, given our assumption of the presence of agents, for this change to take place. Height and Width become more 'sophisticated', so that, for example, Height would disqualify itself except when all other things are equal. This would mean that Height would only step forward to judge by height those things that have equal cross sections. Second, there could be a change in 'seniority', in prerogative: History could become the dominant voice. Neither of these two modes of change is impossible. But there is a third mode that produces the same effect in a simpler way. Its key idea is that Height and Width neutralize one another by giving contradictory opinions. The idea is attractive (and close to Piaget's own concept of group-like compositions of operations) but raises some problems. Why do all three agents not neutralize one another so that the child has no opinion at all? The question is answered by a further postulate (which has much in common with Piaget's idea that intellectual operators be organized into groupements). The principle of neutralization becomes workable if enough structure is imposed on the agents for Height and Width to be in a special relationship with one another but not with History. We have seen that the technique of creating a new entity works powerfully in programming systems. And this is the process we postulate here. A new entity, a new agent comes into being. This is agent Geometry, which acts as a supervisor for Height and Width. In cases where Height and Width agree, Geometry passes on their message with great 'authority'. But if they disagree, Geometry is undermined and the voices of the underlings are neutralized. It must be emphasized that Geometry is not meant to 'understand' the reasons for decision making by Height and Width. Geometry knows nothing except whether they agree and, if so, in which direction.

The essential and profound point in Papert's story about computational agents is that epistemological complementarity of components permits the growth of structure.[20] Among the many issues left unresolved by Papert's Piagetian reformulation, my work pursues the question of how such a change, the elevation of control, might come to pass through the child's interactions with her everyday world of experience. It goes on to uncover a second form of such a change − but one with no immediate procedural impact − which I have named the correlation of perspectives.

PAPERT: ON CLASSIFYING THEORIES OF LEARNING[21]

On the complexity of developmental mechanisms

One can classify developmental theories according to how much of the complexity of the human mind they attribute to S_0 (the initial state) and S_t (the terminal state) and to the component of mental function responsible for development. For example, Skinner believes it is possible to explain the passage from S_0 to S_t by a very simple general developmental mechanism (GDM). Both Chomsky and Piaget have used forceful arguments to persuade us that S_t is certainly more complex than Skinner believes, and probably too complex for a simple GDM to guide its growth from the kind of S_0 Skinner would admit. The difficulty facing Skinner is a mismatch between his simple S_0 and the putatively complex S_t. There are in principle three (nonexclusive) reactions to this apparent mismatch: one can postulate that S_0 is more complex than Skinner thought, which is the route taken by Chomsky; one can postulate, as Piaget does, that the GDM must be more

20 This idea is witnessed in force by the studies of Chapter 2 and 4.
21 These excerpts are from *Language and Learning*, (Piatelli-Palmerini, 1980).

powerful than Skinner believed; finally, one could deny the mismatch, for example, arguing as Herbert Simon does that ST really is structurally simple after all and thus that S0 and the GDM can both be simple as well (although, of course, Simon's GDM and S0 are radically different from Skinner's).

On Piaget

A naive perception of Piaget sees him as saying: nothing is innate, everything emerges from development. Of course, this is absurd if pushed undialectically to the limit; but what he does teach us is this: if you make a list of structures and notions and rules (or whatever you call them) found in adult intelligence, and if you ask which of them is innate, the answer will be *none*. The point behind the apparent contradiction is simple enough: everything has a developmental history through which it emerges from other, very different things. Whatever it is that is innate, we can at least be sure that it is *not* (and probably does not even resemble) any discrete part of the adult mind. The principle might seem quite obvious, but whereas it is exemplified in a deep and subtle way in Piaget's total work, it is violated by the very form of Chomsky's suggestions that developed entities, such as 'the specified subject condition' or 'the notion of bound anaphor' (these are his actual words) might be 'properties' of the initial state. In fact, one can see a large part of Piaget's work as the search for *intermediate entities,* which can play the role of precursors of the structures we find in the adult, or even of the child of any particular age. Thus, the question 'Is the notion of number innate?' is displaced by seeing how it grows out of various precursors whose existence was not recognized by Aristotle or any other pre-Piagetian psychologists. . . . I argue. . . that the power of Piaget's contribution would scarcely be altered if the intermediate objects he has discovered are proved to be 'innate'; the hard and deep work was discovering the precursors.

Through locating *intermediate entities,* structural precursors to that organization of mind which exhibits the well recognized skills of the developing child, and their interactions, I have tried to illuminate as precisely as possible how the mind becomes more complex through its interactions with a world of considerable variety. I need take no position on the initial state (S_0) — beginning my analysis in the middle of things. In those cases examined here, it is possible to represent simply significant changes among the complex structures of the mind. Further, the role of serendipity in learning is clearly important. The complexity of the world — through continuous interaction over long periods of time — significantly augments whatever is a person's initial knowledge state so that eventually, in the happiest outcomes, the human mind becomes an entity of untraceable complexity.

LÉVI-STRAUSS: ON BRICOLAGE

In his attempt to appreciate the significant achievements of pre-scientific thought — among which may be counted all human civilizations — Claude Lévi-

Strauss sought to distinguish between modern science and the science of the concrete. To explicate his ideas with a system of examples, he contrasted the methods of the engineer and of the bricoleur.[22]

There still exists among ourselves an activity which on the technical plane gives us quite a good understanding of what a science we prefer to call 'prior' rather than 'primitive', could have been on the plane of speculation. This is what is commonly called 'bricolage' in French. In its old sense the verb 'bricoler' applied to ball games and billiards, to hunting, shooting, and riding. It was however always used with reference to some extraneous movement: a ball rebounding, a dog straying or a horse swerving from its direct course to avoid an obstacle. And in our own time the 'bricoleur' is still someone who works with his hands and uses devious means compared to those of a craftsman.[23] The characteristic feature of mythical thought is that it expresses itself by means of a heterogeneous repertoire which, even if extensive, is nevertheless limited. It has to use this repertoire, however, whatever the task in hand because it has nothing else at its disposal. Mythical thought is therefore a kind of intellectual 'bricolage' — which explains the relation which can be perceived between the two.

The analogy is worth pursuing since it helps us to see the real relations between the two types of scientific knowledge we have distinguished. The bricoleur is adept at performing a large number of diverse tasks; but, unlike the engineer, he does not subordinate each of them to the availability of raw materials and tools conceived and procured for the purpose of the project. His universe of instruments is closed and the rules of his game are always to make do with 'whatever is at hand', that is to say, with a set of tools and materials which is always finite and is also heterogeneous because what it contains bears no relation to the current project, or indeed to any particular project, but is the contingent result of all the occasions there have been to renew or enrich the stock or to maintain it with the remains of previous constructions or destructions. The set of the bricoleur's means cannot therefore be defined in terms of a project. . . . It is to be defined only by its potential use or, putting it another way and in the language of the bricoleur himself, because the elements are collected and retained on the principle that 'they may always come in handy'. Such elements are specialized up to a point, sufficiently for the bricoleur not to need the equipment and knowledge of all trades and professions, but not enough for each of them to have only one definite and determinate use...

Consider him (the bricoleur) at work and excited by his project. His first practical step is retrospective. He has to turn back to an already existent set made up of tools and materials, to consider or reconsider what it contains and, finally and above all, to engage in a sort of dialogue with it and,

---

22 These citations are drawn from pages 16 through 21 in *The Savage Mind,* University of Chicago Press, 1966.

23 The 'bricoleur' has no precise equivalent in English. He is a man who undertakes odd jobs and is a jack-of-all-trades or a kind of professional do-it-yourself man, but, as the text makes clear, he is of a different standing from, for instance, the English 'odd-job man' or handyman. [Translator's note.]

before choosing between them, to index the possible answers which the whole set can offer to his problem. He interrogates all the heterogeneous objects of which his treasury is composed to discover what each of them could 'signify' and so contribute to the definition of a set which has yet to materialize but which will ultimately differ from the instrumental set only in the internal disposition of its parts. . . . The engineer no doubt also cross-examines his resources. . . . In his case, his means, power and knowledge are never unlimited and in this negative form he meets resistance with which he has to come to terms. It might be said that *the engineer questions the universe, while the bricoleur addresses himself to a collection of oddments left over from human endeavors,* that is, only a sub-set of the culture.

The difference is therefore less absolute than it might appear. It remains a real one, however, in that the engineer is always trying to make his way out of and go beyond the constraints imposed by a particular state of civilization while the bricoleur by inclination or necessity always remains within them.

In the continual reconstruction from the same materials, it is always earlier ends which are called upon to play the part of means. . . . This formula, which could serve as a definition of '*bricolage*', explains how an implicit inventory or conception of the total means available must be made. . . so that a result can be defined which will always be a compromise between the structure of the instrumental set and that of the project. Once it materializes, the project therefore must be inevitably at a remove from the initial aim (which was moreover a mere sketch), ... Further, the bricoleur also, and indeed principally, derives his poetry from the fact that he does not confine himself to accomplishment and execution: he speaks not only with things, as we have seen, but also through the medium of things: giving an account of his personality and life by the choices he makes between limited possibilities. The bricoleur may not ever complete his purpose but he always puts something of himself into it.

There are several advantages in adopting the image of bricolage as a central characterization of human activity. With respect to the issue of the psychological reality of our descriptions, the first advantage is verisimilitude. The bricoleur is not a dumb engineer; he is a person doing a different thing. If thinking is a form of bricolage, it is more like other natural human activities than is Simon's descriptions of thought as the serial search within a problem space of an agent whose specification is as a subset of an expert. The second advantage is that bricolage, as a characterization of behavior, is more nearly compatible with a view of mind as a process controlled by the contention of multiple objectives competing for resources than is planning, for example. Most importantly, bricolage can provide us with an image for the process of mind under self-construction.

JACOB: ON BRICOLAGE IN EVOLUTION[24]

Nature functions by integration. Whatever the level, the objects analyzed by natural sciences are always organizations, or systems. Each system at a given level uses as ingredients some systems of the simpler level, but some only. The hierarchy of complexity of objects is thus accompanied by a series of restrictions and limitations. At each level, new properties may appear which impose new constraints on the system. But these are merely additional constraints. Those that operate at any given level are still valid at the more complex level. Every proposition that is true for physics is also true for chemistry, biology, or sociology. Similarly, every proposition that is valid for biology holds true for sociology. But as a general rule, the statements of greatest importance at one level are of no interest at the more complex ones. The law of perfect. gases is no less true for the objects of biology or sociology than for those of physics. It is simply irrelevant in the context of the problems with which biologists, and even more so sociologists, are concerned.

This hierarchy of successive integrations, characterized by restrictions and by the appearance of new properties at each level, has several consequences. . . . [One] concerns the nature of the restrictions and limitations found at every step of increasing complexity. Can one explain why, among all the possible interactions at one level, only certain are observed at the more complex one? . . . There is no general answer to such questions, and it seems doubtful that there will ever be a specific answer for any one particular complexity. Complex objects are produced by evolutionary processes in which two factors are paramount: the constraints that at every level control the systems involved, and the historical circumstances that control the actual interactions between the systems. The combination of constraints and history exists at every level, although in different proportions. Simpler objects are more dependent on constraints than on history. As complexity increases, history plays a greater part.

How do constraints and history interact? Jacob develops this theme by applying to the question the Lévi-Strauss metaphor of bricolage (for which word he, a Frenchman, prefers the English 'tinkering'), in his vision of evolution.

This mode of operation has several aspects in common with the process of evolution. Often, without any well-defined long-term project, the tinkerer [sic] gives his materials unexpected functions to produce a new object. . . . Similarly evolution makes a wing from a leg or a part of an ear from a piece of jaw. Naturally, this takes a long time. Evolution behaves like a tinkerer who, during eons upon eons, would slowly modify his work, unceasingly retouching it, cutting here, lengthening there, seizing the opportunities to adapt it progressively to its new use. . . . The lung of vertebrates was formed in the following way. Its development started in certain fresh water fishes living in stagnant pools with insufficient oxygen. They adopted the habit of

24 These excerpts are drawn from the article 'Evolution as tinkering' (*Science*, 1974); that article appears also in *The Possible and the Actual* (Jacob, 1982).

swallowing air and absorbing oxygen through the walls of the esophagus. Under these conditions, enlargement of the surface area of the esophagus provided a selective advantage. Diverticula of the esophagus appeared and, under continuous selective pressure, enlarged into lungs. . . . To make a lung with a piece of esophagus sounds very much like tinkering.

Unlike engineers, tinkerers who tackle the same problem are likely to end up with different solutions. This also applies to evolution, as exemplified by the variety of eyes found in the living world. It is obviously a great advantage under many conditions to possess light receptors, and the variety of photoreceptors in the living world is amazing. . . . Eyes appeared a great many times in the course of evolution, based on at least three principles — pinhole, lens, and multiple tubes. Lens eyes, like ours, appeared both in mollusks and vertebrates. Nothing looks so much like our eye as the octopus eye. Both work in almost exactly the same way. Yet they did not evolve in the same way. Whereas in vertebrates photoreceptor cells of the retina point away from light, in mollusks they point toward light. Among all solutions found to the problem of photoreceptors, these two are similar but not identical. In each case, natural selection did what it could with the materials at its disposal.

At the molecular level

It is at the molecular level that the tinkering aspect of natural selection is perhaps most apparent. . . . It is not biochemical novelties that generated diversification of organisms. . . . What distinguishes a butterfly from a lion, a hen from a fly, or a worm from a whale, is much less a difference of chemical constituents than in the organization and the distribution of these constituents. . . . The genetic program is executed through complex regulatory circuits that switch the different biochemical activities of the organism on or off. Very little is known as yet about the regulatory circuits that operate in the development of complex organisms. It is known, however, that among related organisms such as mammals, the first steps of embryonic development are remarkably similar, with divergences showing up only progressively as development proceeds. These divergences concern much less the actual structure of cellular or molecular types than their number and position. . . . Small changes modifying the distribution in time and space of the same structures are sufficient to affect deeply the form, the functioning, and the behavior of the final product — the adult animal. It is always a matter of using the same elements, and of adjusting them, of altering here or there, of arranging various combinations to produce new objects of increasing complexity. It is always a matter of tinkering.

A final example: the human brain

Although our brain represents the main adaptive feature of our species, what it is adapted to is not clear at all. What is clear, however, is that, like the rest of our body, our brain is a product of natural selection, that is of differential reproductions accumulated over millions of years under the pressure of various environmental conditions. . . . But curiously enough, brain development in mammals was not as integrated a process as, for example, the transformation of a leg into a wing. The human brain was formed by the superposition of new structures on old ones. . . . The formation of a dominating neocortex coupled with the persistence of a nervous hormonal system partially, but not totally, under the rule of the neocortex — strongly resembles the tinkerer's procedure. It is somewhat like adding a jet engine to an old horse cart. It is not surprising, in either case, that accidents, difficulties, and conflicts can occur.

It is hard to realize that the living world as we know it is just one among many possibilities; that its actual structure results from the history of the earth. Yet living organisms are historical structures: literally, creations of history. They represent, not a perfect product of engineering, but a patchwork of odd sets pieced together when and where opportunities arose. For the opportunism of natural selection is not simply a matter of indifference to the structure and operation of its products. It represents the nature of a historical process full of contingency.

The interplay of local opportunities — physical, ecological, and constitutional — produces a net historical opportunity which in turn determines how genetic opportunities will be exploited. It is this net historical opportunity that mainly controls the direction and pace of adaptive evolution.

Jacob's use of the Lévi-Strauss metaphor, presented crisply with a profound appliction, is primary evidence of the fecundity of the point of view. If we ask more precisely what are the interrelation of constraints and history in human cognitive developement, we must look to a kind and level of exploration represented by my attempt in the four analytical chapters of this work.

TVERSKY AND KAHNEMANN: ON ANCHORING WITH VARIATION

We are all taught how we should think. How do people think, really, no matter what they are supposed to do? Tversky and Kahnemann addressed this issue through the study of how people solved calculation problems that were beyond their capacity in a limited period of time. They concluded that people rely on heuristics — rules of estimation that provide good but not perfect answers to hard questions. Of the three they discuss, representativeness, availability, and adjustment and anchoring, these citations focus on the last — which I consider the most important:[25]

> In many situations, people make estimates by starting from an initial value that is adjusted to yield the final answer. The initial value, or starting point, may be suggested by the formulation of the problem, or it may be the

25 These citations are drawn from an article in *Science* (September 1974), 'Judgement under uncertainty: heuristics and biases'. The authors' work has been extended and is now represented by a more extensive book, *Judgement under Uncertainty* (Kahnemann, Slovic and Tversky, 1983).

result of a partial computation. In either case, *adjustment are typically insufficient.* That is, different starting points yield different estimates, which are biased toward the initial value. We call this phenomenon *anchoring.*

Insufficient adjustment: In a demonstration of the anchoring effect, subjects were asked to estimate various quantities, stated in percentages (for example, the percentage of African countries in the Unitied Nations). For each quantity, a number between 0 and 100 was determined by spinning a wheel of fortune in the subjects' presence. The subjects were instructed to indicate first whether that number was higher or lower than the value of the quantity, and then to estimate the value of the quantity by moving upward or downward from the given number. Different groups were given different numbers for each quantity, and these arbitrary numbers had a marked effect on estimates. For example, the median estimates of the percentage of African countries in the United Nations were 25 and 45 for groups that received 10 and 65, respectively, as starting points. Payoffs for accuracy did not reduce the anchoring effect.

Anchoring occurs not only when the starting point is given to the subject, but also when the subject bases his estimate on the result of some incomplete computation. . . .

Biases in the evaluation of conjunctive and disjunctive events: Studies of choice among gambles and of judgements of probability indicate that people tend to overestimate the probability of conjunctive events and to underestimate the probability of disjunctive events. These biases are readily explained as the effects of anchoring. The stated probability of the elementary event (success at any one stage) provides a natural starting point for the estimation of the probabilities of both conjunctive and disjunctive events. Since adjustment from the starting point is typically insufficient, the final estimates remain too close to the probabilities of the elementary events in both cases. Note that the probability of a conjunctive event is lower than the probability of each elementary event, whereas the overall probability of a disjunctive event is higher than the probability of each elementary event. As a consequence of anchoring, the overall probability will be overestimated in conjunctive problems and underestimated in disjunctive problems.

By collecting subjective probability distributions for many different quantities, it is possible to test the judge for proper calibration. . . . Several investigators have obtained probability distributions for many quantities from a large number of judges. These distributions indicated large and systematic departures from proper calibration. In most studies, the actual values of the assessed quantities are either smaller than $X(01)$ or greater than $X(99)$ for about 30% of the problems. That is, the subjects state overly narrow confidence intervals which reflect more certainty than is justified by their knowledge about the assessed quantities. This bias is common to naive and sophisticated subjects and is not eliminated by introducing proper scoring rules. . . .The reliance on heuristics and the prevalence of biases are not restricted to laymen. Experienced researchers are also prone to the same biases — when they think intuitively. For example the tendency to predict the outcome that best represents the data, with insufficient regard for prior probability, has been observed in the intuitive judgements of individuals who have had extensive training in statistics. Although the statistically sophisticated avoid elementary errors, such as the gambler's fallacy,[26] their intuitive judgments are liable to similar fallacies in more intricate and less transparent problems.

If, as Goodman suggests, worlds differ not only in categorization (their assignment of what's what) but also in the relative salience of one element in comparison with another (what's primary), the observation that anchoring with variation is a common process of thought among both naive and sophisticated problem solvers argues that it is a natural process of thought as well. This process is one I take as a given in my analyses.[27] If thought begins or eventually comes down to processing of concrete models of particular past experience, then anchoring with variation and its implications of the characteristic processes of thinking are of central importance in studying learning.

THE TEXTURE OF BEHAVIOR

Taking behavior seriously does not always permit the development of an explicit model of the behavior, as this vignette from *Midwest and its Children* (Barker and Wright, 1955) should convince you:

> On June 2, 1949, four-year-old Margaret Reid spent 28 minutes in the Midwest behavior setting, Home Meal (lunchtime). . . . her behavior was consistent with the standing behavior pattern of the lunchtime setting. But this is by no means all. Margaret did 42 clearly discriminable and different things on the level of behavior episodes during the 28 minutes. Here are 21 of the 42 actions, just half the total:
>
>> Rejecting lemonade; Recollecting pancakes eaten for breakfast; Cutting tomato; Helping self to noodles; Forecasting Bible School picnic; Challenging little brother to lunch eating race; Appraising combination of lemon juice and milk; Inquiring about Valentine's day; Coping with dropped napkin; Commenting on play of neighbor friend; Playing on words about Bible School picnic; Wiping something out of eye; Reporting little brother's capers; Dunking cookies in cocktail sauce; Telling about imaginary friends; Putting box of Kleenex on bench; Inviting parents to look into stomach; Soliciting mother's opinion on brother's eating; Using spoon as airplane; Chanting 'Bones to Be, Bones to Be'; Reporting on birthday greetings at Bible School. . . .

Barker and Wright then expand one of these incidents — Cutting tomato — into fifteen even more detailed action descriptions. How information processing

---

26 The gambler's fallacy is the expectation that preceding events affect what are in fact independent probabilities.

27 See the discussion of elaboration in Chapter 1 and of Miriam's mental calculations in Chapter 2.

models of today should approach material exhibiting such volatility is far from clear. In some instances, as Anzai and Simon (1979) demonstrate in their article 'The theory of learning by doing', the analysis of limited-scope case material may proceed with admirable specificity. However, the orderliness of thought shown by their subject, a liberal arts college graduate, is not characteristic of the less regular thought of the child from whom every adult develops.

My study has taken a middle course between the analysis of limited scope experimental protocols and the overwhelming detail of a complete ecological study. By following the *child's* main interests and activities, the primary themes of her development were permitted to emerge sufficiently early on that they could serve as foci of documentation. Thus I could follow the learning of a single mind on its natural scale of development — that of months and years — while still preserving a sufficiency of material for detailed analysis where the pattern of development indicates the effort is justified; from these main developmental themes, I have chosen for extended analysis those which engage what I take to be central issues of the nature of mind. I believe there is no other so rich study of the cognitive development of so mature a child extending over so long a time and so explosive a period of mental growth.

References

Anzai, Y. and Simon, H. A. (1979) The theory of learning by doing. *Pscyhological Review,* **86,** 124–140.

Barker, R. and Wright, H. (1971) *Midwest and its Children.* Hamden, Connecticut: Archon Books (original edition 1955).

Bartlett, F. (1932) *Remembering.* London: Cambridge University Press.

Berrill, N. J. (1965) *Man's Emerging Mind.* Greenwich, Connecticut: Fawcett Publications.

Brown, J. S. and Burton, R. R. (1978) A diagnostic model for procedural bugs in basic mathematical skills. *Cognitive Science,* **2,** 155–192.

Emberley, E. (1972) *Make a World.* Boston and Toronto: Little, Brown, and Co.

Fann, K. T. *Peirce's Theory of Abduction.*

Flavell, J. (1963) *The Developmental Psychology of Jean Piaget.* New York: Van Nostrand.

Ginsberg, H. (1977) *Children's Arithmetic: the learning process.* New York: Van Nostrand.

Goodman, N. (1978) *Ways of Worldmaking.* Indianapolis: Hackett Publishing Company.

Inhelder, B. and Piaget, B. (1958) *The Growth of Logical Thinking from Childhood to Adolescence.* New York: Basic Books.

Inhelder, B. and Piaget, J. (1964) *The Early Growth of Logic in the Child.* Translated by E. A. Lunzer and D. Papert. New York: W. W. Norton.

Inhelder, B., Sinclair, H. and Bovet, M. (1974) *Learning and the Development of Cognition.* Cambridge, Mass.: Harvard University Press.

Jacob, F. (1982) Evolution and tinkering. *Science,* **196,** 1161–1166, 10 June 1977. Republished in *The Possible and the Actual.* New York: Pantheon Books, 1982.

Kuhn, T. (1962) *The Structure of Scientific Revolutions.* Chicago: University of Chicago Press.

Langer, S. (1967) *Mind: an Essay on Human Feeling,* Vol. 1. Baltimore: Johns Hopkins Press.

Lawler, R. (1980) Introducing writing with a computer. *SIGCUE,* 1980 (Special interest group, computer users in education; Association for Computing Machinery).

Lawler, R. (1981) The progressive construction of mind. *Cognitive Science,* **5,** 1–30.

Lawler, R. (1982) Extending a powerful idea. *The Journal of Mathematical .Behavior,* Summer.

Lenat, D. (1976) AM: an artificial intelligence approach to discovery in mathematics as heuristic search. Standford Artificial Intelligence Laboratory Memo 286. July.

Lenat, D. and Brown, J. (1983) Why AM and Eurisko appear to work. In *Proceedings of the National Conference on Artificial Intelligence, 1983.*

Lévi-Strauss, C. (1966) *The Savage Mind.* Chicago: University of Chicago Press.

Lewin, K. (1935) The conflict between Aristotelian and Galilean modes of thought in contemporary psychology.' In Lewin, K., *A Dynamic Theory of Personality – Selected Papers* (translated by Adams and Zener). New York and London: McGraw-Hill.

Lewin, R. (1983) How did vertebrates take to the air? *Science,* July 1.

Minsky, M. (1975) A framework for representing knowledge. In *The Psychology of Computer Vision* (ed. P. Winston). New York: McGraw-Hill.

Minsky, M. and Papert, S. (1974) The '72 Progress Report. Published as *Artificial Intelligence (the Condon Lectures).* Eugene, Oregon: Oregon System of Higher Education.

Moore, J. and Newell, A. (1973) How can Merlin understand? In *Knowledge and Cognition* (ed. L. Gregg). Potomac, Maryland: L. Erlbaum Associates.

Newell, A. and Simon, H. (1972) *Human Problem Solving.* Englewood Cliffs, New Jersey: Prentice-Hall.

Newell, A. (1973) Production systems: models of control structures. In *Visual Information Processing* (ed. W. G. Chase). New York: Academic Press.

Noton, D. and Stark, L. (1971a) Scan paths in eye movements during pattern perception. *Science,* **171,** 308–310.

Noton, D. and Stark, L. (1971b) Eye movements and visual perception. *Scientific American,* **224,** 6.

Papert, S. (1980) *Mindstorms: Children, Computers, and Powerful Ideas.* New York: Basic Books.

Peirce, C. (1956) *Chance, Love, and Logic: Philosophical Essays* (ed. M. Cohen). New York: George Braziller, Inc.

Piaget, J. (1974) *The Language and Thought of the Child.* (translated by Marjorie Gabain). New York: New American Library (original edition 1926).

Piaget, J. (1965) *The Child's Concept of Number.* New York: W. W. Norton &

Co. (original French edition 1941; first published in English in 1952).

Piaget, J. (1963) *The Origins of Intelligence in Children.* New York: W. W. Norton & Co. (originally published in 1952).

Piaget, J. (1972) Intellectual evolution from adolescence to adulthood. *Human Development,* **15**, 1–12.

Piaget, J. (1976a) *The Psychology of Intelligence.* Totowa, New Jersey: Littlefield, Adams & Co (originally published in 1947).

Piaget, J. (1976b) *The Grasp of Consciousness.* Cambridge, Mass.: Harvard University Press (originally published in 1974).

Piaget, J. and Inhelder, B. (1975) *The origin of the Idea of Chance in Children.* New York: W. W. Norton & Co., 1975 (originally published in 1951).

Piatelli-Palmerini, M. (1980) *Language and Learning.* Cambridge, Mass.: Harvard University Press.

Schmandt-Besserat, D. (1978) The earliest precursors of writing. *Scientific American,* June.

Simon, D. P. and Simon, H. (1973) Alternative uses of phonemic information in spelling. Pittsburgh: Learning Research and Development Centre Report.

Sussman, G. A. (1975) *Computational Model of Skill Acquisition.* New York: Elsevier.

Toulmin, S. (1972) Norbert Wiener and Warren McCulloch. In *Markers of Modern Thought.* New York: American Heritage Publishing Co.

Tversky, A. and Kahneman, D. (1983) Judgement under uncertainty: heuristics and biases. *Science,* 1974, **185**, 1124–1131. Republished in *Judgement under uncertainty: heuristics and biases,* by Kahnemann, Slovic, and Tversky. Cambridge: Cambridge University Press.

Valett, R. A. *Profile for the Stanford–Binet (L–M).* Palo Alto, Calif.: Consulting Psychologists Press.

Wertz, H. (1982) An integrated, interactive, and incremental programming environment for the development, of complex systems. Paris: Laboratoire Informatique Théoretique et Programmation, University Paris 7.

Winston, P. (1975) Learning structural descriptions from examples. In *The Psychology of Computer Vision* (ed. P. Winston). New York: McGraw-Hill.

Unpublished Works

Czerny and von Glaserfeld, E. A dynamic approach to the recognition of triangularity. University of Georgia, Athens, Ga.

Lawler, R. (1979) One child's learning: an intimate study. Unpublished doctoral dissertation. MIT.

Minsky, M. (1985) *The Society Theory of Mind.* Forthcoming.

Suggested readings not specifically cited

Berliner, H. (1978) A chronology of computer chess and its literature. *Artificial Intelligence,* **10**, 201–214.

Dawkins, R. (1976) *The Selfish Gene.* New York: Oxford University Press.

Freud, S. (1938) *Selected Works* (Translated by A. A. Brill). New York: The Modern Library.

Goodall, J. (1971) *In the Shadow of Man.* Boston: Houghton Mifflin Co.

Gruber, H. (1974) *Darwin on Man.* London: Wildwood House, Ltd. Republished, Chicago: Chicago University Press, 1981.

Gruber, H. and Voneche, J. (1977) *The Essential Piaget.* New York: Basic Books.

Karp, W. (1972) Isaac Newton. In *Makers of Modern Thought.* New York: American Heritage Publishing Company, Inc. (N.B. The conflicts between Newton and Hooke continued. See 'Newton's discovery of gravity' by I. Cohen. *Scientific American,* March, 1981.)

Kohler, W. (1976) *The Mentality of Apes* (translated by E. Winter). New York: Liveright (original edition 1925).

Langer, S. (1942, 1951) *Philosophy in a New Key.* New York: The New American Library.

Lawler, R. (1982b) In the lap of the machine. *Boston Review,* June.

Lawler, R. (1982c) Designing computer microworlds. *Byte Magazine,* August, 1982. Republished in *New Horizons in Educational Computing* (ed. M. Yazdani). Chichester, England: Ellis Horwood, 1984.

May, R. (1958) *Existence.* New York: Simon & Schuster.

Neisser, U. (1967) *Cognitive Psychology.* Englewood Cliffs, N. J.: Prentice-Hall.

Neisser, U. (1976) *Cognition and Reality.* San Francisco: W. H. Freeman.

Piaget, J. (1965) *Insights and Illusions of Philosophy* (translated by Wolfe Mays). New York: The New American Library.

Piaget, J. (1971) *Biology and Knowledge* (translated by Beatrix Walsh). Chicago: University of Chicago Press.

Piaget, J. (1970) *Structuralism* (translated by Chaninah Maschler). New York: Harper Colophon Books.

Putnam, H. (1981–1982) Convention: a theme in philosophy. *New Literary History.*

Putnam, H. (1983) Foreword to the Fourth Edition. In *Fact, Fiction, and Forecast* by Nelson Goodman. Cambridge, Mass.: Harvard University Press.

Rogers, C. (1961) *On Becoming a Person.* Boston: Houghton Mifflin Co.

Simon, H. (1974) How big is a chunk? *Science,* **183,** 482–488.

Tinbergen, N. (1960) *The Herring Gull's World.* New York: Harper Torchbooks.

White, R. W. (1952) *Lives in Progress.* New York: Henry Holt.

Acknowledgments

The person who has done the most for this work and so far has received entirely inadequate credit is my son Rob. For two years before Miriam began to join me at MIT, Rob had been my helper, my subject, and my inspiration. From him, I learned how essential it is to follow a child's lead if you want to know his mind. From him, I learned that seemingly complex problems may have simple answers if you ask and listen understandingly. From him, I learned that the world of the child's everyday experience informs his judgments and theories about what things are and how they work. Furthermore, my relationship with Rob contributed significantly to my embarking in mid-life on a scientific career. On my 32nd birthday, as I balanced my opportunities and responsibilities, I asked what I, as his father, owed Rob; the reply that shaped my choice was to provide him through my life an example in action of the values I believe in, and to try to do so in an environment wherein he and his sister could participate in my working life. Within a few years, Rob had joined me as a junior colleague at MIT. He was a terrific kid at six and seven, energetic, imaginative and friendly. If he and his friends Sam Lewis and Danny Moore were noisy and rambunctious on occasion, they were no more trouble than one might expect of such lads.

Why didn't The Intimate Study deal with Rob? It did, in fact, in the specific senses that he participated in all the experiments and Logo sessions and that his output and mechanical recordings were saved. Let me thank Hal Abelson here for proposing this as the solution to the problem we both recognized, that of Rob's feeling displaced in my life by his younger sister; the solution was not perfect, but it made the best outcome of a difficult choice. I have not analyzed Rob's work so thoroughly as Miriam's because I believed I was not capable of doing so. As the labor of these past eight years shows, I did have to make a choice. I believed I could not analyze Rob's work so well as Miriam's because he had, during the preceding 18 months, entered upon a phase of explosive intellectual growth which took him at depth into domains of experience beyond my knowledge. For example, at seven, he knew more about the military history of the Pacific campaign that I will ever know. I believed that Miriam's more limited range of experiences was still, albeit only barely, within my grasp. This choice and my consequent focus on the analysis of Miriam's learning should not obscure either the generative role of Rob's earlier experiments with me or the elegance of his work during the study itself [1]. Without Rob's earlier work, the experiments with Miriam could not have been so focussed as they are: without him, my endeavor would never have begun.

The experimental work done here was mainly my own, but it was richly supplemented by the aid of others at need. This was especially true for experiments in the Piagetian repertoire. I had the able assistance of three researchers who had studied in Piaget's Center of Genetic Epistemology at Geneva. Papert worked with Piaget for years, and performed two experiments for me. Lawrence Miller, who studied with Guy Cellerier, and Sheldon Wagner, who worked with Barbel Inhelder, both performed experiments drawn from descriptions in *The Grasp of Consciousness*. Howard Austin helped shape and then videotape our 'physical skills' experiment. Gretchen Lawler was frequently called on to help, was often willing, and did help even when she was not happy to do so.

Before accepting admission to MIT, I discussed with Papert what being a research student at the Logo project would be like. He replied, 'Everyone agrees that at some point in life a person should be responsible for his continuing education; people may argue about the age at which this should happen, but you, in your mid-thirties, are surely old enough to focus your own studies and direct your own research. Your responsibility would be to do your best work on the most profound problem you are able to address'. Despite his commitment to a myriad of projects, Seymour reviewed the progress of The Intimate Study and my analyses of the corpus. His responses were less suggestive then gently critical. If as an adviser Seymour was somewhat transcendental, he has been to me like the good daemon of Socrates, who warned him when he was going wrong but never told him what to do. This was an entirely suitable relationship between a learned man and a mature, serious student.

When I presented my thesis on The Intimate Study to MIT, both my faculty committee (Seymour Papert, Marvin Minsky, and Susan Carey) and external readers helped me to appreciate the value of and understand the limitations of the work. John Andrea of Cambridge University in New Zealand, Howard Gruber of Rutgers, Donald Norman of UCSD, all gave me encouraging but critical reactions. Professor Hermine Sinclair of Geneva was especially generous with her time. I valued her knowledge of Piagetian literature and

---

1   Rob's most attractive significant single piece of work has been published as *Extending a Powerful Idea*.

experiment and her willingness to read and discuss my work from her perspective. Other scholars I met later, I think here of Robert Davis, Heinrich Bauersfeld, Guy Cellerier, and Barbel Inhelder, have inspired and heartened me by their quick and deep penetration of analyses and their appreciation of my scientific objectives. Of those in the extended community of scholars, the support of Sheldon White has been more encouraging than any other. Even as early as the data collection phase of The Intimate Study, he recognized that mine was not a commitment to a 'mindless empiricism' but a pursuit of the appropriate level of particular detail needed for a scientific comprehension of how an individual mind changes with specific experiences. Over the intervening years, he has honored me by serious discussion of how themes in my analyses relate to the classic problems of psychology. The discussions have borne fruit in this work, especially in Chapter 5, for Sheldon White raised to salience for me the issue of the multi-modal character of mind. Without his guidance, this book would not be what it is. Without his longstanding encouragement, it might not exist at all.

John Flavell's book on Piaget directed me to Barker and Wright. Hilary Putnam urged me to take Nelson Goodman especially seriously. Similarly, Howard Gruber advocated the centrality of the vision of Kurt Lewin to the research and analyses I had done and do. Meetings with Howie in Cambridge and with those of his colleagues at Rutgers especially interested in case study methodology were often an opportunity for reflecting on how the computational representations of artificial intelligence require the kinds of concrete information that can only come from exquisitely detailed empirical studies.

R. W. White's book *Lives in Progress* uses case study to exemplify the application of psychological theories. From his example, I reasoned that if AI ideas were potentially important in understanding mind, their application to the concrete case would be an important and worthwhile endeavor. Further, Jane Goodall's trek into the jungle to study chimpanzee behavior and Tinbergen's study of the herring gull were major arguments for the fecundity of detailed empirical work. But they were more, they were inspirations as well. If a young woman could have the courage to go off to live in the jungle with chimpanzees for two years, and if scientists need have the patience to lie in a cold, wet blind for days watching bird behavior, the chore of observing human children in one's own family came to seem less onerous than the obvious labor requirement of analysis meant it must inescapably be. Lives of such folks still remind us we can make our works sublime; what greater gift than such examples could one ever hope to find?

The individual chapters of this book have developed over many years; during that time, I have presented the work and discussed it in seminars and as papers. The criticisms I received have generally been supportive and helpful. Lawrence Miller read a draft of Chapter 1 enthusiastically. Papert's quick grasp of my proposal that bricolage was a primary metaphor for conceiving of the self-construction of mind was very gratifying. While preparing the materials of Chapter 2 for publication as an article, I presented it at seminars at MIT's Division for Study and Research in Education and at a colloquium of the Yale AI project. Among the many helpful comments from these communities, those by C. Reisbeck at Yale and by A. DiSessa stand out now in my memory. John Seeley Brown read an early draft of Chapter 4 as an article reviewer. John's critical comments and Donald Norman's later advice convinced me that I should not break up this work as journal articles but prepare the whole thing as what it is, an integrated vision of a fragmentary view of mind. My deepest and most thorough discussion of Chapter 4 has been with Cellerier. Chapter 5 was discussed at a seminar at The World Center for Computers and Human Development ('CMI', an acronym for 'Le Centre Mondial l'Informatique.'). I recall distinctly helpful comments from E. Akermann, E. Marti, A. DiSessa, and G. Cellerier. Without question, the most fruitful reactions were from Hilary Putnam; he recognized immediately the congeniality of my point of view and philosophical commitments with those of Nelson Goodman; he recommended *Ways of Worldmaking*. Goodman's first footnote cited a translation by Susanne Langer, a thinker whose works I had known and read repeatedly over two decades. Langer, the seminal modern philosopher, the friend of my best Yale professor (David James), the favorite of the friend and mentor of my undergraduate days at Caltech, Hunter Mead. Only Charles Bures, successor to his responsibilities at Mead's untimely death, with his advocacy of the importance of Peirce's contributions to modern philosophy has equally influenced these philosophical commitments.

Artificial Intelligence is now the latest fashion in the commercial world, but the computer culture of which my family was a part during the Intimate Study was then considered an esoteric speciality of academia. Those involved with the Logo project as students who most sharply influenced my own developing ideas were Howard Austin and Lawrence Miller. Throughout the last decade, there has been no one with whom I have spent more time in serious discussion than Howard. His early arguments about the disparateness of skill components and his use of detailed videotape analysis in his own work were major influences on my own choices. No one could have had a more helpful, generous, and effective friend than Howard has been to me and my family during these years. Laurie Miller came to Cambridge to study at Harvard and MIT from studies with Cellerier and Karmiloff-Smith at Geneva. With his guidance and help, I first began micro-analysis of videotaped experiments with my children — replicating some experiments of Karmiloff-Smith and Inhelder ('If you want to get ahead, get a theory'. *Cognition* **3**, 3). Laurie also raised casually in conversation an issue Cellerier had discussed: what are the appropriate primitives in terms of which to discuss the operation of the body's various sensory systems; he also invited me to join him at some of Sheldon White's lectures on psychology at Harvard. Beyond these directly formative pulses provided to my work, discussions with Laurie have been a constant opportunity to review, evaluate, and broaden my research and its relation to important currents and issues in the study of mind. Without the frequent, familiar conversations with Austin and Miller, this book would have been a different and a lesser work than it is.

When I first came to MIT, I was hired as a research assistant by the AI lab; subsequently I received a fellowship through the Division for Research and Study in Education. These grants were welcome and valued. However, since I had a family to support during those student years, we used up our savings,

Gretchen's dowry, and her salary for several years. Subsequently, largely through Papert's advocacy of my work, I was employed as a researcher by MIT. After a writing grant from the Spencer Foundation enabled me to develop significantly the material of Chapters 3 and 5, I returned to my research, again with Papert, at CMI (The World Center for Informatics) in Paris. In my first month there, I completed the writing promised under the Spencer Foundation grant. I finished this book after my return from France, and before joining the Fundamental Research Laboratory of GTE — although final editing and galley correction seems an interminable process.

Within the Logo sub-culture of the AI lab, most of the people were at least tolerant of children and many were interested in them; Rob and Miriam were made a part of that culture as much as I was. Henry Lieberman, Paul Goldenberg, and Greg Gargarian at various times have been close friends of Rob, Miriam, and me. Jose Valente, whose period as a grad student at MIT was most nearly coextensive with my own, became a firm friend whose conversation and hospitality were enormously valuable during several difficult years. The younger members of the Logo group were a delight and an inspiration: Margaret Minsky, Danny Hillis, Ellen Hildreth, Gary Drescher, Brian Silverman, Gloria Rudisch, a pediatrician and mother, a member of the larger lab family, was like a good angel to many of us, always friendly, interested, and thoughtful. There were times when I worked at MIT while my family was not with me. I started early and worked late. Maybe because I was once a hacker myself, I feel friendship for the fellows who work late and fix hard problems. Some of them made the first TI sprite Logo and MIT Logo for the Apple; they showed my children computer games and introduced me to microcomputers. Ed Hardebeck, Mark Gross, Pat Soblavero, Lee Klotz are all surely acquaintences well met. And I know Rob got advice from people I never knew on how to play with the games available on the AI lab's Altos (in a casual encounter with Gene Roddenberry, he offered to show him how to play Star Trek).

It has been my privilege, at the Logo project and later at CMI, to meet and become friends with people from Europe, Africa, and South America. Gunther Albers has been a perceptive reader and active advocate of my work in the European Cognitive Science community. Horacio Reggini, Antonio Battro, and Jose Ripper, of Argentina and Brazil, and colleagues from Senegal, Bouna Gaye, Mohamadou Diallo, Mamadou Niang, Moussa Gning, and especially Fatimata Sylla, urged me to believe that my research might support the goals of human development in Africa and South America. Many colleagues from Europe, met through OECD, UNESCO, or CMI, believe that this study of my children will help them understand the potential benefits and limitations to the value of computer experience for children of their societies. Let me thank such friends for their encouragement and hope their beliefs are justified.

Many of my colleagues at MIT and some of the myriad visitors to the Logo project have surely affected this labor in ways they don't know and I can't describe. The publisher is knocking at the door for corrected galleys. I hope any serious debts passing unnoticed will be forgiven.

The Logo Project of the MIT AI lab was a unique intellectual crossroads. The reputation of MIT, in general, and of Minsky and Papert in particular, created this environment, one where good work could be done and would be noticed. Let this be my final thanks then, that there are such places and such people.

Index